Real Survival Stories

Shah Rukh

Published by Shah Rukh, 2024.

REAL SURVIVAL STORIES

First edition. May 10, 2024.

ISBN: 979-8224589449

Written by Shah Rukh.

Table of Contents

Prologue

Survival is a word that carries a weight much heavier than its eight simple letters. It's a battle cry, a testament to the human spirit's unyielding will to live, and a journey marked by unimaginable challenges. Throughout history, people have been thrust into situations that test the very limits of their endurance, resilience, and ingenuity. From the frozen expanses of the Antarctic to the scorching deserts of Africa, from the heart of a sinking ship to the eerie silence of outer space, these stories of survival reveal the incredible depths of human courage and the extraordinary lengths to which people will go to stay alive.

In this book, *Real Survival Stories*, we delve into the gripping accounts of those who faced the unthinkable and lived to tell their tales. Each chapter is a window into a different world—a world where the rules of everyday life are stripped away, and the primal instinct to survive takes over. You will read about Steve Callahan, who survived 76 days adrift on a tiny raft in the vast Atlantic Ocean, and Poon Lim, who fought off sharks and starvation while stranded at sea. You'll journey with Aron Ralston, who performed the unimaginable to free himself from a deadly canyon, and feel the chilling cold of the Antarctic alongside the crew of Shackleton's Endurance expedition.

These stories are not just tales of hardship and endurance; they are narratives of hope, determination, and the unbreakable human spirit. They remind us that even in the darkest moments, when all seems lost, there is always a glimmer of hope—a chance to fight, to endure, and to survive.

As you turn these pages, you will discover the incredible resourcefulness and tenacity that define us as human beings. You will see how ordinary people, when faced with extraordinary circumstances, can become heroes of their own stories. These accounts are not just about survival against the elements or against incredible odds—they are about survival against the limits we often set for ourselves, proving time and again that the human spirit is capable of remarkable things.

So, brace yourself for a journey through some of the most harrowing and inspiring survival stories ever told. Each chapter is a testament to the strength of the human spirit, a powerful reminder that in the face of adversity, we are all capable of more than we can ever imagine. Welcome to *Real Survival Stories*—a tribute to those who refused to give up, even when the odds were stacked against them.

Chapter 1: Steve Callahan's 76 Days Adrift

Steve Callahan's extraordinary tale of survival, chronicled in his harrowing 76-day ordeal adrift in the Atlantic Ocean, stands as one of the most remarkable survival stories in modern history. It is a testament to human resilience, resourcefulness, and the indomitable will to survive against insurmountable odds. The story begins in January 1982, when Callahan, an experienced sailor and boat designer, embarked on a solo transatlantic journey aboard his small sailboat, the *Napoleon Solo*. Little did he know that this voyage would soon turn into a nightmare that would push him to the very limits of his endurance.

The Fateful Night: A Catastrophic Event

Callahan's journey began without incident as he sailed from the Canary Islands toward the Caribbean. However, just six days into his voyage, disaster struck. In the middle of the night, while Callahan was asleep in his bunk, a mysterious force—believed to be a whale or a large shark—punched a hole through the hull of his boat. The sudden impact jolted Callahan awake, and he quickly realized that his vessel was taking on water. In a matter of minutes, the *Napoleon Solo* was sinking beneath him.

With no time to waste, Callahan grabbed essential supplies, including a survival kit, and scrambled into a six-foot inflatable life raft, which he had named *Rubber Ducky*. As he watched his beloved sailboat disappear beneath the waves, he was left alone in the vast expanse of the Atlantic Ocean, with only his small raft as a lifeline. Thus began his epic fight for survival.

Life on the Raft: The Struggle for Survival

Life on the raft was grueling from the outset. Callahan had to contend with a host of challenges, from extreme weather conditions to the constant threat of dehydration, starvation, and exposure. The life raft, designed for short-term use, was woefully inadequate for a long-term survival situation. It provided minimal protection from the elements, and its small size made it difficult for Callahan to move around or find a comfortable position to sleep.

One of the most pressing issues Callahan faced was the lack of fresh water. He had only a limited supply of water in his survival kit, and he knew it would quickly run out. Desperate to find a solution, Callahan relied on a solar still—a device that uses the sun's heat to evaporate seawater, leaving behind drinkable fresh water. However, the solar still was temperamental and produced only small amounts of water each day, barely enough to keep him alive.

In addition to the scarcity of water, Callahan faced the challenge of finding food. With no fishing gear, he improvised by fashioning a spear from a metal rod and using it to catch small fish that swam near the raft. Over time, he became proficient at spearfishing, providing himself with a steady, albeit meager, supply of food. He also scavenged whatever he could from the ocean, including barnacles and other marine life that attached themselves to the raft.

The physical toll of the ordeal was immense. Callahan lost a significant amount of weight, his body weakened by the lack of proper nutrition and the harsh conditions. His skin became raw and blistered from constant exposure to saltwater and the sun's relentless rays. Yet, despite the physical hardships, Callahan's mental resilience remained unshaken. He was determined to survive, driven by the hope that he would eventually be rescued.

Battling the Elements: Storms, Sharks, and Solitude

The Atlantic Ocean is a place of extremes, and Callahan experienced it all during his time adrift. He endured violent storms that threatened to capsize his fragile raft, with towering waves crashing down on him, soaking him to the bone and nearly drowning him in the process. During these storms, he clung to the raft for dear life, praying that it would hold together under the onslaught of the elements.

Sharks were another constant threat. The smell of fish attracted these apex predators, and they would often circle the raft, bumping it with their noses or gnashing their teeth against its rubber sides. Callahan had to remain vigilant at all times, using his spear to fend off the sharks whenever they got too close. The presence of these predators added to the psychological strain of his ordeal, as he knew that a puncture in the raft's thin walls would spell certain death.

Isolation was perhaps the greatest challenge Callahan faced. Alone in the vastness of the ocean, with no land in sight and no other human beings to communicate with, he struggled with the crushing loneliness and despair that threatened to overwhelm him. To combat the mental toll, Callahan focused on maintaining a daily routine, setting goals for himself, and keeping his mind occupied. He recorded his thoughts and observations in a journal, which would later become the basis for his bestselling book, *Adrift: Seventy-six Days Lost at Sea*.

The Turning Point: Signs of Hope

As the days turned into weeks and then months, Callahan's situation grew increasingly dire. His supplies were dwindling, his body was deteriorating, and the psychological strain was mounting. Yet, he refused to give up. He continued to ration his food and water carefully, cking out every last bit of sustenance from his dwindling supplies.

A turning point came when Callahan began to notice signs that he was approaching land. He observed changes in the ocean currents, the appearance of more bird life, and even the occasional piece of debris floating by—indications that he might be nearing the Caribbean, where he had originally been headed. These signs renewed his hope and gave him the strength to continue fighting for survival.

The Rescue: A Miraculous Ending

On April 21, 1982, after 76 days adrift and having covered over 1,800 miles of ocean, Callahan's ordeal finally came to an end. He was spotted by a group of fishermen off the coast of Marie-Galante, a small island in the Caribbean. The fishermen initially mistook his raft for a piece of debris, but when they saw movement, they realized it was a person. They quickly moved in to rescue him, pulling him aboard their boat and bringing him to safety.

Callahan was emaciated, dehydrated, and weak, but he was alive. His survival was nothing short of a miracle, a testament to his incredible determination and resourcefulness. He had endured 76 days alone at sea, surviving on little more than fish, rainwater, and sheer willpower.

Aftermath and Legacy: A Story for the Ages

In the aftermath of his rescue, Callahan's story captured the world's attention. He became an international sensation, and his memoir, *Adrift: Seventy-six Days Lost at Sea*, became a bestseller. The book is a gripping account of his ordeal, offering readers a vivid and detailed recounting of his time adrift, as well as insights into the psychological and emotional challenges he faced.

Callahan's experience also had a profound impact on his life. He continued to sail and design boats, but his time at sea left him with a deep respect for the power of nature and the fragility of human life.

He became an advocate for survival training and ocean safety, using his experience to educate others on the importance of preparation and self-reliance in extreme situations.

The legacy of Steve Callahan's 76 days adrift lives on as one of the greatest survival stories of all time. His ordeal is a reminder of the incredible strength of the human spirit and the lengths to which we can go to stay alive, even in the face of overwhelming odds. It is a story that continues to inspire and captivate, serving as a powerful testament to the enduring will to survive.

Chapter 2: The Story of Poon Lim

The story of Poon Lim is a remarkable tale of endurance, ingenuity, and the human spirit's unyielding will to survive against seemingly insurmountable odds. Poon Lim, a Chinese seaman, holds the extraordinary record of surviving the longest alone on a life raft in the open sea, an astonishing 133 days. His ordeal began during World War II, a time of global conflict and perilous maritime conditions, making his survival even more incredible.

The Background: Life Before the Ordeal

Poon Lim was born on March 8, 1918, in Hainan, a large island off the southern coast of China. Growing up in a region known for its fishing and maritime traditions, Poon Lim was no stranger to the sea. However, he did not initially set out to become a sailor. In 1932, at the age of 14, Poon Lim left home to join his brother in Hong Kong, where he worked in a shipyard. It was here that he gained the skills and knowledge that would later prove crucial to his survival. As World War II escalated, Poon Lim found work as a steward on British merchant ships, a job that eventually led him into the heart of his harrowing survival story.

In 1942, the global situation was dire. The Axis powers, including Germany and Japan, were making significant advances, and the seas were perilous due to the presence of German U-boats (submarines) and other enemy vessels. British merchant ships, which played a critical role in supplying the Allies, were prime targets for these U-boats. Poon Lim found himself aboard one such ship, the *SS Ben Lomond*, a British merchant vessel tasked with carrying vital supplies across the Atlantic Ocean.

The Sinking of the SS Ben Lomond

On November 23, 1942, the *SS Ben Lomond* was en route from Cape Town, South Africa, to Paramaribo in Dutch Guiana (now Suriname). The ship, which was sailing unescorted, was suddenly attacked by a German U-boat, the U-172, under the command of Captain Carl Emmermann. The U-boat fired two torpedoes at the *Ben Lomond*, and within minutes, the ship was struck, resulting in a catastrophic explosion. The ship began to sink rapidly, leaving the crew with little time to react.

In the chaos that ensued, many of the crew members perished in the explosion or drowned as the ship went under. Poon Lim, however, managed to grab a life jacket and leap overboard. As he struggled to stay afloat amidst the debris and oil-slicked waters, he spotted a wooden life raft and swam toward it. Exhausted but alive, Poon Lim climbed aboard the raft, not realizing that he was about to begin a grueling ordeal that would last for months.

Life on the Raft: The Struggle for Survival

Poon Lim's life raft was a simple, rectangular wooden structure measuring about 8 feet by 8 feet. It was equipped with basic survival supplies, including several tins of biscuits, some water, a few flares, and a flashlight. There was also a small canvas canopy for protection from the sun. However, these supplies were only intended to sustain someone for a few days, not the months that lay ahead.

From the outset, Poon Lim faced a daunting battle for survival. The Atlantic Ocean was vast, and the chances of being rescued were slim, especially during wartime when ships avoided the open seas for fear of being attacked by submarines. Poon Lim's first challenge was to ration his limited supplies carefully. He calculated that he had enough biscuits and water to last him for a short period, but he knew that he would need to find alternative sources of food and water if he were to survive for any extended length of time.

As the days turned into weeks, Poon Lim's resourcefulness became his most valuable asset. He constructed a makeshift fishing line using the wire from the flashlight and fashioned a hook out of a nail. He used small pieces of biscuit as bait and was able to catch fish, which provided him with much-needed sustenance. To conserve his limited supply of fresh water, Poon Lim devised a method to collect rainwater using a canvas tarpaulin. He would funnel the rainwater into empty biscuit tins, which he carefully rationed.

One of the most harrowing challenges Poon Lim faced was the constant threat of exposure. The sun beat down mercilessly during the day, and the nights were often cold and damp. To protect himself from sunburn and dehydration, Poon Lim used the canvas canopy to create shade during the day and wrapped himself in it at night to stay warm. Despite his efforts, the harsh conditions took a toll on his body. His skin became blistered and cracked from the sun and saltwater, and he began to lose weight rapidly.

Battling the Elements: Storms and Sharks

Life on the open sea is unpredictable, and Poon Lim had to contend with the full range of the ocean's moods. He endured violent storms that threatened to capsize his small raft. The waves would swell to terrifying heights, tossing the raft like a toy on the surface of the water. During these storms, Poon Lim would cling to the raft with all his strength, praying that it would hold together.

In addition to the storms, Poon Lim had to deal with the constant presence of sharks. The fish he caught often attracted these predators, which would circle the raft, sometimes bumping it with their noses. Poon Lim knew that if a shark managed to puncture the raft, it could spell the end of his survival. He fashioned a makeshift spear from a piece of wood and metal, using it to fend off the sharks whenever they got too close. This constant battle with nature's fiercest predators added another layer of psychological strain to his ordeal.

The Psychological Toll: Loneliness and Despair

As the weeks stretched into months, the psychological toll of isolation and uncertainty weighed heavily on Poon Lim. He was completely alone, with no means of communicating with the outside world. The vastness of the ocean around him, with no land in sight, was a constant reminder of his isolation. The fear of never being found and the possibility of dying alone at sea was always present in his mind.

To maintain his sanity, Poon Lim kept himself busy with routine tasks. He cleaned the raft regularly to prevent the buildup of salt and debris, fished for food, and checked his water supply. He also kept a mental record of the days he had been adrift, though as time passed, the days began to blur together. Despite the bleakness of his situation, Poon Lim never lost hope. He remained determined to survive and kept his spirits up by imagining the day he would be rescued.

Encounters with Passing Ships: Hope and Disappointment

During his time adrift, Poon Lim had several encounters with passing ships. On more than one occasion, he spotted a ship on the horizon and desperately signaled for help using his flares and flashlight. However, the ships either did not see him or chose not to stop, perhaps fearing a German U-boat attack. Each time a ship passed without rescuing him, Poon Lim's hope would falter, but he refused to give in to despair.

On one occasion, a German U-boat surfaced near his raft. The crewmen saw Poon Lim but, for reasons unknown, chose not to harm him. They simply looked at him from a distance and then sailed away, leaving him alone once more. This encounter was a stark reminder of the dangers that surrounded him, but it also reinforced his determination to survive against all odds.

The Final Stretch: Nearing the End of the Ordeal

As Poon Lim's ordeal dragged on, his physical condition continued to deteriorate. He was losing weight rapidly, his body weakened by the lack of proper nutrition, and his skin was covered in sores from prolonged exposure to the elements. Yet, his will to survive remained unbroken. He continued to catch fish and collect rainwater, eking out a meager existence on the open sea.

By the fourth month, Poon Lim's supplies were nearly exhausted, and his body was severely emaciated. He had drifted over 1,200 miles across the Atlantic Ocean, and his raft was showing signs of wear and tear. Despite the overwhelming odds, Poon Lim's determination to survive never wavered. He knew that he had come too far to give up now.

The Rescue: A Miraculous End to the Ordeal

On April 5, 1943, after 133 days adrift, Poon Lim's ordeal finally came to an end. He was spotted by a group of Brazilian fishermen off the coast of Brazil, near the mouth of the Amazon River. The fishermen initially mistook his raft for a piece of debris, but when they realized there was a man aboard, they quickly moved to rescue him. Poon Lim was barely conscious, weak from months of starvation and exposure, but he was alive.

The fishermen brought Poon Lim ashore, where he was taken to a hospital in Belém, Brazil. He was severely malnourished and weighed only 125 pounds, but after receiving medical treatment, he began to recover. News of his incredible survival quickly spread, and Poon Lim became an international sensation. His story was celebrated around the world as a testament to the strength of the human spirit and the will to survive.

Aftermath and Legacy: A Heroic Tale of Survival

After his rescue, Poon Lim was taken to the British Consulate in Brazil, where he recounted his ordeal to officials. He was eventually repatriated to the United Kingdom, where he received a hero's welcome. The British government awarded him the British Empire Medal for his bravery and resilience. Despite the accolades, Poon Lim remained humble, insisting that he was just an ordinary man who did what he had to do to survive.

Poon Lim's record for the longest survival at sea on a life raft remains unbroken to this day. His story has been the subject of numerous books, documentaries, and articles, and it continues to inspire people around the world. Poon Lim's incredible journey is a powerful reminder of the human capacity to endure even the most extreme circumstances and the unyielding will to live.

In the years following his ordeal, Poon Lim returned to civilian life and eventually emigrated to the United States, where he became a naturalized citizen. He lived a quiet life, working in various jobs and raising a family. Poon Lim passed away on January 4, 1991, at the age of 72, but his legacy lives on as one of the greatest survival stories in history.

Conclusion: A Timeless Tale of Endurance

The story of Poon Lim is more than just a tale of survival; it is a testament to the power of the human spirit. Faced with the unimaginable challenges of being alone at sea for over four months, Poon Lim demonstrated extraordinary resourcefulness, courage, and determination. His ability to adapt to his environment, find food and water, and fend off threats is a testament to his ingenuity and resilience. But perhaps most importantly, Poon Lim's story is a reminder that hope and the will to survive can sustain us even in the darkest of times.

14

Chapter 3: The Survival of Mauro Prosperi

The story of Mauro Prosperi is one of the most extraordinary survival tales of modern times, showcasing the incredible endurance, resilience, and sheer willpower of a man who found himself in one of the most inhospitable environments on Earth—the vast and unforgiving Sahara Desert. Prosperi's ordeal began in 1994 during the Marathon des Sables, an extreme endurance race through the Sahara, and it would become a harrowing 10-day journey of survival against all odds. His experience is not just a story of physical endurance, but also a profound exploration of the human spirit's capacity to confront fear, despair, and the will to live.

The Background: Who Is Mauro Prosperi?

Mauro Prosperi was born in 1955 in Rome, Italy. By the time of his fateful race in 1994, Prosperi was a seasoned endurance athlete and an accomplished policeman. His background as a pentathlete—competing in events that require both physical stamina and mental toughness—made him particularly well-suited for extreme challenges. The Marathon des Sables, often touted as the world's most difficult foot race, was an event that attracted only the most daring and physically fit athletes. It is a six-day, 250-kilometer (155-mile) race across the Sahara Desert, where participants must carry their own supplies and face the relentless heat, sandstorms, and treacherous terrain.

Prosperi entered the Marathon des Sables in 1994 with confidence, having prepared meticulously for the race. He had trained extensively, ensuring he was in peak physical condition, and had carefully planned his nutrition and hydration strategies. However, no amount of preparation could have prepared him for the ordeal that awaited him in the desert—a series of events that would push him beyond the limits of human endurance.

The Marathon des Sables: The Beginning of the Ordeal

The Marathon des Sables began as planned, with Prosperi among the 00 competitors who set out to conquer the grueling course. The first few days of the race went relatively smoothly for Prosperi. He managed the intense heat, averaging 50 degrees Celsius (122 degrees Fahrenheit) during the day, and navigated the challenging terrain with skill. The competitors were guided by race organizers and provided with checkpoints to replenish their water supplies and rest. However, the Sahara is a place of unpredictability, and the desert's true dangers soon made themselves known.

On the fourth day of the race, disaster struck. A violent sandstorm suddenly descended upon the racers, engulfing the desert in a blinding whirlwind of sand and wind. The storm was so severe that it obscured visibility and forced the race organizers to halt the event temporarily. For the participants, the storm was a terrifying experience; they could barely see their hands in front of their faces, and the howling winds drowned out all other sounds. It was during this sandstorm that Mauro Prosperi became separated from the rest of the group—a critical moment that marked the beginning of his incredible ordeal.

Lost in the Sahara: The Realization of Isolation

When the sandstorm finally subsided, Prosperi found himself alone in the vast expanse of the desert, disoriented and with no clear sense of direction. His compass was useless, and the landscape around him offered no landmarks to guide him. The desert stretched out in all directions, a seemingly endless sea of sand and rocky outcrops, with no sign of civilization or even the other racers.

Initially, Prosperi attempted to backtrack to the last checkpoint, but the shifting sands had erased any traces of the race route. Realizing that he was hopelessly lost, Prosperi made the fateful decision to continue moving, hoping to stumble upon a village or an oasis. He knew that staying in one place was not an option; in the Sahara, immobility could mean death by dehydration or heatstroke. His training as an athlete kicked in, and he focused on maintaining his stamina, rationing his water, and conserving his energy.

However, the reality of his situation soon set in. The Sahara Desert is one of the harshest environments on Earth, with extreme temperatures that can fluctuate drastically between day and night, minimal vegetation, and scarce water sources. Prosperi's supplies—intended to last only for the duration of the race—were quickly running out. He had only a small amount of food, a limited supply of water, and minimal equipment. As the days passed, the enormity of his predicament became increasingly clear: he was alone in the desert, with no means of communication and no way of knowing if or when he would be rescued.

The Struggle for Survival: Ingenious and Desperate Measures

As the days dragged on, Prosperi's situation became increasingly dire. The harsh desert conditions began to take a toll on his body and mind. He suffered from severe dehydration, his lips cracked, and his tongue swelled in his mouth. The relentless sun burned his skin, and the lack of food left him weak and disoriented. But despite these challenges, Prosperi's survival instincts kicked in, and he began to employ a series of ingenious and desperate measures to stay alive.

One of the first survival strategies Prosperi employed was to ration his remaining water meticulously. He knew that dehydration was his greatest enemy, and he took small, measured sips of water, trying to make it last as long as possible. When his water supply eventually ran out, Prosperi resorted to extreme measures: he began drinking his urine. While the thought of doing so is repulsive to most, in survival situations, urine can provide some hydration and help stave off dehydration, although it is not a long-term solution.

In addition to his water problems, Prosperi also faced the challenge of finding food in the barren desert. He was forced to eat anything he could find, including insects, snakes, and even small birds that he managed to catch. On one occasion, Prosperi stumbled upon a bat, which he caught and consumed raw, desperate for any source of protein. These unconventional meals provided him with some energy, but they were far from sufficient to sustain him over the long term.

As the days wore on, Prosperi's body began to break down. He lost a significant amount of weight, his muscles atrophied, and he became increasingly weak. The intense heat during the day and the freezing temperatures at night added to his physical suffering. But perhaps the greatest challenge he faced was the psychological toll of his isolation. The Sahara is a place of profound silence, and the lack of human contact began to weigh heavily on Prosperi's mind. He was plagued by feelings of loneliness, fear, and despair, and he struggled to maintain his sanity in the face of overwhelming odds.

The Abandoned Shrine: A Beacon of Hope

After several days of wandering through the desert, Prosperi stumbled upon what seemed like a mirage—a small, abandoned Muslim shrine known as a marabout. The shrine, a simple stone structure, was a relic of a bygone era, used by travelers as a place of worship and rest. For Prosperi, finding the shrine was a turning point in his ordeal. It offered him shelter from the blistering sun during the day and the cold at night, and it became a focal point for his efforts to survive.

Inside the shrine, Prosperi found a few relics left behind by previous visitors, including a small well. However, the well was dry, offering no immediate respite from his dire water situation. Undeterred, Prosperi continued to search the surrounding area for any sign of water, digging in the sand and exploring nearby crevices. His efforts were in vain, and the realization that the well was dry was a crushing blow to his morale.

Despite the setback, the shrine became a place where Prosperi could rest and regroup. He used his time there to gather his strength and plan his next move. Knowing that he could not stay at the shrine indefinitely, Prosperi began to prepare for the possibility of leaving and continuing his search for civilization. However, his physical condition was rapidly deteriorating, and he knew that he was running out of time.

The Darkest Moment: Contemplating Suicide

As the days passed and Prosperi's situation became increasingly desperate, he reached what he later described as the darkest moment of his ordeal. Faced with the overwhelming likelihood of dying alone in the desert, Prosperi began to contemplate suicide. He reasoned that it would be better to end his suffering on his own terms rather than succumb to the slow, agonizing death that seemed inevitable.

Prosperi's thoughts turned to his family—his wife and children—whom he feared he would never see again. The despair and hopelessness he felt in those moments were almost overwhelming. He considered using the knife he had brought with him to slit his wrists, hoping that his body would be found and that his family would at least have closure.

But even in this moment of despair, Prosperi's will to live proved stronger than his desire to end his suffering. He made a small cut on his wrist but quickly realized that he could not go through with it. The survival instinct that had kept him alive thus far prevailed, and Prosperi resolved to keep fighting, no matter how bleak his situation seemed. This decision marked a turning point in his ordeal—his determination to survive was rekindled, and he found the strength to carry on.

The Rescue: A Miraculous End to the Ordeal

On the tenth day of his ordeal, Prosperi's fortunes finally changed. Weak, emaciated, and barely able to move, he stumbled upon a group of Tuareg nomads, a desert-dwelling people known for their deep knowledge of the Sahara and their ability to survive in its harsh conditions. The Tuaregs were astonished to find a man in such a dire state wandering alone in the desert, and they immediately took him in.

The Tuaregs provided Prosperi with water, food, and shelter, nursing him back from the brink of death. They recognized the severity of his condition and understood that he needed more help than they could provide in their remote location. After stabilizing him, they transported Prosperi to a nearby Algerian military camp, where he received medical attention. The soldiers were amazed that he had survived so long in the desert under such extreme conditions.

From the military camp, Prosperi was eventually taken to a hospital, where he began the slow process of recovery. He was severely dehydrated, malnourished, and had lost over 40 pounds (about 18 kilograms) during his ordeal. His kidneys were damaged, and he was suffering from severe physical and psychological exhaustion. Despite the trauma he had endured, Prosperi's body and spirit proved resilient, and he gradually regained his strength.

News of Mauro Prosperi's incredible survival spread quickly, and he became an international sensation. His story captivated people around the world, not just because of the physical feats he accomplished, but because of the mental toughness and indomitable willpower he displayed. He had survived in one of the harshest environments on Earth, relying on a combination of survival skills, resourcefulness, and sheer determination.

Aftermath: Reflections on Survival

In the years following his ordeal, Mauro Prosperi reflected on the experience and what it had taught him about life, survival, and the human spirit. He spoke openly about the physical and mental challenges he faced, and how close he came to giving up. But he also emphasized the importance of hope, resilience, and the will to survive.

Prosperi's story is a powerful reminder of the incredible strength that lies within each of us, often untapped until we are faced with the most extreme circumstances. His ability to adapt to his environment, make difficult decisions, and keep moving forward despite overwhelming odds is a testament to the human capacity for endurance.

After his recovery, Prosperi returned to his normal life, but he was forever changed by his experience in the Sahara. He continued to participate in endurance events, but with a new perspective on life and survival. He also shared his story with others, hoping to inspire people to face their own challenges with the same determination and courage that had seen him through his darkest days.

Legacy: An Enduring Tale of Survival

Mauro Prosperi's survival story remains one of the most remarkable in modern history. It is not just a tale of physical endurance, but also a profound exploration of the human spirit's capacity to confront fear, despair, and the will to live. His journey through the Sahara Desert is a testament to the power of the mind and body to endure even the most extreme conditions.

Prosperi's ordeal has been recounted in numerous documentaries, books, and interviews, ensuring that his story continues to inspire new generations. He has been invited to speak at events around the world, where he shares his experiences and the lessons he learned from his time in the desert.

The story of Mauro Prosperi is a reminder that survival is not just about physical strength or skill—it is about the mental fortitude to keep going when all seems lost. It is about the will to live, even when the odds are stacked against you, and the ability to find hope in the most hopeless of situations. His story is a beacon of inspiration, demonstrating that the human spirit is capable of overcoming even the most daunting challenges.

Conclusion: The Triumph of the Human Spirit

Mauro Prosperi's survival in the Sahara Desert is a story of extraordinary human endurance, a testament to the power of the human spirit to overcome adversity. His journey is a vivid example of how, even in the face of overwhelming odds, the will to survive can carry us through the most harrowing of trials. Prosperi's tale is not just about surviving in the desert; it is about the resilience of the human mind and body, the importance of hope, and the unbreakable will to live.

His experience in the Sahara has left an indelible mark on the world, reminding us all of the incredible strength we possess within ourselves. It is a story that continues to resonate, inspiring people to face their own challenges with courage and determination. Mauro

Prosperi's survival is a timeless example of the triumph of the human spirit, a story that will be remembered and revered for generations to come.

23

Chapter 4: The Survival of Rick Allen

The story of Rick Allen's survival is one of the most remarkable tales of perseverance, resilience, and triumph in the face of overwhelming adversity. Rick Allen, the drummer for the iconic British rock band Def Leppard, not only survived a life-altering accident but also managed to defy all odds by continuing his music career despite losing his left arm. His journey is a testament to the strength of the human spirit and the power of determination in overcoming the most daunting challenges.

The Accident: A Life Shattered in Seconds

Rick Allen's life changed forever on December 31, 1984. At just 21 years old, Allen was enjoying the success of Def Leppard, a band that was quickly rising to fame in the rock music scene. The band had recently released their third album, "Pyromania," which had catapulted them into international stardom. On that fateful New Year's Eve, Rick Allen and his girlfriend at the time, Miriam Barendsen, were driving in his Corvette Stingray to a New Year's Eve party in Sheffield, England.

As they were driving along a winding road, another car attempted to pass them at high speed. Allen, who was driving, lost control of his vehicle as he tried to let the other car pass. The car skidded off the road and flipped several times before crashing into a field. The force of the crash was so severe that Allen was thrown from the car because he was not wearing his seatbelt. His left arm got caught in the seatbelt, and the force of the ejection severed the limb from his body.

Allen was rushed to a nearby hospital, where doctors fought to save his life and his arm. Initially, they managed to reattach the limb, but it soon became apparent that the damage was too severe, and the arm had to be amputated. For a young man whose life revolved around drumming, the loss of his arm was not just a physical blow but a psychological one as well. The future of his career, his passion, and his identity as a musician seemed to have been taken away in an instant.

The Aftermath: A Journey Through Darkness

The period following the accident was incredibly difficult for Rick Allen. The physical pain was intense, but the emotional and psychological toll was even greater. Allen faced a devastating reality—he was a one-armed drummer in a world where drumming was synonymous with having two fully functioning arms. The thought of never being able to play the drums again was unbearable.

Depression, anger, and frustration consumed Allen as he grappled with his new reality. He had to come to terms with the loss of his arm and the impact it would have on his life and career. The future seemed bleak, and for a time, Allen considered giving up on drumming altogether. The prospect of returning to Def Leppard, a band that was at the peak of its success, seemed impossible. How could he, with only one arm, continue to be the drummer for one of the biggest rock bands in the world?

During this dark period, Allen was supported by his bandmates, family, and friends, who encouraged him to keep fighting. They refused to let him give up on his passion for music and drumming. Their support, combined with his own inner strength, gradually helped Allen to emerge from the depths of despair. Instead of surrendering to his circumstances, Allen began to search for ways to overcome his physical limitations and continue doing what he loved most—playing the drums.

The Comeback: Redefining the Art of Drumming

Rick Allen's determination to return to drumming led him on a remarkable journey of innovation and adaptation. With the help of his bandmates and a team of engineers, Allen began to explore the possibility of drumming with one arm. The key to his comeback lay in the development of a custom-designed electronic drum kit that would allow him to play with his feet as well as his right arm.

The electronic drum kit was a revolutionary piece of equipment. It featured a series of foot pedals that could trigger different drum sounds, essentially allowing Allen to play the parts that he would normally play with his left arm using his feet instead. The kit was designed to be highly sensitive, responding to even the slightest touch, which enabled Allen to perform complex drumming patterns despite his physical limitations.

Learning to play with this new setup was no easy task. It required an entirely new approach to drumming, and Allen had to retrain his body and mind to adapt to the new techniques. The process was grueling and took months of intense practice and dedication. There were moments of frustration and doubt, but Allen's resolve never wavered. He was determined to prove that he could still be a world-class drummer, despite his disability.

Returning to the Stage: Def Leppard's Triumphant Return

The true test of Rick Allen's comeback came when he rejoined Def Leppard for their live performances. The band was about to embark on the recording of their next album, "Hysteria," and Allen was determined to be part of it. The support of his bandmates was unwavering—they had never considered replacing him, and they were ready to work with him as he adapted to his new drumming style.

In 1986, just two years after his life-altering accident, Rick Allen made his triumphant return to the stage. His first major performance was at the Monsters of Rock festival at Castle Donington in England. It was an emotional moment, not just for Allen but for the thousands of fans who had gathered to see Def Leppard perform. The crowd erupted in cheers and applause as Allen took his place behind the drum kit, a symbol of his incredible resilience and determination.

The performance was a resounding success. Allen's new drumming technique was flawless, and the band delivered a powerful set that left no doubt that Def Leppard was back and stronger than ever. For Allen, it was a deeply personal victory—a moment of redemption that proved to the world, and to himself, that he was still capable of greatness.

The Hysteria Album: A Testament to Perseverance

Def Leppard's "Hysteria" album, released in 1987, became one of the most successful albums in rock history. It was a testament to the band's perseverance and Allen's extraordinary comeback. The album featured hit singles like "Pour Some Sugar on Me," "Love Bites," and "Armageddon It," and went on to sell over 20 million copies worldwide.

Rick Allen's drumming on "Hysteria" was nothing short of remarkable. Despite his physical limitations, he delivered a performance that was both powerful and precise, showcasing his incredible adaptability and skill. The album's success was a validation of Allen's hard work and determination to overcome the odds. It solidified his place as one of the greatest drummers in rock history, not just for his technical abilities, but for his indomitable spirit.

Life After the Accident: An Inspiration to Millions

In the years following his accident, Rick Allen has continued to inspire millions of people around the world. His story is not just about surviving a horrific accident, but about thriving in its aftermath. Allen has become a symbol of hope and resilience, showing that it is possible to overcome even the most devastating challenges and emerge stronger on the other side.

Allen has used his platform to raise awareness about disability and to advocate for others who face similar challenges. He founded the Raven Drum Foundation, a nonprofit organization that helps veterans and people in crisis through healing arts programs. The foundation's mission is to empower individuals facing trauma and adversity, offering them the tools and support they need to heal and thrive.

In addition to his work with the Raven Drum Foundation, Allen has also become an accomplished artist. He began painting as a form of therapy after his accident and has since developed a unique style that has garnered international acclaim. His art, much like his music, is a reflection of his journey—a celebration of life, resilience, and the human spirit.

Legacy: The Unbreakable Rick Allen

Rick Allen's survival story is one of the most inspiring in the world of music and beyond. It is a story of a man who refused to let a life-changing accident define him, who fought against the odds to reclaim his passion and his purpose. Allen's journey from the brink of despair to the heights of rock stardom is a powerful reminder that no obstacle is insurmountable, and that with determination, creativity, and the support of those around us, we can overcome even the most daunting challenges.

Today, Rick Allen continues to perform with Def Leppard, and his drumming remains as powerful as ever. His story is a beacon of hope for anyone facing adversity, a shining example of what it means to be unbreakable. Through his music, his art, and his advocacy, Allen has left an indelible mark on the world, proving that the human spirit is capable of extraordinary things, even in the face of unimaginable hardship.

In the end, Rick Allen's survival is not just about the physical act of surviving a tragic accident—it is about the triumph of the human spirit over adversity, the power of resilience, and the unyielding belief that anything is possible. His story will continue to inspire generations to come, reminding us all that no matter what challenges we face, we have the strength within us to overcome them and achieve greatness.

Chapter 5: Aron Ralston's Survival

Aron Ralston's survival story is one of the most extraordinary tales of human endurance, willpower, and the relentless drive to live against all odds. His harrowing experience in Utah's Blue John Canyon, where he was trapped alone for more than five days, has become a symbol of resilience and the power of the human spirit. Ralston's ordeal, which involved one of the most extreme acts of self-preservation, captivated the world and has since been immortalized in books, documentaries, and the feature film "127 Hours." To fully appreciate the magnitude of his survival, it's essential to delve deeply into the details of his life before the incident, the events that led to his entrapment, his time in the canyon, and the incredible journey that followed.

The Man Behind the Legend: Aron Ralston's Background

Aron Lee Ralston was born on October 27, 1975, in Marion, Ohio. Raised in a family that valued education and achievement, Ralston was an intelligent and ambitious young man. His family moved to Denver, Colorado, when he was 12 years old, and it was here, surrounded by the majestic Rocky Mountains, that his love for the outdoors began to flourish. Ralston was an avid outdoorsman from a young age, developing a passion for hiking, mountain climbing, and all forms of wilderness adventure. His zest for life and love for nature were evident in his pursuits; he was always seeking new challenges and pushing his physical and mental limits.

After graduating from Cherry Creek High School in Colorado, Ralston went on to attend Carnegie Mellon University in Pittsburgh, Pennsylvania, where he earned a degree in mechanical engineering and French. Despite his academic success, the mountains of Colorado continued to call him. After college, he worked briefly as a mechanical engineer at Intel but soon realized that the corporate world was not for him. Ralston decided to leave his job to pursue his true passion—mountaineering.

By the time of his fateful trip to Blue John Canyon, Ralston had already established himself as a skilled and experienced outdoorsman. He had climbed nearly all of Colorado's 59 "fourteeners" (mountains over 14,000 feet) and had a wealth of knowledge about survival techniques and backcountry navigation. However, no amount of experience could have fully prepared him for the ordeal that lay ahead.

The Fateful Trip to Blue John Canyon

On April 26, 2003, Aron Ralston set out alone on what was supposed to be a routine day hike in Utah's Canyonlands National Park. His destination was Blue John Canyon, a remote and narrow slot canyon known for its stunning beauty and challenging terrain. Ralston, who was an experienced solo hiker, did not see any particular danger in his plan to explore the canyon alone. He was confident in his abilities and believed that he was fully prepared for the adventure.

However, Ralston made a critical decision that would later prove to be nearly fatal—he did not inform anyone of his plans. He did not leave a note or tell friends or family where he was going. This meant that when things went terribly wrong, no one knew where to look for him, significantly complicating any potential rescue efforts.

Ralston arrived at Blue John Canyon in the early afternoon and began his descent into the labyrinthine canyon. As he navigated the narrow passageways and drop-offs, he marveled at the natural beauty around him, unaware that his life was about to take a dramatic turn. After a few hours of exploring, Ralston attempted to descend a narrow slot where a large boulder was wedged between the canyon walls. As he carefully lowered himself, disaster struck—the 800-pound boulder shifted, trapping his right arm against the canyon wall.

Trapped: The Fight for Survival Begins

In an instant, Aron Ralston's life was irrevocably changed. The boulder had pinned his right arm, leaving him trapped in a remote section of the canyon with no one aware of his predicament. The realization of his situation dawned on him quickly—he was alone, stuck, and miles from help. Ralston's first instinct was to free himself by any means necessary, but despite his best efforts, the boulder would not budge. He tried using his ropes, his body weight, and every ounce of strength he could muster, but the massive rock was immovable.

Hours turned into days as Ralston remained trapped in the canyon, his arm still pinned beneath the boulder. He rationed the small amount of food and water he had brought with him—a burrito, two burritos, and a small amount of water. However, it quickly became apparent that his supplies would not last long. As the days passed, Ralston's situation grew increasingly dire. The hot desert sun beat down on him during the day, while the cold nights sapped his strength and morale.

During this time, Ralston began to experience intense physical and psychological challenges. Dehydration set in, causing him to become weak and delirious. His trapped arm began to lose circulation, and he realized that he was facing the very real possibility of death. Despite these harrowing circumstances, Ralston remained remarkably calm and focused. He used his engineering background to analyze his situation and consider all possible options for escape.

He attempted to chip away at the boulder with a multi-tool knife but quickly realized that this would take far too long.

Ralston also began to document his experience on his camcorder, recording video messages to his family and friends. In these messages, he expressed his love for them and his acceptance of the possibility that he might not survive. These recordings served as a form of catharsis for Ralston, allowing him to process the gravity of his situation and prepare himself mentally for what might come next.

A Desperate Decision: The Choice to Amputate

As the days wore on, Ralston's physical condition deteriorated further. He was severely dehydrated, weak, and in excruciating pain. He had exhausted all other options for freeing himself, and it became clear that there was only one way out—he would have to amputate his own arm. The decision was not made lightly. Ralston spent several days contemplating the idea, knowing that it was an extreme and dangerous course of action. However, he also knew that if he did not act soon, he would die in the canyon.

On the morning of May 1, 2003, after five days of being trapped, Ralston made the decision to go through with the amputation. Using the dull blade of his multi-tool, he began to cut through the flesh, muscle, and tendons of his trapped arm. The process was agonizingly slow and painful, but Ralston remained determined. The most difficult part of the procedure was cutting through the bone, which Ralston eventually managed by using the leverage of the boulder to snap the radius and ulna bones in his forearm.

After hours of excruciating effort, Ralston successfully severed his arm and freed himself from the boulder. He immediately applied a makeshift tourniquet to his arm to stop the bleeding and began the long and arduous journey out of the canyon.

The Escape: A Grueling Journey to Safety

Although Aron Ralston had freed himself from the boulder, his ordeal was far from over. Weak, dehydrated, and suffering from significant blood loss, he faced the daunting task of finding his way out of the canyon and reaching help. Ralston knew that he was still miles away from civilization and that his chances of survival depended on his ability to navigate the treacherous terrain and reach safety before his strength gave out.

Ralston's escape from Blue John Canyon is a testament to his incredible resilience and resourcefulness. Despite his weakened state, he managed to rappel down a 65-foot cliff using his one good arm. The descent was dangerous and physically demanding, but Ralston's years of climbing experience paid off. Once on the canyon floor, he began the arduous hike toward his vehicle, which was parked several miles away.

The journey was grueling. Ralston had to navigate through rugged terrain under the scorching desert sun, all while battling extreme dehydration and blood loss. He sipped from a small remaining amount of water and continued to document his progress on his camcorder, determined to survive against all odds. Along the way, he encountered a family of hikers who were exploring the area. The hikers immediately recognized the severity of Ralston's condition and provided him with water and first aid.

The hikers quickly alerted authorities, and a rescue helicopter was dispatched to the scene. Ralston was airlifted to a hospital in Moab, Utah, where he received emergency medical treatment. Despite the severity of his injuries, Ralston's quick thinking and self-amputation had saved his life. Doctors later confirmed that had he not taken the drastic step of amputating his arm, he would have died from dehydration or infection within a matter of hours.

The Aftermath: Recovery and Reflection

Aron Ralston's survival story did not end with his rescue. The physical and emotional recovery process was long and challenging. He underwent multiple surgeries to treat his injuries and faced months of physical therapy to adapt to life with one arm. The psychological toll of the experience was also significant. Ralston had to come to terms with the trauma of his ordeal and the loss of his limb, both of which required immense mental strength.

However, Ralston refused to let his experience define him in a negative way. Instead, he chose to use his story as a source of inspiration and motivation for others. He became a sought-after motivational speaker, sharing his story of survival and resilience with audiences around the world. In 2004, Aron Ralston published a memoir titled *Between a Rock and a Hard Place*, in which he recounted the details of his harrowing ordeal in Blue John Canyon. The book became a bestseller and further solidified Ralston's status as a symbol of perseverance and the human will to survive. His memoir provided readers with an intimate look at the mental and physical challenges he faced during his time trapped in the canyon, as well as the profound insights he gained about life, mortality, and the strength of the human spirit.

Ralston's story also caught the attention of Hollywood, leading to the creation of the critically acclaimed film *127 Hours* in 2010. Directed by Danny Boyle and starring James Franco as Ralston, the film vividly depicted the events of those fateful days in the canyon. The film received widespread praise for its gripping portrayal of Ralston's ordeal and Franco's powerful performance, bringing the story to an even wider audience.

Beyond his speaking engagements and the success of his memoir and film adaptation, Ralston continued to pursue his passion for the outdoors. Remarkably, he returned to mountain climbing, skiing, and other outdoor activities despite the loss of his arm. His determination to continue living life to the fullest, even after such a traumatic experience, served as an inspiration to countless individuals facing their own challenges.

Ralston's survival also sparked discussions about the importance of preparedness and safety in outdoor adventures. His experience underscored the critical need for hikers and climbers to inform others of their plans, carry adequate supplies, and be prepared for the unexpected. His story became a cautionary tale that highlighted the potential dangers of solo adventuring, but it also emphasized the incredible resilience and resourcefulness that can emerge in the face of life-threatening situations.

In the years following his ordeal, Ralston became an advocate for wilderness safety and survival training. He shared his knowledge and experience with others, hoping to prevent similar tragedies from occurring. His story has been used in survival courses, educational programs, and safety campaigns, serving as a powerful reminder of the thin line between life and death in the wilderness.

Aron Ralston's survival story is not just about a man who cut off his arm to save his life; it is about the triumph of the human spirit in the direst of circumstances. It is a story of courage, determination, and the unwavering will to live. Ralston's ability to remain calm under extreme pressure, to make the unimaginable decision to amputate his own arm, and to summon the strength to escape the canyon and seek help, speaks to the extraordinary potential within each of us to overcome even the most insurmountable obstacles.

Ralston's experience also offers valuable lessons about the human capacity for adaptation and recovery. His ability to rebuild his life after such a traumatic event, to find new ways to pursue his passions, and to use his experience to inspire and educate others, is a testament to the resilience of the human spirit. His story reminds us that even in the face of overwhelming adversity, we have the power to choose how we respond, to find meaning in our struggles, and to emerge stronger on the other side.

Today, Aron Ralston's name is synonymous with survival and the indomitable will to live. His story continues to resonate with people around the world, serving as a beacon of hope and inspiration for anyone facing their own challenges. Whether on the mountains or in the canyons of life, Ralston's journey teaches us that with courage, determination, and the will to survive, we can overcome even the most daunting of circumstances.

Chapter 6: The Miracle on the Hudson

The Miracle on the Hudson is one of the most extraordinary and well-known aviation survival stories in modern history. On January 15, 2009, US Airways Flight 1549, piloted by Captain Chesley "Sully" Sullenberger and First Officer Jeffrey Skiles, made an emergency water landing on the Hudson River in New York City. All 155 people aboard the Airbus A320 survived, thanks to the remarkable skills and quick thinking of the flight crew, earning the event the moniker "Miracle on the Hudson." This event is celebrated not only as a triumph of human ingenuity and expertise but also as a testament to the importance of rigorous training, teamwork, and the resilience of the human spirit.

The Flight and the Bird Strike

US Airways Flight 1549 was a regularly scheduled domestic passenger flight from LaGuardia Airport in New York City to Charlotte Douglas International Airport in North Carolina. On that cold January day, the flight was carrying 150 passengers and 5 crew members. The aircraft, an Airbus A320-214, was relatively new and in excellent condition, and the weather was clear with good visibility. At 3:25 PM, the plane took off from LaGuardia's Runway 4, with Captain Sullenberger at the controls and First Officer Skiles handling the radio communications and other flight duties.

Just three minutes after takeoff, as the plane climbed to an altitude of about 2,800 feet, disaster struck. The aircraft flew directly into a flock of Canada geese, a situation that poses a significant risk to airplanes, especially during the critical phases of takeoff and landing. The birds collided with the aircraft at high speed, causing both engines to fail almost simultaneously. The sound of the engines sputtering and shutting down was accompanied by a smell of burning, and passengers later described hearing a loud bang and feeling a sudden loss of power.

With both engines completely disabled, the aircraft lost thrust, leaving Captain Sullenberger and First Officer Skiles with mere seconds to assess the situation and make critical decisions. The plane was too low and too slow to glide to a nearby airport, and the densely populated urban area below offered no safe place for an emergency landing.

The Decision to Land on the Hudson River

As the plane began to descend rapidly, Captain Sullenberger took control of the situation. Understanding the gravity of their predicament, he quickly evaluated their options. Returning to LaGuardia or diverting to Teterboro Airport in New Jersey, the two closest airfields, would have required more altitude and distance than they had available. Sullenberger determined that the only viable option was to attempt a water landing on the Hudson River, a decision that would prove to be both daring and unprecedented.

This decision was made within seconds, showcasing the extraordinary composure and decisiveness of Captain Sullenberger. Water landings, especially on rivers, are extremely risky and rarely attempted because of the high potential for the aircraft to break apart or capsize upon impact. However, Sullenberger, with his extensive experience as a pilot and former Air Force fighter pilot, believed that with precise control and the right angle of descent, they might be able to land the plane safely on the river's surface.

The Emergency Water Landing

Captain Sullenberger and First Officer Skiles communicated their intentions to air traffic control, with Sullenberger calmly informing them, "We can't do it... We're gonna be in the Hudson." These words, delivered with remarkable calmness, conveyed the gravity of the situation while also demonstrating the pilot's focus and control.

As the aircraft descended towards the river, the flight crew worked in unison to prepare for the emergency landing. Skiles followed Sullenberger's instructions meticulously, helping to manage the glide and the descent rate while attempting to restart the engines—a futile effort given the extent of the damage. In the passenger cabin, the flight attendants quickly moved to secure the passengers, instructing them to brace for impact in the emergency landing positions.

Sullenberger guided the aircraft with precision, aiming for a part of the river that was relatively clear of obstacles and near several ferry terminals, which would later prove crucial for the rescue efforts. The approach was critical; the nose of the plane needed to be slightly raised to ensure that the aircraft would not flip over upon contact with the water. This maneuver, known as "flaring," was executed perfectly by Sullenberger.

At 3:31 PM, just over three minutes after the bird strike, Flight 1549 made contact with the Hudson River. The plane touched down smoothly, with the tail hitting the water first and the rest of the aircraft following in a controlled descent. The impact was jarring, but the aircraft remained intact, and the fuselage did not rupture—a critical factor that prevented the plane from quickly sinking.

The Immediate Aftermath

After the successful water landing, the plane floated on the Hudson's surface, gradually taking on water but remaining buoyant enough to allow for an orderly evacuation. The water temperature was just above freezing, and the air temperature was around 20°F (-6°C), creating a dire situation for anyone exposed to the elements for too long. The passengers and crew had to evacuate quickly to avoid hypothermia.

Captain Sullenberger and the flight attendants immediately began the evacuation process, instructing passengers to exit onto the wings through the over-wing exits and into the inflatable life rafts. The crew's prior emergency training became invaluable during these moments, as they worked to keep everyone calm and organized. Despite the chaotic situation, there was no panic among the passengers, who later credited the crew's professionalism and the miraculous landing for their composed behavior.

The evacuation was complicated by the fact that the water was rapidly rising inside the fuselage, and some passengers found themselves wading through waist-deep water to reach the exits. The freezing water and the listing of the aircraft added to the challenge, but within minutes, all 155 individuals were out of the plane and either on the wings or in the life rafts.

The Rescue Efforts

Almost immediately after the plane landed, nearby ferries, tugboats, and emergency response vessels began converging on the scene. The proximity of the crash site to Manhattan, one of the busiest areas in the world, played a critical role in the swift response. The New York Waterway ferries were among the first to arrive, with crews springing into action to rescue the passengers from the plane's wings and the frigid water.

The rescuers faced challenging conditions, with ice floating in the river and the constant threat of hypothermia. However, their quick and coordinated efforts ensured that all passengers were rescued within 24 minutes of the crash landing. Many passengers were treated for hypothermia, minor injuries, and shock, but remarkably, there were no fatalities.

Captain Sullenberger was the last to leave the aircraft, walking through the plane twice to ensure that no one was left behind. His actions during the evacuation and his decision to stay aboard until everyone was safe further cemented his status as a hero.

Aftermath and Investigation

The successful emergency landing of Flight 1549 was hailed as a "miracle" by the media, the public, and aviation experts. The event was unprecedented in aviation history; never before had a large commercial jet made an emergency landing on water with all passengers surviving. The National Transportation Safety Board (NTSB) launched an investigation to determine the causes of the accident and to assess the actions taken by the flight crew.

The investigation confirmed that the bird strike had caused both engines to fail and that Captain Sullenberger's decision to land on the Hudson River was the best and only option available. The NTSB praised Sullenberger and Skiles for their exemplary performance under extreme pressure, noting that their actions saved the lives of everyone on board.

The incident also led to changes in aviation safety procedures, particularly in how pilots are trained to handle dual engine failures and other critical emergencies. The success of the landing and evacuation was attributed not only to the skill of the pilots but also to the advancements in aircraft design, which allowed the Airbus A320 to remain afloat long enough for everyone to evacuate.

Legacy and Impact

The Miracle on the Hudson has left a lasting legacy in the fields of aviation, emergency response, and public consciousness. Captain Sullenberger became a national hero, receiving numerous awards and accolades for his actions. He was invited to speak at various events, including President Barack Obama's inauguration, and his story was widely covered in the media.

In 2016, the story was adapted into a major motion picture titled "Sully," directed by Clint Eastwood and starring Tom Hanks as Captain Sullenberger. The film brought the story to an even broader audience, highlighting the intense pressures faced by Sullenberger and the scrutiny that followed the event.

The Miracle on the Hudson also served as a powerful reminder of the importance of preparedness, training, and calmness in the face of disaster. It underscored the need for continuous improvement in aviation safety and the critical role that quick thinking and teamwork play in averting catastrophe.

For the survivors, the event was a life-changing experience. Many have spoken about how the incident gave them a new perspective on life, deepening their appreciation for each day and the importance of resilience. The bond formed between the passengers, crew, and rescuers is a testament to the strength of the human spirit in times of crisis.

Conclusion

The Miracle on the Hudson is a story of hope, heroism, and the triumph of the human spirit. It is a tale of an extraordinary emergency landing that defied the odds, showcasing the best of what people can achieve when faced with seemingly insurmountable challenges. Captain Sullenberger's quick thinking, exceptional piloting skills, and the professionalism of his crew, combined with the rapid response of New York's emergency services, ensured that what could have been a devastating tragedy turned into a miraculous survival story. The legacy of that cold January day in 2009 continues to inspire and remind us of the incredible power of determination, courage, and resilience in the face of adversity.

Chapter 7: The Survival of Robert Falcon Scott's Expedition

The survival story of Robert Falcon Scott's expedition to the South Pole is one of the most harrowing and tragic tales in the history of polar exploration. This ill-fated journey, which took place during the early 20th century, is marked by extraordinary bravery, unimaginable suffering, and ultimately, the demise of Scott and his team. Despite their failure to return from the Antarctic, the expedition left a profound legacy and provided invaluable contributions to scientific knowledge, making their story one of both tragic loss and enduring significance.

Background: The Race to the South Pole

The early 20th century was a period of intense exploration, often referred to as the "Heroic Age of Antarctic Exploration." During this time, nations and explorers vied for the glory of being the first to reach the South Pole, the last unclaimed geographical prize on Earth. Among these explorers was Captain Robert Falcon Scott, a British Royal Navy officer who had already made a name for himself as an Antarctic explorer during the Discovery Expedition (1901–1904). Scott was determined to claim the South Pole for Britain and solidify his place in history.

In 1909, Scott began planning his next Antarctic expedition, known as the Terra Nova Expedition (1910–1913). His primary goal was to be the first to reach the South Pole, but he also aimed to conduct scientific research and gather extensive geological, biological, and meteorological data. Unbeknownst to Scott, the Norwegian explorer Roald Amundsen was also planning an expedition to the South Pole, setting the stage for a dramatic and ultimately tragic race.

The Terra Nova Expedition: Preparation and Journey to Antarctica

Scott's expedition was named after the ship Terra Nova, a former whaling vessel that had been refitted for the journey. The expedition was a massive undertaking, involving a team of 65 men, including scientists, naval officers, and seamen. The expedition was well-funded, with financial support from the British government, private donors, and the public, and was equipped with the latest technology and supplies for polar exploration.

Scott's team departed from Cardiff, Wales, on June 15, 1910, aboard the Terra Nova, and after a stop in New Zealand, they reached the Antarctic coast on January 4, 1911. The expedition established a base camp on Ross Island, at a place they named Cape Evans, where they spent the winter months preparing for their journey to the Pole. During this time, the team conducted scientific research, laid supply depots along the route to the Pole, and acclimated themselves to the harsh Antarctic conditions.

The expedition faced numerous challenges from the outset. The Terra Nova encountered pack ice and severe storms during the voyage, which delayed their arrival in Antarctica. The winter months at Cape Evans were marked by extreme cold, darkness, and isolation, conditions that took a toll on the men both physically and mentally. Additionally, Scott's decision to rely on a combination of motor sledges, ponies, and dogs for transportation proved problematic. The motor sledges broke down early in the journey, and the ponies, ill-suited to the Antarctic climate, struggled in the deep snow and eventually had to be shot.

The Push to the Pole: A Grueling Journey

On November 1, 1911, Scott and his team set out from Cape Evans on their journey to the South Pole. The initial party consisted of 16 men, who took turns hauling heavy sledges loaded with supplies and scientific equipment. The conditions were brutal, with temperatures plummeting to -40 degrees Fahrenheit (-40 degrees Celsius) and fierce winds whipping across the barren landscape. Progress was slow, and the men quickly realized that the journey would be far more difficult than they had anticipated.

As they advanced, Scott began to make critical decisions about the composition of the final polar party. He gradually reduced the number of men as they neared the Pole, sending some back to base camp while others continued onward. On January 3, 1912, Scott selected the final five men who would make the push to the South Pole: himself, Lieutenant Henry "Birdie" Bowers, Dr. Edward Wilson, Captain Lawrence "Titus" Oates, and Petty Officer Edgar Evans. The rest of the team was sent back to Cape Evans.

The final stretch to the South Pole was grueling. The men were exhausted, their supplies were dwindling, and the extreme cold was taking a severe toll on their bodies. On January 17, 1912, after a journey of more than two months, the team finally reached the South Pole, only to be met with devastating news: they were not the first to arrive. Roald Amundsen and his Norwegian team had beaten them to the Pole by 34 days. The Norwegians had left a small tent and a note confirming their victory, which Scott's team found upon their arrival.

The discovery was a crushing blow to Scott and his men. They had endured immense hardships, only to arrive second. In his diary, Scott wrote of the "horrible day" when they reached the Pole and saw Amundsen's flag flying there. The men's morale was shattered, but they still faced the daunting task of returning to base camp, a journey that would prove even more deadly than the trek to the Pole.

The Tragic Return: A Fight for Survival

The return journey from the South Pole began on January 19, 1912, and it quickly became a fight for survival. The men were physically and mentally exhausted, their supplies were running low, and the harsh Antarctic environment offered no respite. As they retraced their steps back towards Cape Evans, they encountered even more severe weather conditions, with blizzards, extreme cold, and treacherous terrain impeding their progress.

The first member of the team to succumb to the elements was Petty Officer Edgar Evans. Evans, who had been suffering from frostbite and a head injury sustained during a fall, began to deteriorate rapidly. He became delirious and struggled to keep up with the rest of the team. Despite the efforts of his comrades to support him, Evans collapsed and died on February 17, 1912, at the foot of the Beardmore Glacier. His death marked the beginning of the end for the expedition.

The remaining four men continued their desperate march northward, but their situation grew increasingly dire. Captain Oates, who was suffering from severe frostbite and gangrene, became a significant concern for the team. His condition worsened to the point where he could barely walk, and he knew that his presence was slowing the group down and diminishing their chances of survival. In a final act of self-sacrifice, Oates famously told his companions, "I am just going outside and may be some time," before walking out of the tent into a blizzard on March 16, 1912. His body was never found.

Now reduced to three men—Scott, Wilson, and Bowers—the team pressed on, but their situation was becoming increasingly hopeless. They were starving, suffering from frostbite and exhaustion, and the weather continued to worsen. In early March, they reached the final supply depot, just 11 miles (18 kilometers) from their planned rendezvous with a relief party. However, they were trapped by a fierce blizzard that raged for days, preventing them from making any further progress.

In his final diary entries, Scott described the desperate conditions they faced. The men were confined to their tent, unable to move due to the blizzard, and their supplies were almost entirely depleted. On March 29, 1912, Scott made his last entry, acknowledging that they were close to death. He wrote of his sorrow for the families they would leave behind and expressed his gratitude for the loyalty and courage of his companions.

The three men died in their tent, succumbing to the cold, hunger, and exhaustion. Their bodies, along with Scott's diaries and other personal effects, were discovered eight months later, in November 1912, by a search party from Cape Evans. The searchers erected a cairn over the tent and marked the site with a cross, paying tribute to the men who had perished in one of the most tragic episodes of Antarctic exploration.

Legacy and Impact: A Story of Tragedy and Heroism

The story of Robert Falcon Scott's expedition is one of the most poignant and enduring tales of human endurance and tragedy. Although Scott and his men failed to return from their journey, their story has been celebrated for its bravery, determination, and the spirit of exploration that drove them to attempt such a perilous endeavor.

Scott's diaries, which were recovered from the tent, provided a detailed account of the expedition's final days and have since become a key historical document. The diaries offer a window into the thoughts and emotions of the men as they faced almost certain death, and they have been widely studied and published, ensuring that their story would not be forgotten.

The scientific achievements of the Terra Nova Expedition should not be overlooked, despite the tragedy that befell the polar party. The expedition collected valuable geological, biological, and meteorological data that contributed to the understanding of the Antarctic environment. The scientific work carried out by the team, particularly by Dr. Edward Wilson, who was both a medical doctor and a naturalist, remains an important part of the legacy of the expedition.

In the years following the tragedy, Scott became a national hero in Britain, and his story was celebrated as an example of British courage and endurance. Memorials were erected in his honor, including a statue in his hometown of Plymouth and a memorial in St. Paul's Cathedral in London. However, as time passed, some historians and scholars began to critically examine the decisions and preparations that led to the disaster, questioning whether the tragedy could have been avoided with better planning and judgment.

The story of Scott's expedition has also inspired countless books, films, and documentaries, ensuring that the tale of the Terra Nova Expedition continues to captivate and move audiences around the world. The tragedy of Scott and his men serves as a reminder of the dangers and uncertainties of exploration, as well as the enduring human spirit that drives individuals to push the boundaries of the known world, even at the cost of their own lives.

Conclusion: A Tragic Chapter in the History of Exploration

The survival story of Robert Falcon Scott's expedition to the South Pole is not one of triumph, but rather of endurance in the face of overwhelming adversity. It is a story of men who ventured into one of the harshest environments on Earth, driven by a desire to explore and to achieve greatness, only to be met with unimaginable suffering and loss. While Scott and his men did not survive their journey, their story continues to resonate as a powerful testament to human courage, determination, and the pursuit of knowledge, even in the most extreme circumstances. The legacy of Scott's expedition endures, not only as a cautionary tale of the perils of exploration but also as a symbol of the enduring spirit of adventure that compels humanity to explore the unknown.

Chapter 8: Alexander Selkirk's Marooning

The story of Alexander Selkirk's marooning is one of the most remarkable tales of survival in the annals of maritime history. Selkirk, a Scottish sailor, was cast away on a remote island in the South Pacific in the early 18th century. His ordeal lasted for more than four years, during which he survived alone on the island, enduring the harsh conditions of isolation, and relying on his resourcefulness and resilience. Selkirk's extraordinary experience not only captivated the imagination of his contemporaries but also inspired one of the most famous novels in English literature, Daniel Defoe's "Robinson Crusoe." The story of Alexander Selkirk is a testament to human endurance, the will to survive, and the capacity to adapt to even the most extreme circumstances.

Background: The Age of Exploration and Piracy

The early 18th century was a period of intense exploration and maritime activity, particularly in the Atlantic and Pacific Oceans. European powers were vying for control of trade routes, colonies, and resources in the New World, leading to frequent conflicts at sea. This era also saw the rise of privateers and pirates, who were often sanctioned by governments to attack and plunder the ships of rival nations. Alexander Selkirk was born into this world of seafaring adventure and danger.

Selkirk was born in 1676 in Lower Largo, a small fishing village in Fife, Scotland. As a young man, he was known for his rebellious nature and adventurous spirit, which eventually led him to a life at sea. By the early 1700s, Selkirk had joined a crew of privateers, essentially state-sanctioned pirates, who were authorized by the

British government to attack and loot Spanish ships and settlements in the Americas.

In 1703, Selkirk signed on as the sailing master of the *Cinque Ports*, a privateering ship under the command of Captain Thomas Stradling. The *Cinque Ports* was part of an expedition led by the notorious privateer William Dampier, who was already famous for his circumnavigations and exploits in the Pacific. The goal of the expedition was to capture Spanish ships and treasures along the west coast of South America, a region rich in silver and gold.

The Marooning: Selkirk's Decision to Stay Behind

The *Cinque Ports* set sail from England in 1703, and after several months of dangerous and grueling voyages, the ship arrived off the coast of South America. The conditions aboard the *Cinque Ports* were harsh, with the crew enduring overcrowding, limited supplies, and the constant threat of disease. The ship itself was in poor condition, with leaks and a deteriorating hull that made it increasingly unseaworthy.

By 1704, tensions between Captain Stradling and his crew had reached a breaking point. Selkirk, who had become increasingly concerned about the seaworthiness of the *Cinque Ports*, argued with Stradling, urging him to repair the ship or abandon it altogether. Selkirk was convinced that continuing the voyage in such a decrepit vessel would lead to disaster. However, Stradling refused to listen to Selkirk's warnings, and the situation quickly escalated.

In a dramatic and fateful decision, Selkirk announced that he would rather be left on an uninhabited island than continue aboard the *Cinque Ports*. He believed that his chances of survival on land were better than on the sinking ship. Captain Stradling, eager to rid himself of the troublesome sailor, agreed to Selkirk's request. On

September 2, 1704, Selkirk was marooned on the uninhabited island of Más a Tierra, part of the Juan Fernández Archipelago, located some 400 miles off the coast of Chile.

Selkirk was left on the island with only a few basic supplies: a musket, a knife, a cooking pot, a Bible, some clothing, bedding, tobacco, and a small amount of food. As the *Cinque Ports* sailed away, Selkirk was suddenly alone, abandoned on a remote and inhospitable island with no clear hope of rescue. The reality of his situation quickly set in—he was completely isolated, with only his wits and survival skills to sustain him.

Survival on the Island: Adapting to Isolation

Selkirk's initial days on the island were filled with despair and regret. The realization that he was utterly alone, with no way to communicate with the outside world, was overwhelming. The island, though lush and green, was wild and untamed, with dense forests, steep cliffs, and rugged terrain. Selkirk had to quickly adapt to his new environment if he was to survive.

One of Selkirk's first challenges was finding food. Fortunately, the island was home to a variety of animals and plants that provided sustenance. Wild goats, which had been introduced to the island by earlier sailors, roamed freely, and Selkirk soon became adept at hunting them. He used his musket to kill goats, providing him with meat, which he cooked using the fire he made with flint. He also utilized the goats for their milk, skins, and horns, which he used to make clothing and tools.

In addition to goats, Selkirk foraged for other food sources. The island's forests were abundant with wild fruits, such as plums, pomegranates, and berries. He also gathered edible plants and roots, supplementing his diet with whatever he could find. Over time,

Selkirk learned to fish in the island's streams and along the coast, using handmade lines and hooks.

Water was another critical concern, but Selkirk was fortunate to find fresh water streams on the island. He constructed simple containers to collect and store water, ensuring he had a steady supply. Shelter was also a priority, and Selkirk initially used caves and natural rock formations to protect himself from the elements. However, as he became more familiar with the island, he built a more permanent shelter using wood, leaves, and other materials he found.

Isolation was perhaps the greatest challenge Selkirk faced. The lack of human contact weighed heavily on him, and he struggled with loneliness and fear. However, he found solace in his faith, regularly reading the Bible, which became a source of comfort and strength. Selkirk also maintained his physical and mental well-being by establishing a daily routine. He hunted, foraged, maintained his shelter, and took care of his clothing and tools. This routine not only helped him survive but also kept him focused and mentally resilient.

As time passed, Selkirk became increasingly self-sufficient and resourceful. He repaired his clothing using goat skins and learned to make new garments. He fashioned tools and weapons from wood, bone, and stone, improving his ability to hunt and fish. He even managed to domesticate some of the wild goats, using them as a steady source of milk and meat.

Selkirk's isolation also forced him to confront his own thoughts and emotions. With no one to talk to, he spent long hours reflecting on his life, his decisions, and his future. The solitude allowed him to develop a deep sense of self-awareness and introspection. Despite the harshness of his environment, Selkirk gradually found a sense of peace and acceptance in his situation.

Rescue and Return to Civilization

After more than four years of living in isolation, Selkirk's ordeal finally came to an end. In February 1709, a British privateering ship, the *Duke*, commanded by Captain Woodes Rogers, arrived at the Juan Fernández Islands. The *Duke* was part of a privateering expedition, and its crew was astonished to discover a lone man living on the island.

When the sailors first encountered Selkirk, they were shocked by his appearance. He was dressed in goatskins, his hair and beard were long and unkempt, and he had become somewhat wild in his mannerisms. However, once Selkirk began speaking, it became clear that he was not a madman but rather a castaway who had survived against all odds. Selkirk was overjoyed to see the sailors and eagerly shared his story with them.

Captain Rogers was impressed by Selkirk's resilience and resourcefulness. Recognizing the value of having such a skilled and experienced sailor on board, Rogers invited Selkirk to join the crew of the *Duke*. Selkirk accepted the offer, and he was soon back aboard a ship, heading toward the familiar world of civilization. His return to society was a significant adjustment, as he had to relearn social norms and reintegrate into the company of others after years of solitude.

Selkirk's story quickly spread among the crew and later reached England, where it became a sensation. His remarkable survival tale was celebrated as an example of human endurance and the triumph of the human spirit over adversity. Upon his return to England, Selkirk became something of a celebrity, with people eager to hear firsthand accounts of his time on the island.

Legacy and Inspiration: The Story of "Robinson Crusoe"

The story of Alexander Selkirk's marooning had a profound impact on popular culture, most notably inspiring Daniel Defoe's novel "Robinson Crusoe," published in 1719. Defoe's novel, which tells the fictional story of a man stranded on a deserted island for 28 years, is widely regarded as one of the first English novels and remains a classic of world literature.

While "Robinson Crusoe" is a work of fiction, Defoe drew heavily on Selkirk's real-life experiences. The novel explores themes of survival, self-reliance, and the human ability to adapt to and overcome extreme circumstances, all of which were central to Selkirk's story. Defoe's depiction of Crusoe's ingenuity, his struggle against loneliness, and his eventual mastery of his environment mirrors many aspects of Selkirk's own life on the island.

However, "Robinson Crusoe" also diverges from Selkirk's story in significant ways. While Crusoe's time on the island is marked by encounters with indigenous people and other castaways, Selkirk's experience was one of complete isolation, with no contact with other humans for over four years. Despite these differences, the novel captured the imagination of readers and solidified the image of the castaway as a symbol of human resilience and survival.

Alexander Selkirk's legacy extends beyond literature. His story has been retold in numerous books, articles, and documentaries, and his name has become synonymous with survival against the odds. The island where he was marooned was eventually renamed Robinson Crusoe Island in his honor, a testament to the enduring impact of his story.

Conclusion: A Testament to Human Endurance

The story of Alexander Selkirk's marooning is a powerful reminder of the human capacity for endurance, adaptability, and survival.

Faced with seemingly insurmountable odds, Selkirk not only survived but thrived in one of the most isolated and challenging environments on Earth. His ability to adapt to his circumstances, maintain his physical and mental well-being, and find meaning in his solitude is a testament to the strength of the human spirit.

Selkirk's experience also highlights the unpredictable and often dangerous nature of maritime exploration during the Age of Sail. The decision to maroon him on a remote island could easily have led to his death, yet it ultimately resulted in one of the most remarkable survival stories in history. His tale serves as both a cautionary example of the risks of exploration and an inspiring account of human resilience.

Today, Alexander Selkirk's story continues to resonate as a symbol of survival and self-reliance. His legacy lives on in literature, history, and the enduring fascination with tales of castaways and marooned sailors. The story of Selkirk's marooning on the island of Más a Tierra is not just a tale of survival—it is a celebration of the indomitable human spirit that drives individuals to persevere, no matter the odds.

Chapter 9: The Chilean Miners

The story of the Chilean miners is one of the most harrowing and inspiring survival tales of modern times. It revolves around the dramatic rescue of 33 miners who were trapped deep underground for 69 days in the San José copper-gold mine in Chile's Atacama Desert. This event captured global attention, drawing in millions who anxiously watched and waited for news of the miners' fate. The ordeal began on August 5, 2010, and culminated in their successful rescue on October 13, 2010. The miners' remarkable story is a testament to human endurance, the power of hope, and the extraordinary efforts of rescuers, engineers, and experts from around the world.

Background: The San José Mine and Its Conditions

The San José mine, located near the town of Copiapó in northern Chile, has a long history dating back to the 19th century. The mine was primarily known for its copper and gold deposits and was one of many such mines in the region. However, it was also notorious for its challenging and often dangerous working conditions. The mine's steep and narrow tunnels, along with its aging infrastructure, made it a hazardous place for workers.

In the years leading up to the 2010 disaster, there had been several incidents at the San José mine that raised concerns about its safety. Workers had reported frequent collapses, unstable rock formations, and inadequate safety measures. Despite these warnings, the mine continued to operate, driven by the demand for its valuable minerals. The miners, many of whom came from poor backgrounds, relied on the mine for their livelihoods, despite the known risks.

The Collapse: A Sudden Catastrophe

On August 5, 2010, the miners at the San José mine were going about their usual work deep within the mine, approximately 700 meters (2,300 feet) below the surface. Suddenly, without warning, a massive section of the mine's rock ceiling gave way, causing a catastrophic collapse. The collapse blocked the main access tunnel, trapping 33 miners inside. The debris, consisting of thousands of tons of rock, created an impenetrable barrier between the miners and the surface, cutting off their escape route.

The collapse sent shockwaves through the mine and the surrounding community. Initial attempts by the miners to contact the surface through their radio system failed, as the collapse had damaged the communication lines. Panic quickly set in among the trapped miners as they realized the gravity of their situation. They were entombed in a hot, humid, and dark space, with limited supplies and no immediate way to signal for help.

Initial Reactions: Despair and Determination

In the immediate aftermath of the collapse, the miners faced a grim reality. They were trapped in a small refuge chamber, designed as a temporary safe haven in case of emergencies. However, this refuge was not intended for long-term survival. It had limited oxygen, food, and water, and the conditions inside were dire. The temperature in the mine exceeded 30 degrees Celsius (86 degrees Fahrenheit), and the humidity levels were stifling.

The miners knew that their chances of survival depended on their ability to remain calm and work together. Under the leadership of Luis Urzúa, the shift foreman, the group quickly organized themselves. They rationed their limited food supplies, which consisted of a few cans of tuna, biscuits, and small amounts of water. Each miner was given just a spoonful of tuna and a small sip of water each day in a desperate attempt to stretch their provisions.

Despite their dire circumstances, the miners did not give up hope. They knew that the surface crews would be working to rescue them, but they also understood that it would be a monumental task. The rock collapse had created a barrier that was nearly impossible to penetrate, and the mine's unstable conditions made rescue operations extremely dangerous. The miners also faced the psychological challenge of coping with the uncertainty of their fate, as days turned into weeks with no sign of rescue.

The Rescue Efforts: A Global Response

As news of the collapse spread, it quickly became a major international story. The Chilean government, led by President Sebastián Piñera, took immediate action, launching a massive rescue operation. The collapse of the San José mine became a national emergency, and the entire country rallied behind the effort to save the trapped miners.

The initial days of the rescue operation were filled with uncertainty and challenges. The rescue teams faced the daunting task of locating the exact position of the miners, who were trapped deep within the mine's complex network of tunnels. The rescuers used drilling equipment to bore small holes into the mine, hoping to make contact with the miners and determine their condition.

The breakthrough came on August 22, 17 days after the collapse, when one of the drilling probes reached the refuge chamber. Attached to the probe was a note written by the miners that read, "Estamos bien en el refugio, los 33" ("We are well in the refuge, the 33 of us"). This message sent waves of relief and jubilation across Chile and around the world. The miners were alive, but the challenge of bringing them to the surface was far from over.

Life Underground: Coping with the Unimaginable

With the knowledge that the miners were alive, the focus of the rescue operation shifted to keeping them alive and planning for their eventual extraction. Through the small borehole, rescuers were able to send down food, water, medical supplies, and letters from the miners' families. This lifeline became the miners' only connection to the outside world.

The miners' resilience was remarkable. They established a daily routine to maintain their physical and mental health. They exercised to keep their bodies strong, held prayer sessions to boost their spirits, and supported each other through the darkest moments. Psychologists on the surface provided guidance on how to manage the stress and anxiety of their prolonged entrapment.

The physical conditions in the mine remained challenging. The air was thick with dust and moisture, and the heat was oppressive. Despite these hardships, the miners displayed extraordinary courage and solidarity. They celebrated small victories, such as receiving fresh clothes or messages from their loved ones, and they remained focused on the hope of rescue.

The Plan for Rescue: Engineering a Miracle

While the miners coped with life underground, the rescue teams above were working around the clock to devise a plan to bring them to the surface. The challenge was immense. The miners were trapped nearly half a mile underground, and the surrounding rock was unstable and prone to further collapses.

The rescue plan that eventually emerged was known as "Plan B," which involved drilling a rescue shaft large enough to accommodate a specially designed capsule that could lift the miners to the surface one by one. This plan required precision drilling, as the shaft had to be perfectly aligned with the refuge chamber where the miners were located. Any mistake could have catastrophic consequences.

The drilling process was fraught with difficulties. The rescuers encountered hard rock formations that slowed progress, and there were constant concerns about the stability of the mine. Despite these challenges, the drilling teams, composed of experts from around the world, persevered. They worked tirelessly, knowing that the lives of 33 men depended on their success.

Finally, on October 9, 2010, after more than two months of intense effort, the rescue shaft was completed. The next step was to lower the specially designed capsule, named "Fénix" (Phoenix), into the mine. The capsule was equipped with oxygen, communication devices, and a harness system to safely transport each miner to the surface.

The Rescue: A Global Celebration

The rescue operation began on October 12, 2010, amid a global outpouring of support and anticipation. The eyes of the world were on the San José mine as the first miner, Florencio Ávalos, was brought to the surface in the Fénix capsule. The moment he emerged from the mine, after 69 days underground, was met with cheers, tears, and celebrations around the world. It was a powerful symbol of human endurance and the triumph of the human spirit.

One by one, the miners were brought to the surface in the Fénix capsule. Each rescue took about 15 minutes, and the process continued throughout the night and into the next day. The operation was meticulously coordinated, with medical teams standing by to assess the miners' health and provide immediate care.

The final miner to be rescued was Luis Urzúa, the shift foreman who had played a crucial role in keeping the group together during their ordeal. As he emerged from the mine, the entire rescue operation came to a triumphant conclusion. All 33 miners had been saved, and not a single life was lost.

Aftermath: The Legacy of the Chilean Miners

The successful rescue of the Chilean miners was a moment of immense pride for Chile and a source of inspiration for people around the world. The miners became national heroes, and their story was celebrated as a triumph of human resilience, teamwork, and the power of hope. The rescue operation itself was hailed as a remarkable achievement, demonstrating the capabilities of modern engineering and the effectiveness of international cooperation.

In the months and years that followed, the miners' story continued to resonate. Several of the miners wrote books, gave interviews, and traveled the world to share their experiences. Their ordeal highlighted the dangers faced by miners and the need for improved safety standards in the industry. It also sparked discussions about the psychological and emotional challenges of long-term survival in extreme conditions.

For the miners themselves, life after the rescue was a mix of challenges and opportunities. While they were celebrated as heroes, many struggled with the psychological aftermath of their ordeal. Some faced difficulties adjusting to normal life, grappling with post-traumatic stress disorder (PTSD) and other mental health issues. Others used their newfound fame to advocate for better working conditions for miners and to raise awareness about the importance of mental health support for survivors of traumatic events.

Conclusion: A Story of Hope and Human Spirit

The story of the Chilean miners is one of the most compelling survival tales of the 21st century. It is a story of human endurance, the power of hope, and the extraordinary efforts of rescuers and experts who refused to give up in the face of overwhelming odds. The miners' survival was not just a physical achievement but also a testament to the strength of the human spirit in the darkest of times.

Their story continues to inspire people around the world, reminding us that even in the most desperate circumstances, hope and perseverance can lead to miraculous outcomes. The legacy of the Chilean miners lives on as a powerful example of what can be achieved when people come together with determination, compassion, and unwavering resolve.

Chapter 10: Yossi Ghinsberg's Lost in the Amazon

Yossi Ghinsberg's ordeal in the Amazon rainforest is one of the most harrowing survival stories ever told. It is a tale of incredible endurance, resourcefulness, and the sheer will to survive against overwhelming odds. Ghinsberg's story, which took place in the early 1980s, has captivated audiences worldwide and was later chronicled in his memoir *Jungle*, which was also adapted into a feature film. His experience highlights the dangers of venturing into uncharted territories, the unpredictability of nature, and the profound resilience of the human spirit.

Background: The Journey into the Unknown

Yossi Ghinsberg was a young Israeli adventurer who, like many others, sought to explore the unknown and experience the thrill of the wild. In 1981, at the age of 22, he set off on what he thought would be the adventure of a lifetime: a trek deep into the Amazon rainforest. He had recently finished his service in the Israeli Navy and was eager to see the world. After traveling through South America, he found himself in La Paz, Bolivia, where he met a few other travelers with similar dreams of exploration.

Ghinsberg was drawn to the idea of exploring a part of the Amazon that was still largely uncharted. His goal was to find a remote indigenous tribe and discover hidden treasures of the forest, such as gold. It was a journey inspired by the tales of explorers and adventurers who had come before him, but it was also fraught with danger.

In La Paz, Ghinsberg met three other travelers: Marcus Stamm, a Swiss teacher; Kevin Gale, an American photographer; and Karl

Ruprechter, an Austrian geologist. Karl claimed to have knowledge of the area and convinced the others to join him on an expedition into the Bolivian Amazon, promising an adventure that would lead them to an indigenous tribe living deep in the jungle, untouched by modern civilization.

The Expedition: Into the Heart of Darkness

The four men set off on their journey, driven by the promise of adventure and discovery. They were excited and optimistic, unaware of the true dangers that awaited them. The plan was to spend a few weeks trekking through the jungle, reaching the indigenous tribe, and then making their way back. However, the Amazon rainforest is one of the most inhospitable environments on Earth, filled with venomous creatures, dense foliage, and treacherous rivers.

As they ventured deeper into the jungle, the reality of the situation began to set in. The group quickly realized that Karl Ruprechter, who had presented himself as an experienced guide, was not as knowledgeable as he had claimed. The terrain was far more challenging than they had anticipated, and the group struggled to find their way through the dense undergrowth and across the fast-flowing rivers.

The physical toll of the journey became evident as the men grew increasingly exhausted. They were plagued by hunger, fatigue, and the constant threat of dangerous wildlife. The rainforest, with its oppressive heat and relentless humidity, began to take its toll on their bodies and minds. The camaraderie that had initially bonded the group started to fray as tensions rose and doubts about Karl's leadership grew.

Marcus, in particular, began to struggle with the harsh conditions. He developed trench foot from the constant exposure to wet conditions, and his physical state deteriorated rapidly. The group was forced to slow their pace, which only increased the strain on their supplies and morale.

The Split: A Fateful Decision

After weeks of arduous travel, the group reached a point where they were forced to make a difficult decision. They were running out of food, and the terrain was becoming increasingly impassable. The jungle was relentless, and the men were physically and mentally exhausted. Karl proposed that they split up into two groups: he would lead Marcus back to civilization via a known route along the river, while Yossi and Kevin would continue their journey downriver on a makeshift raft, hoping to reach a town further downstream.

The decision to split up was a turning point in the expedition. Yossi and Kevin were reluctant to leave Marcus behind, but they ultimately agreed to the plan, believing it was the best chance for everyone to survive. They constructed a simple raft out of logs and set off down the river, while Karl and Marcus began the arduous trek back through the jungle.

The Raft: A Descent into Chaos

Yossi and Kevin's journey down the river was fraught with danger from the very beginning. The river was wild and unpredictable, filled with rapids and submerged rocks that threatened to capsize their fragile raft at any moment. The two men clung to the raft as it was tossed about by the powerful currents, desperately trying to navigate the treacherous waters.

Their journey quickly turned into a nightmare. At one point, the raft struck a rock and began to break apart. Yossi and Kevin were thrown into the river, and in the chaos, they became separated. Yossi managed to grab onto a piece of the raft and was carried further downstream by the current, while Kevin was left behind.

Now alone in the vast and unforgiving jungle, Yossi faced the terrifying reality that he was lost. He had no food, no map, and no idea how to get back to civilization. The dense jungle surrounded him on all sides, and the river, which had seemed like a lifeline, had become a menacing force that had swallowed up his only companion.

Alone in the Jungle: A Struggle for Survival

For the next three weeks, Yossi Ghinsberg endured a hellish ordeal as he struggled to survive in one of the most hostile environments on Earth. The Amazon rainforest, while teeming with life, offered little in the way of sustenance for a lone human. Yossi was forced to rely on his wits and instincts to survive, facing a series of near-death experiences that tested his resolve to the limit.

Without food or shelter, Yossi scavenged for whatever he could find. He attempted to catch fish with his bare hands, dug up roots, and ate whatever edible plants he could identify. But the jungle was not kind to him. He accidentally consumed toxic plants that made him violently ill, and he was constantly under attack by swarms of insects that left his skin covered in painful bites.

Water, which was essential for his survival, was both a blessing and a curse. While he had access to the river, drinking from it was risky due to the presence of parasites and other contaminants. At times, he resorted to drinking rainwater collected in leaves. His body became increasingly weak and emaciated as he struggled to find enough nourishment to sustain himself.

The psychological toll of being alone in the jungle was perhaps even more devastating than the physical challenges. Yossi was haunted by the knowledge that no one knew where he was and that his chances of rescue were slim. He was isolated in a vast and indifferent wilderness, with no way of knowing if he would ever see another human being again.

In the depths of despair, Yossi began to experience vivid hallucinations. He imagined that he was accompanied by a woman who spoke to him, offering him comfort and encouragement. These hallucinations, while disorienting, provided him with a sense of companionship that helped him maintain his sanity in the face of overwhelming loneliness.

Encounters with Danger: The Perils of the Amazon

The Amazon rainforest is home to some of the most dangerous creatures on the planet, and Yossi encountered many of them during his ordeal. He had close calls with venomous snakes, jaguars, and other predators that could easily have ended his life. One particularly terrifying encounter involved a colony of fire ants that attacked him while he was sleeping, covering his body with painful stings.

In another instance, Yossi came face to face with a jaguar while trying to gather food near the riverbank. With no weapon to defend himself, he was forced to rely on his instincts. Remembering a technique he had heard about, he lit a match and waved it in front of the jaguar's face, hoping to scare it away. Miraculously, the tactic worked, and the jaguar retreated into the jungle, leaving Yossi unharmed.

These encounters with the jungle's deadly inhabitants reinforced the precariousness of Yossi's situation. He was a foreigner in an environment that was utterly indifferent to his survival, and he had to rely on his ingenuity and luck to stay alive.

The Turning Point: A Glimmer of Hope

As the days turned into weeks, Yossi's condition deteriorated. He was severely malnourished, dehydrated, and covered in sores from insect bites and exposure to the elements. He had lost a significant amount of weight, and his strength was waning. Yet, despite the dire circumstances, he refused to give up hope.

A turning point came when Yossi stumbled upon a riverbank where he found a small footprint. The sight of the footprint gave him a renewed sense of hope, as it indicated that there were people nearby. He began to follow the river in the hope of finding human habitation or at least signs of rescue.

Yossi's perseverance paid off when, after several more days of agonizing travel, he was discovered by a group of indigenous people from the area. The group, known as the Curipaco tribe, had been hunting along the river when they came across the emaciated and delirious Ghinsberg. They immediately took him in, providing him with food, water, and shelter, and nursed him back to health.

Rescue and Aftermath: A Story of Survival

After being cared for by the Curipaco tribe, Yossi was eventually brought back to civilization. His ordeal had lasted 21 days, during which he had survived alone in one of the most hostile environments on Earth. When he was finally rescued, he was in a dire state, having lost nearly 40 pounds and suffering from severe malnutrition and dehydration.

Yossi's survival was nothing short of miraculous. His ability to endure such extreme conditions was a testament to his mental and physical resilience. After his rescue, he was reunited with Kevin Gale, who had also survived the ordeal after being found by local fishermen. Unfortunately, Marcus Stamm and Karl Ruprechter were never found, and it is believed that they perished in the jungle.

Legacy: A Tale of Endurance and Inspiration

Yossi Ghinsberg's story of survival in the Amazon is a powerful reminder of the strength of the human spirit. His experience in the jungle tested him in ways he could never have imagined, pushing him to the very limits of his endurance. Yet, through it all, he maintained a sense of hope and determination that ultimately saved his life.

After his ordeal, Yossi returned to Israel and later wrote a memoir titled *Jungle*, which detailed his harrowing experience. The book became a bestseller and was later adapted into a feature film starring Daniel Radcliffe as Yossi. His story has inspired countless people around the world, serving as a reminder of the resilience and courage that lie within all of us.

Yossi Ghinsberg went on to become a motivational speaker, sharing his story with audiences around the world. He has dedicated his life to spreading a message of hope, perseverance, and the importance of respecting the natural world. His experience in the Amazon has left an indelible mark on him, shaping his outlook on life and inspiring others to overcome their own challenges, no matter how insurmountable they may seem.

The story of Yossi Ghinsberg's survival in the Amazon is a timeless tale of adventure, endurance, and the unbreakable human spirit. It serves as a powerful reminder that even in the face of the most daunting obstacles, the will to survive can overcome almost anything.

Chapter 11: The Survival of Andi Hatch

Andi Hatch's survival story is a gripping tale of resilience, determination, and the incredible power of human endurance in the face of life-threatening circumstances. While not as widely known as some other survival stories, Hatch's ordeal in the wilderness is a compelling account of how one individual can overcome seemingly insurmountable odds through sheer willpower, resourcefulness, and the will to live.

The Background: A Passion for Adventure

Andi Hatch was a woman with a deep passion for the outdoors and adventure. Born and raised in a small town, she grew up with a love for nature, often spending her free time hiking, camping, and exploring the wilderness. Her affinity for the natural world was more than just a hobby; it was a way of life. As an experienced hiker and camper, Andi was well-versed in outdoor survival skills and was no stranger to the challenges that the wilderness could present.

In the summer of 2005, Andi planned a solo backpacking trip into the rugged mountains of the Pacific Northwest. She had always found solace in the solitude of nature and often sought out the peace and tranquility that could only be found in the remote wilderness. This particular trip was intended to be a week-long retreat, a chance to disconnect from the chaos of everyday life and reconnect with the natural world.

The Journey Begins: Into the Wilderness

Andi set out on her journey with a carefully packed backpack containing all the essentials: food, water, a tent, a sleeping bag, a map, a compass, and other necessary gear. She had meticulously planned her route, choosing a remote trail that would take her deep into the mountains, far from the beaten path. The trail was known for its breathtaking scenery but also for its challenging terrain, with steep climbs, dense forests, and narrow ridges.

The first few days of the trek went smoothly. Andi reveled in the beauty of the wilderness, the fresh mountain air, and the sense of freedom that came with being alone in nature. She followed the trail as planned, taking her time to enjoy the sights and sounds of the forest. The weather was perfect, with clear skies and mild temperatures, making for ideal hiking conditions.

However, as Andi ventured deeper into the mountains, the terrain became increasingly difficult. The trail narrowed, winding through dense thickets and across rocky ridges. The elevation gain was more significant than she had anticipated, and the physical demands of the hike began to take their toll. Despite the challenges, Andi pressed on, confident in her abilities and determined to complete the journey.

The Unexpected: A Turn for the Worse

On the fourth day of her hike, Andi encountered an unexpected and dangerous situation that would change the course of her journey. As she was navigating a particularly steep and rocky section of the trail, she lost her footing and tumbled down a steep embankment. The fall was violent and disorienting, and when she finally came to a stop, she found herself at the bottom of a ravine, injured and disoriented.

The fall had left Andi with a broken leg and several deep gashes on her arms and legs. The pain was excruciating, and she quickly realized that she was in a dire situation. The remote location of the ravine meant that there was little chance of anyone finding her, and she was unable to walk due to her injury. Her supplies, including food and water, were scattered across the ravine, and she knew that she would have to act quickly if she was to survive.

The Struggle for Survival: Alone and Injured

Andi's first priority was to assess her injuries and take stock of her situation. Her leg was badly broken, and she knew that she would need to stabilize it if she had any hope of moving. Using a few sturdy branches and strips of fabric torn from her clothing, she fashioned a makeshift splint to immobilize the leg. The pain was intense, but she knew that she had to push through it if she was to survive.

With her leg splinted, Andi began the painstaking task of gathering her scattered supplies. Crawling on her hands and knees, she managed to recover her backpack, which fortunately contained some food and water. However, she quickly realized that her situation was far more precarious than she had initially thought. The fall had destroyed most of her food supply, and her water had been contaminated with dirt and debris from the ravine. She was now faced with the prospect of surviving in the wilderness with limited resources, a broken leg, and no way to call for help.

Despite the dire circumstances, Andi refused to give in to despair. She knew that her survival depended on her ability to stay calm, think clearly, and make the best use of the resources at her disposal. She rationed her remaining food and water, eating only small amounts to conserve her supplies. She also used her knowledge of the wilderness to identify edible plants and berries, supplementing her diet with whatever she could find in the ravine.

The Psychological Battle: Fighting Despair

One of the most challenging aspects of Andi's ordeal was the psychological toll it took on her. The isolation, the pain, and the uncertainty of her situation all weighed heavily on her mind. As the days turned into weeks, she struggled to maintain hope and keep her spirits up. The constant pain from her injuries, coupled with the fear of never being found, made it difficult to stay positive.

Andi knew that maintaining a strong mental attitude was crucial to her survival. She kept herself busy by setting small goals each day, such as gathering food, purifying water, or finding a more comfortable place to rest. These tasks helped her stay focused and gave her a sense of purpose, even in the face of overwhelming odds.

To combat the loneliness and isolation, Andi would talk to herself and even to the surrounding trees and animals, finding comfort in the sound of her own voice. She also kept a journal, documenting her experiences, thoughts, and feelings. Writing became a way for her to process her emotions and maintain a sense of connection to the outside world.

The Physical Battle: Enduring the Elements

In addition to the psychological challenges, Andi had to contend with the harsh physical realities of surviving in the wilderness. The weather, which had been mild at the start of her journey, began to deteriorate as the days went on. Heavy rainstorms swept through the mountains, turning the ravine into a muddy quagmire. The cold temperatures at night made it difficult to stay warm, especially with her limited mobility and the lack of proper shelter.

To protect herself from the elements, Andi used her tent and sleeping bag, but the wet conditions made it difficult to stay dry. She built a small lean-to using branches and leaves to provide additional shelter from the rain, but it offered little protection from the biting cold at night. Hypothermia became a constant threat, and she knew that she needed to find a way to stay warm if she was to survive.

Fire became Andi's lifeline in the wilderness. Despite her injuries, she managed to gather enough dry wood and kindling to start a fire using her matches. The fire provided much-needed warmth and a sense of security, but it was a constant struggle to keep it going in the damp conditions. Andi would spend hours each day gathering wood and tending to the fire, knowing that it was essential to her survival.

The Search and Rescue: A Glimmer of Hope

As the days turned into weeks, Andi's situation grew increasingly desperate. Her food supplies were dwindling, and her injuries showed no signs of healing. The isolation and the constant pain took a toll on her mental and physical health, and she began to wonder if she would ever be found.

Unbeknownst to Andi, a search and rescue operation had been launched after she failed to return from her trip as scheduled. Her family and friends had raised the alarm when she missed her return date, and a team of rescuers had been dispatched to search the area. However, the remote location of the ravine and the challenging terrain made the search difficult, and weeks passed with no sign of Andi.

As hope began to fade, Andi continued to cling to life, refusing to give up. She knew that if she could survive long enough, there was a chance that someone would find her. Her determination and resilience kept her going, even as her body weakened and the days grew colder.

The Miracle: A Rescue Against the Odds

After more than three weeks alone in the wilderness, Andi Hatch's ordeal finally came to an end when she was spotted by a search helicopter. The rescuers, who had been combing the area for weeks, had nearly given up hope of finding her alive. But Andi's fire, which she had kept burning day and night, was the beacon that led them to her.

The helicopter landed in the ravine, and the rescuers were stunned to find Andi alive, albeit severely injured and emaciated. She was immediately airlifted to a hospital, where she received treatment for her injuries, dehydration, and malnutrition. The doctors were amazed at her resilience and ability to survive in such harsh conditions for so long.

The Aftermath: Recovery and Reflection

Andi's recovery was slow and arduous. Her injuries required extensive medical treatment, and it took months for her to regain her strength. However, the psychological scars of her ordeal were just as deep as the physical ones. She struggled with nightmares, flashbacks, and feelings of anxiety long after she was rescued. The experience had changed her in profound ways, and it took time for her to come to terms with what she had been through.

Despite the trauma, Andi found solace in the fact that she had survived against all odds. Her experience taught her valuable lessons about resilience, the power of the human spirit, and the importance of never giving up, no matter how dire the circumstances. She became an advocate for outdoor safety and survival training, sharing her story with others to help them prepare for the unexpected challenges that can arise in the wilderness.

Legacy: A Story of Endurance and Hope

Andi Hatch's survival story is a testament to the strength of the human spirit and the will to survive. Her ordeal in the wilderness serves as a powerful reminder that, even in the face of overwhelming adversity, it is possible to endure and overcome. Her story has inspired countless people, both for her courage and for the valuable lessons she learned along the way.

In the years following her rescue, Andi has dedicated herself to helping others develop the skills and knowledge needed to survive in the wilderness. She has become a respected voice in the outdoor community, sharing her experiences and advocating for greater awareness of the risks and challenges that come with outdoor adventures. Through her work, she has helped countless others prepare for their own journeys into the wild, ensuring that they have the tools and mindset needed to stay safe and survive.

Andi Hatch's survival story is more than just a tale of endurance; it is a story of hope, resilience, and the unbreakable human spirit. Her experience in the wilderness has left an indelible mark on her, shaping her outlook on life and inspiring others to face their own challenges with courage and determination. Her legacy is one of strength and perseverance, a reminder that, no matter how difficult the journey, it is always possible to find a way through.

Chapter 12: Apollo 11's Return

The return of Apollo 11, the mission that marked the first successful manned landing on the Moon, is a monumental chapter in human history. This event encapsulates the culmination of years of intense planning, innovation, and determination by NASA and the broader scientific community. The safe return of astronauts Neil Armstrong, Edwin "Buzz" Aldrin, and Michael Collins was not merely the final step in a historic journey but a critical and complex operation that required flawless execution under immense pressure. The successful return of Apollo 11 remains a testament to human ingenuity, courage, and the relentless pursuit of knowledge.

Background: The Context of Apollo 11

Apollo 11 was the fifth crewed mission in NASA's Apollo program, launched on July 16, 1969. It was a direct result of the challenge set by President John F. Kennedy in 1961, who declared that the United States should commit to landing a man on the Moon and returning him safely to Earth before the decade's end. This bold goal was driven by the intense Cold War competition with the Soviet Union, which had already achieved significant milestones in space exploration, including the launch of the first artificial satellite, Sputnik, and sending the first human, Yuri Gagarin, into space.

The Apollo program was NASA's response to this challenge, involving a series of progressively complex missions aimed at developing the technology and experience needed to land humans on the Moon. By 1969, NASA had successfully tested the lunar module in space and conducted other essential preparatory missions, paving the way for Apollo 11. The mission itself involved multiple stages: launching from Earth, traveling to the Moon, landing on the lunar surface, returning to lunar orbit, and then making the long journey back to Earth.

The Moon Landing: A Historic Achievement

On July 20, 1969, after four days of travel through space, the Apollo 11 lunar module, Eagle, touched down on the Moon's surface in the Sea of Tranquility. Neil Armstrong and Buzz Aldrin became the first humans to walk on the Moon, while Michael Collins orbited above in the command module, Columbia. Armstrong's first steps on the lunar surface and his iconic words, "That's one small step for man, one giant leap for mankind," were broadcast live to millions of people around the world, marking an unprecedented achievement in human history.

For several hours, Armstrong and Aldrin conducted scientific experiments, collected lunar soil and rock samples, and planted the American flag. They left behind various items, including a plaque commemorating the landing, a patch honoring the Apollo 1 crew who had perished in a launch pad fire, and a disc containing messages from world leaders. These activities, though brief, were meticulously planned and executed, demonstrating the precision and coordination that defined the entire mission.

Preparing for the Return Journey: Critical Decisions and Challenges

While the landing on the Moon was a monumental achievement, the safe return of the astronauts to Earth was the ultimate goal of the mission. Every aspect of the return journey was fraught with challenges, uncertainties, and the potential for disaster. The process of returning from the Moon began as soon as Armstrong and Aldrin rejoined Collins in the command module, a critical and delicate maneuver.

One of the first significant tasks was the lunar ascent. After spending about 21 hours on the Moon, Armstrong and Aldrin had to launch the upper stage of the lunar module, Eagle, from the lunar surface to rendezvous with the command module, Columbia, in lunar orbit. This required precise timing and navigation, as the two spacecraft needed to dock smoothly to transfer the astronauts and the precious lunar samples back to Columbia. Failure in this maneuver could have left Armstrong and Aldrin stranded on the Moon, a risk that weighed heavily on the minds of the mission controllers and the astronauts themselves.

The ascent from the lunar surface was executed flawlessly. The lunar module's ascent engine fired successfully, and Eagle was guided back into lunar orbit, where it docked with Columbia. Once the astronauts and their samples were safely transferred, the now-empty lunar module was jettisoned, and Columbia began preparations for the journey back to Earth.

The Return Trip: Re-entry and Splashdown

The journey from lunar orbit to Earth, known as the transearth injection (TEI), was another critical phase of the mission. This involved firing the command module's service propulsion system (SPS) engine to leave lunar orbit and set a course for Earth. The timing and accuracy of this burn were crucial; any miscalculation could have sent the spacecraft off course, with potentially disastrous consequences.

The SPS engine burn took place on July 21, 1969, just hours after the lunar module was jettisoned. The engine fired for several minutes, propelling the spacecraft out of lunar orbit and on a trajectory back to Earth. This burn had to be precise not only in timing but also in duration and direction to ensure that Columbia would intersect with Earth's atmosphere at the correct angle and speed. Too steep an angle could cause the spacecraft to burn up during re-entry, while too shallow an angle might result in it skipping off the atmosphere and being lost in space.

Once the TEI burn was completed, the astronauts began the three-day journey back to Earth. During this time, they conducted a few final experiments, continued to monitor their trajectory, and prepared the spacecraft for re-entry. One of the key preparations was jettisoning the service module, which housed the main engine, fuel tanks, and other systems that were no longer needed. This left only the command module, a small, cone-shaped capsule that would carry the astronauts through the fiery re-entry into Earth's atmosphere and protect them from the extreme heat generated during the descent.

Re-entry was one of the most dangerous phases of the mission. As Columbia re-entered Earth's atmosphere on July 24, it encountered temperatures of up to 5,000 degrees Fahrenheit due to the friction between the spacecraft and the air. The command module's heat shield, made of an ablative material that would burn away and absorb the intense heat, was crucial in protecting the astronauts from incineration. Any failure of this shield would have resulted in the loss of the crew.

The command module entered the atmosphere at a precise angle of 6.24 degrees, within the narrow corridor necessary for a safe descent. The astronauts experienced intense G-forces as the capsule decelerated rapidly, and communication with Mission Control was temporarily lost during the re-entry blackout, a period when the ionization of the air around the spacecraft interfered with radio signals. This period of silence, lasting about four minutes, was tense for both the crew and the mission controllers, who waited anxiously for the re-establishment of contact.

When communication was finally restored, the astronauts were on the final leg of their journey. Parachutes deployed to slow the capsule's descent, and at 12:50 PM EDT on July 24, 1969, Columbia splashed down in the Pacific Ocean, approximately 900 miles southwest of Hawaii. The splashdown was the culmination of years of effort, innovation, and planning, and it marked the successful completion of the Apollo 11 mission.

The Recovery Operation: Ensuring the Crew's Safety

Following the splashdown, the recovery operation began immediately. The U.S.S. Hornet, an aircraft carrier, had been stationed in the Pacific near the splashdown point to retrieve the astronauts. Helicopters were dispatched from the Hornet to locate the floating command module and ensure that the astronauts were safely extracted.

Once the helicopters arrived at the splashdown site, divers were deployed to secure flotation devices around the command module to prevent it from sinking. The astronauts, still inside the capsule, were then hoisted aboard the helicopters using a special recovery harness. This process was completed efficiently, and within minutes, Armstrong, Aldrin, and Collins were safely aboard the helicopters, which then transported them to the U.S.S. Hornet.

Upon arriving on the Hornet, the astronauts were immediately placed in a mobile quarantine facility (MQF). This precaution was taken because, at the time, there were concerns about the possibility of the astronauts bringing back unknown pathogens from the Moon. The MQF was a specially designed trailer equipped with living quarters, medical facilities, and communication systems, allowing the astronauts to be monitored and communicate with the outside world while remaining isolated.

The quarantine period lasted for 21 days, during which time the astronauts were monitored for any signs of illness or contamination. Fortunately, no pathogens or harmful effects were found, and the astronauts were eventually released, having been declared free of any lunar germs. The quarantine facility itself was later displayed in museums, becoming a symbol of the extraordinary measures taken to ensure the safety of the crew and the public.

The Aftermath: Global Celebration and Legacy

The successful return of Apollo 11 marked the triumphant conclusion of one of the most ambitious and daring undertakings in human history. The mission's success was celebrated around the world, with the astronauts receiving a hero's welcome upon their return. Parades, ceremonies, and receptions were held in their honor, and they were hailed as symbols of human achievement and perseverance.

The legacy of Apollo 11 is profound and far-reaching. It demonstrated the incredible potential of human ingenuity and collaboration, showing what could be achieved when people from different backgrounds, disciplines, and countries worked together towards a common goal. The mission also inspired generations of scientists, engineers, and explorers, many of whom would go on to contribute to subsequent space missions and other groundbreaking endeavors.

In the broader context of history, Apollo 11 represented a turning point in the space race, effectively ending the competition between the United States and the Soviet Union with a decisive American victory. It also paved the way for future space exploration, including the Apollo 12-17 missions, which continued to explore the Moon and bring back valuable scientific data. The knowledge and experience gained from Apollo 11 have continued to influence space exploration to this day, including current missions to the Moon, Mars, and beyond.

Reflections: The Human Element of Apollo 11

While the technical achievements of Apollo 11 are often highlighted, the mission was also a deeply human story. It was a story of bravery, teamwork, and the pursuit of knowledge in the face of immense challenges and dangers. The astronauts, engineers, scientists, and support staff involved in the mission were driven by a shared belief in the importance of exploration and the desire to push the boundaries of what was possible.

For the astronauts themselves, the return to Earth was a time of reflection. After experiencing the desolation of the lunar surface and the vastness of space, they returned to a planet that suddenly seemed both fragile and precious. This perspective, often referred to as the "overview effect," profoundly impacted the astronauts, leading them to appreciate the interconnectedness of life on Earth and the importance of protecting our planet.

In the years following the mission, the Apollo 11 astronauts continued to inspire people around the world through their stories, their work, and their contributions to science and exploration. Neil Armstrong, in particular, became a symbol of quiet strength and humility, often avoiding the spotlight but always embodying the spirit of exploration that had driven him to take that historic first step on the Moon.

Conclusion: A Legacy of Exploration and Discovery

The return of Apollo 11 was not just the end of a journey; it was the beginning of a new era of exploration and discovery. The mission's success proved that humanity could reach beyond the confines of Earth and explore other worlds, setting the stage for future generations to continue this legacy of exploration. Apollo 11 remains a defining moment in human history, a reminder of what we can achieve when we dare to dream and work together to turn those dreams into reality.

As we look back on the mission today, we are reminded of the courage, determination, and ingenuity that made it possible. The safe return of the Apollo 11 astronauts was a victory not just for NASA or the United States, but for all of humanity. It showed us that the sky is not the limit, and that with vision, perseverance, and a commitment to exploration, there are no bounds to what we can achieve.

Chapter 13: Louis Zamperini's Ordeal

Louis Zamperini's ordeal is one of the most extraordinary survival stories of the 20th century. His life, marked by athletic success, wartime heroism, unimaginable suffering, and an ultimate journey of forgiveness, reads like an epic tale. Born on January 26, 1917, in Olean, New York, Zamperini grew up in Torrance, California, where he quickly developed a reputation as a troublemaker before discovering his talent for running. This talent would lead him to the 1936 Berlin Olympics and later help him survive some of the most brutal conditions a human being can endure.

Early Life and Athletic Success

Louis Zamperini was the son of Italian immigrants and the youngest of four children. His early years were tough—he spoke little English and was frequently bullied because of his heritage. In response, he became a rebellious child, often getting into fights and committing petty thefts. His older brother, Pete, recognized Louis's potential and encouraged him to channel his energy into running. This advice changed the trajectory of Louis's life.

Zamperini's natural talent for running became apparent in high school, where he broke several records in the mile and two-mile races. His remarkable speed earned him the nickname "The Torrance Tornado." He eventually qualified for the 1936 Berlin Olympics at the age of 19, the youngest American qualifier in the 5,000 meters. Although he didn't win a medal, Zamperini's final lap in the 5,000-meter race was so fast that it caught the attention of Adolf Hitler, who requested a personal meeting with him. This moment in the spotlight marked the beginning of Zamperini's fame, but the most significant chapters of his life were yet to come.

World War II: Enlistment and Bombardier Duty

With the outbreak of World War II, Zamperini's running career was put on hold as he enlisted in the United States Army Air Corps in 1941. After completing training, he was assigned to a B-24 Liberator bomber as a bombardier in the Pacific Theater. The B-24, nicknamed "The Flying Coffin" due to its high casualty rate, was a notoriously difficult aircraft to fly, with numerous mechanical problems and a reputation for being hard to control.

Zamperini's squadron was based in the Pacific, where they carried out bombing missions against Japanese targets. These missions were perilous, with the constant threat of anti-aircraft fire, mechanical failures, and the vast, unforgiving ocean below. On one such mission, Zamperini's plane, the "Green Hornet," experienced mechanical difficulties and crashed into the Pacific Ocean on May 27, 1943. Of the eleven men aboard, only Zamperini, pilot Russell Allen "Phil" Phillips, and tail gunner Francis "Mac" McNamara survived.

Adrift in the Pacific: 47 Days of Desperation

The crash marked the beginning of an unimaginable ordeal for the three men. Clinging to life in two small inflatable rafts, they were adrift in the vast Pacific Ocean with no rescue in sight. The days turned into weeks as they faced relentless exposure to the sun, saltwater sores, and the constant threat of shark attacks. The men had no provisions other than a few bars of chocolate and some half-pint cans of water. These meager supplies were quickly consumed, and they were forced to rely on their ingenuity to survive.

They caught rainwater when it fell, which was infrequent, and attempted to catch fish and birds to eat. Zamperini's resourcefulness came into play when he managed to catch a few birds that landed on their raft. He would break their necks and use their meat for food while using their intestines as bait to catch fish. This grisly process was necessary to stave off starvation. However, dehydration and the psychological toll of being lost at sea began to weigh heavily on the men.

On the sixth day, Mac McNamara, who had initially panicked and eaten all the chocolate rations, began to lose hope. His mental state deteriorated rapidly, and despite Zamperini and Phillips' efforts to keep his spirits up, Mac died on the 33rd day. His death was a devastating blow to Zamperini and Phillips, who buried him at sea with a prayer. The two survivors continued to drift, their bodies wasting away and their willpower being tested to the extreme.

Zamperini and Phillips faced additional threats beyond hunger and thirst. They endured countless shark attacks, with the predators circling their rafts day and night. At one point, a Japanese bomber flew overhead and strafed their rafts with bullets, puncturing one and leaving the other barely afloat. Remarkably, neither man was hit, but they were left to repair the raft with what little materials they had.

Their situation became increasingly dire as the days wore on. They had drifted over 2,000 miles from their crash site, and their chances of being found seemed slim. Both men were on the brink of death when, on the 47th day, they spotted a Japanese patrol boat. They were no longer lost at sea, but their ordeal was far from over.

Captivity: The Japanese POW Camps

Zamperini and Phillips were taken aboard the Japanese ship, where they were immediately separated and sent to different prisoner-of-war (POW) camps. Zamperini was transported to the island of Kwajalein, a place known as "Execution Island" because most of the prisoners sent there were executed. For 42 days, he endured near-starvation, constant beatings, and interrogations. He was tormented by the guards, who viewed American prisoners with disdain and treated them with unimaginable cruelty.

Despite being constantly on the brink of death, Zamperini refused to give up any military information to his captors. His resilience and refusal to break under torture became a defining aspect of his character. After six weeks on Kwajalein, he was transferred to the mainland of Japan, where he was placed in various POW camps over the next two years. These camps were brutal; prisoners were subjected to forced labor, starvation, disease, and frequent beatings.

One of the most notorious of Zamperini's captors was Mutsuhiro Watanabe, a sadistic camp guard known as "The Bird." Watanabe singled out Zamperini for particularly harsh treatment, likely because of his status as an Olympian and a symbol of American resilience. The Bird's treatment of Zamperini was relentless—he beat him daily, sometimes multiple times a day, and forced him to perform degrading tasks. Watanabe's cruelty knew no bounds, and he seemed to take pleasure in breaking prisoners both physically and mentally. Yet, despite the incessant abuse, Zamperini's spirit remained unbroken.

In one particularly harrowing incident, Zamperini was forced to hold a heavy wooden beam above his head for an extended period. The Bird threatened to kill him if he dropped it. Though the beam was crushingly heavy and Zamperini was already weakened from starvation and disease, he managed to hold it up for 37 minutes until he collapsed from exhaustion. This act of defiance became emblematic of Zamperini's indomitable will to survive.

Liberation and Return to Civilization

As the war neared its end, the conditions in the camps worsened. The Japanese guards, realizing they were losing the war, began to escalate their brutality against the prisoners. Food became even scarcer, and disease ran rampant. However, the tide of war was turning, and by the summer of 1945, the Allied forces had gained the upper hand in the Pacific.

Zamperini and the other POWs were liberated in August 1945, following the atomic bombings of Hiroshima and Nagasaki and Japan's subsequent surrender. Emaciated, sick, and traumatized, Zamperini was finally free after more than two years of captivity. His return home was met with celebration, but also with the profound challenge of reintegrating into society after enduring such unimaginable horrors.

Post-War Struggles: The Battle with PTSD

Upon returning to the United States, Zamperini was hailed as a hero, but his internal battle had just begun. Like many veterans, he suffered from severe post-traumatic stress disorder (PTSD). He was haunted by nightmares of his time in the camps, particularly of The Bird, whose face and voice plagued his dreams. Zamperini turned to alcohol to numb the pain, and his once-promising life began to spiral out of control.

He married Cynthia Applewhite in 1946, but his drinking and violent temper put a severe strain on their relationship. Cynthia was on the brink of leaving him when she attended a Billy Graham crusade in 1949. She returned home a changed woman, deeply moved by the message of forgiveness she had heard. She convinced Louis to attend one of the crusade meetings, though he initially resisted.

At the Billy Graham meeting, Zamperini experienced a profound spiritual awakening. He was reminded of a promise he had made to God during his time adrift in the Pacific—if God saved him, he would dedicate his life to serving Him. This moment marked a turning point in Zamperini's life. He embraced Christianity, forgave his captors, and found peace for the first time since the war.

Forgiveness and Redemption

Zamperini's newfound faith led him on a path of forgiveness and redemption. He began speaking publicly about his experiences, sharing his story of survival and the power of forgiveness. In 1950, he traveled to Japan to meet with several of his former guards and forgave them for the suffering they had caused him. His most significant act of forgiveness came later when he sought to meet with Mutsuhiro Watanabe, The Bird, who had evaded prosecution as a war criminal. Though Watanabe refused to meet him, Zamperini publicly forgave him, freeing himself from the hatred and anger that had consumed him for so long.

Zamperini's story of survival and forgiveness became widely known through Laura Hillenbrand's best-selling book, "Unbroken: A World War II Story of Survival, Resilience, and Redemption," published in 2010. The book was later adapted into a film directed by Angelina Jolie, further cementing Zamperini's legacy as an extraordinary figure of resilience and grace.

Legacy of Louis Zamperini

Louis Zamperini's life was a testament to the strength of the human spirit. He faced incredible odds, enduring physical and psychological torture that would have broken most people. Yet, he emerged not just as a survivor, but as a beacon of hope and forgiveness. His journey from rebellious youth to Olympic athlete, from war hero to prisoner, and finally to a man of deep faith and forgiveness, serves as an inspiration to millions.

Zamperini passed away on July 2, 2014, at the age of 97. His life story continues to inspire those who hear it, reminding us of the power of resilience, the importance of forgiveness, and the ability to find redemption even in the darkest of circumstances. His ordeal during World War II, and the remarkable way he overcame it, stands as a powerful example of what it means to be unbroken.

Chapter 14: The Uruguayan Air Force Flight 571

The story of Uruguayan Air Force Flight 571 is one of the most harrowing and extraordinary survival stories in modern history. It is a tale of endurance, hope, and the human spirit's unyielding will to survive in the face of seemingly insurmountable odds. The incident, which occurred in 1972, has become etched in the annals of history as a prime example of survival against the harshest conditions imaginable, testing the limits of human endurance, both physically and mentally.

The Crash

Uruguayan Air Force Flight 571 was a chartered flight carrying 45 passengers, including members of a Uruguayan rugby team, their friends, and family members. The flight was en route from Montevideo, Uruguay, to Santiago, Chile, with a planned stop in Mendoza, Argentina. On October 13, 1972, the Fairchild FH-227D aircraft encountered severe turbulence and poor weather conditions as it attempted to cross the Andes Mountains, one of the most formidable mountain ranges in the world.

The crew, facing deteriorating weather and poor visibility, made a crucial navigational error. Believing they had already cleared the mountains; they began descending prematurely. Tragically, the aircraft struck a mountain peak, shearing off both wings and sending the fuselage hurtling down a steep, snow-covered slope. The crash killed 12 of the 45 passengers instantly. The survivors found themselves stranded at an altitude of over 11,000 feet in the remote Andes, with little food, no source of heat, and only the clothing on their backs to protect them from the freezing temperatures.

Immediate Aftermath and Initial Struggles

In the immediate aftermath of the crash, the survivors faced a grim reality. The frigid temperatures, which often dropped below freezing at night, posed a severe threat. The thin air at high altitude made it difficult to breathe, and the lack of adequate clothing meant that the survivors were ill-prepared for the harsh environment. The survivors salvaged what they could from the wreckage, using aircraft seats as makeshift blankets and insulation, and attempting to create a small shelter within the fuselage of the plane.

The survivors rationed the meager supply of food they had, which consisted of chocolate, a few bottles of wine, and some other small snacks. The realization soon set in that their food supply would not last long, and they were surrounded by nothing but snow and ice, with no vegetation or animals in sight. The group tried to signal for help by laying out large letters in the snow using the remains of the aircraft, hoping that search planes might spot them. However, the search efforts by authorities were hampered by the remote location and the severe weather conditions, and after eight days, the search was called off, with authorities assuming that no one could have survived the crash.

Desperation and the Turn to Cannibalism

As days turned into weeks, the situation grew increasingly dire. The survivors were now faced with the stark reality that they were completely alone, with no rescue on the horizon. Starvation became a very real and pressing threat. With their food supply exhausted, the survivors were forced to make an unthinkable decision: to stay alive, they would have to resort to cannibalism.

This decision did not come easily. For many, it was a moral and religious dilemma. The survivors were Roman Catholics, and the idea of consuming the flesh of their deceased friends and loved ones was abhorrent to them. However, the dire circumstances left them with little choice. They rationalized that in order to survive, they would have to do the unthinkable. The deceased were seen as sacrificing themselves to allow the others to live. It was a decision born out of sheer desperation and the primal instinct to survive.

The group initially consumed only small amounts of flesh, starting with the organs, which they believed had the most nutritional value. Over time, as they grew weaker, they began to consume more. This grim act provided them with the calories and protein they needed to survive in the harsh conditions, but it took a tremendous psychological toll on the survivors. They struggled with guilt, shame, and the fear of being judged by society if they were ever rescued.

The Avalanche

On October 29, 1972, just over two weeks after the crash, another tragedy struck the survivors. An avalanche swept over their makeshift shelter, killing eight more people and burying the fuselage in snow. The survivors who were not buried managed to dig out their companions, but this event further reduced their numbers and morale. The fuselage, now buried, offered even less protection from the elements, and the survivors were forced to endure even harsher conditions.

The avalanche also buried much of the remaining bodies they were using for sustenance, forcing the survivors to venture further into the snow to retrieve the bodies. This increased the risk and difficulty of obtaining food, adding another layer of hardship to their already desperate situation.

The Expedition for Help

As weeks turned into months, the survivors realized that they could not wait for rescue any longer. They had to take matters into their own hands. Nando Parrado and Roberto Canessa, two of the strongest survivors, decided to embark on a perilous journey to find help. On December 12, 1972, after weeks of planning and gathering strength, the two men, along with a third companion, set out on a treacherous journey across the Andes. Their goal was to reach civilization and bring back help for their remaining friends.

The journey was fraught with danger. The men had to climb steep, snow-covered peaks, navigate treacherous ice fields, and endure the relentless cold and thin air at high altitude. They carried with them only a few rations of the flesh of their deceased companions and the hope that they could find help before it was too late. After several days of grueling travel, they finally reached a lower altitude and encountered signs of human life. They found a river and followed it downstream, eventually encountering a Chilean shepherd, who helped them contact authorities.

The Rescue

On December 20, 1972, more than two months after the crash, the first rescue helicopters arrived at the crash site. The rescue operation was extremely challenging due to the remote location and harsh weather conditions, but over the course of two days, all 16 of the remaining survivors were airlifted to safety. Their ordeal had lasted 72 days in total, and by the time they were rescued, they were emaciated, weak, and suffering from severe frostbite and malnutrition.

The news of their survival and the lengths they had gone to in order to stay alive shocked the world. The story of their cannibalism, in particular, became a subject of intense media scrutiny and public debate. The survivors, however, were grateful to be alive and defended their actions as necessary for survival. They had endured unimaginable hardships and had done what they had to do in order to stay alive.

Aftermath and Legacy

The survivors of Uruguayan Air Force Flight 571 returned to a world that struggled to comprehend the full extent of their ordeal. The public's reaction was mixed, with some viewing the survivors as heroes, while others were horrified by the revelations of cannibalism. Over time, however, the survivors' actions came to be understood in the context of survival, and they were largely forgiven for what they had done.

The story of Flight 571 has since been immortalized in books, documentaries, and films, most notably in the 1993 movie "Alive," which was based on a book by Piers Paul Read. The survivors themselves have spoken openly about their experiences, often emphasizing the importance of hope, solidarity, and the will to survive in the face of overwhelming odds.

Today, the story of Flight 571 stands as a testament to the resilience of the human spirit. It serves as a reminder of the extreme lengths to which people will go in order to stay alive, and of the incredible strength that can be found in the most desperate circumstances. The survivors of Flight 571 not only survived one of the most challenging environments on Earth, but they also overcame the psychological and emotional trauma of their ordeal, emerging as living symbols of human endurance and courage.

Chapter 15: The Survival of Arlene Blum

The survival story of Arlene Blum is a remarkable tale of endurance, courage, and determination in the face of extreme adversity. Arlene Blum is not just a survivor; she is a trailblazer in the world of mountaineering, a scientist, and an advocate for environmental health. Her story is one that has inspired countless people around the world, not only because of the physical challenges she overcame but also because of the social barriers she shattered in a male-dominated field. Her survival is not limited to a single event but rather encompasses a lifetime of overcoming obstacles, both on the highest peaks of the world and in the scientific community.

Early Life and Beginnings

Arlene Blum was born in 1945 in Chicago, Illinois, and raised in a Jewish family that had emigrated from Eastern Europe. From an early age, Blum was driven by a deep curiosity about the world around her and a passion for science. Her father passed away when she was young, and her mother, a single parent, worked hard to provide for her. Despite the challenges, Blum excelled in school and developed a keen interest in chemistry. However, she also faced societal expectations that often limited the ambitions of women, particularly in the sciences.

Blum attended Reed College in Portland, Oregon, where she majored in chemistry. It was during her time at Reed that she was introduced to mountaineering, a sport that would come to define much of her life. Initially, she joined a hiking club, where she quickly fell in love with the mountains. The sense of freedom and challenge that mountaineering offered resonated deeply with her, and she soon became an avid climber.

Breaking Barriers in Mountaineering

In the 1960s and 1970s, the world of mountaineering was overwhelmingly dominated by men. Women were often discouraged from pursuing high-altitude climbing, and there were few opportunities for women to participate in major expeditions. However, Arlene Blum was determined to break through these barriers. She began to organize and lead all-women expeditions, challenging the prevailing attitudes of the time.

One of Blum's first significant achievements came in 1970 when she participated in an expedition to climb Denali (then known as Mount McKinley), the highest peak in North America. The climb was grueling, with extreme cold, high winds, and treacherous conditions. Despite the challenges, Blum and her team successfully reached the summit, marking one of the first all-women ascents of Denali. This achievement was a turning point in her mountaineering career and inspired her to set even more ambitious goals.

The Ascent of Annapurna

Arlene Blum's most famous and challenging expedition came in 1978 when she led the American Women's Himalayan Expedition to Annapurna, one of the most dangerous and difficult peaks in the world. Annapurna, standing at 26,545 feet (8,091 meters), is the tenth-highest mountain on Earth and has one of the highest fatality rates among the world's 8,000-meter peaks. The mountain's treacherous conditions, including avalanches, steep ice faces, and unpredictable weather, make it a formidable challenge even for the most experienced climbers.

The expedition was historic not only because it was an all-women team but also because no American team, male or female, had ever summited Annapurna before. The journey to organize the expedition was fraught with difficulties. Blum faced significant resistance from sponsors, who were skeptical of the idea of an all-women team attempting such a dangerous climb. Additionally, the team had to overcome logistical challenges, including securing permits, organizing supplies, and raising funds.

Despite the obstacles, the expedition set out for Annapurna in the spring of 1978. The team consisted of thirteen women, all experienced climbers from the United States. The climb itself was grueling from the outset. The team faced extreme cold, high winds, and the constant threat of avalanches. Several members of the team fell ill due to the altitude, and others suffered from frostbite. The psychological toll of the climb was immense, as the team battled exhaustion, fear, and the ever-present danger of the mountain.

As the team ascended, they were forced to make difficult decisions. At one point, they encountered an impassable ice wall that required them to change their route. This detour added significant time and danger to the climb. Despite these challenges, on October 15, 1978, two members of the team, Irene Miller and Vera Komarkova, along with Sherpas Mingma Tsering and Chewang Ringjing, reached the summit of Annapurna. This achievement marked the first American ascent of Annapurna and the first ascent by an all-women team.

However, the triumph of reaching the summit was overshadowed by tragedy. As the team was descending, an avalanche swept away two members of the expedition, Alison Chadwick-Onyszkiewicz and Vera Watson, killing them instantly. The loss of their teammates was a devastating blow to the team, and the survivors were forced to confront the harsh realities of high-altitude mountaineering. The expedition's success came at a great cost, and Blum and her team were left to grapple with the emotional aftermath of the climb.

Scientific Contributions and Environmental Advocacy

While Arlene Blum is best known for her mountaineering achievements, her contributions to science and environmental advocacy are equally significant. After earning her Ph.D. in biophysical chemistry from the University of California, Berkeley, Blum began researching the health effects of flame-retardant chemicals. Her work in this area had far-reaching implications for public health and consumer safety.

In the 1970s, Blum conducted research on a flame-retardant chemical called Tris, which was widely used in children's pajamas. Her studies revealed that Tris was a mutagen, meaning it could cause genetic mutations, and it was also found to be carcinogenic. Blum's research led to the removal of Tris from children's sleepwear in the United States, a significant victory for public health.

Blum's work on flame retardants continued for decades, as she advocated for stricter regulations on the use of toxic chemicals in consumer products. She founded the Green Science Policy Institute, an organization dedicated to reducing the use of harmful chemicals in everyday products. Her advocacy has had a profound impact on environmental health policy, leading to greater awareness and regulation of toxic chemicals.

Challenges and Discrimination

Throughout her career, Arlene Blum faced significant challenges and discrimination, both as a woman in science and in mountaineering. In the male-dominated world of high-altitude climbing, she often encountered skepticism and resistance. Sponsors were reluctant to fund her expeditions, and she faced criticism from some male climbers who questioned the capabilities of an all-women team. Despite these obstacles, Blum persisted, driven by her passion for climbing and her belief in the abilities of her team.

In the scientific community, Blum also faced gender-based discrimination. During her early career, opportunities for women in chemistry were limited, and she had to work harder to prove herself in a field that was often unwelcoming to women. However, Blum's determination and perseverance allowed her to overcome these barriers and make significant contributions to both science and mountaineering.

Legacy and Influence

Arlene Blum's legacy extends far beyond her personal achievements. She has inspired generations of women to pursue careers in science, mountaineering, and other fields traditionally dominated by men. Her pioneering expeditions demonstrated that women are capable of achieving greatness in the most challenging environments, and her advocacy work has improved public health and safety.

Blum's story is one of resilience and courage in the face of adversity. Whether climbing some of the world's highest peaks or fighting for environmental health, she has consistently demonstrated an unwavering commitment to her goals. Her life is a testament to the power of determination, the importance of breaking down barriers, and the impact that one person can have on the world.

In addition to her accomplishments, Blum has shared her experiences and lessons through her writing and public speaking. Her book, "Annapurna: A Woman's Place," chronicles the 1978 expedition and provides a candid account of the challenges and triumphs of the climb. The book has become a classic in the literature of mountaineering, offering insights into both the physical demands of high-altitude climbing and the psychological and emotional challenges faced by the team.

Blum's influence continues to be felt today, as she remains an active voice in environmental advocacy and a mentor to young scientists and climbers. Her story is a powerful reminder that survival is not just about overcoming physical challenges; it is also about confronting and overcoming societal barriers, pushing the boundaries of what is possible, and making a lasting impact on the world.

Conclusion

The survival and achievements of Arlene Blum are a remarkable example of human endurance, both in the literal sense of surviving extreme conditions in high-altitude mountaineering and in the metaphorical sense of overcoming societal and professional barriers. Blum's story is one of determination, courage, and resilience in the face of adversity. She has not only survived but thrived, breaking new ground in both science and mountaineering, and leaving a legacy that continues to inspire and empower others. Her life's work serves as a powerful reminder of what can be achieved through perseverance, passion, and a commitment to making the world a better place.

Chapter 16: The Miracle on Mount Hood

The Miracle on Mount Hood is one of the most extraordinary survival stories in the history of mountaineering in the Pacific Northwest of the United States. It is a tale that encapsulates the unpredictable dangers of high-altitude climbing, the heroism of rescue teams, and the sheer willpower required to survive in one of the most challenging environments on Earth. The story involves a group of climbers who faced near-death experiences on Mount Hood, the highest mountain in Oregon, and the subsequent rescue efforts that became a defining moment in the history of mountain rescues.

Mount Hood: The Mountain and Its Challenges

Mount Hood, located about 50 miles east-southeast of Portland, Oregon, is an iconic peak in the Cascade Range. Standing at 11,240 feet (3,426 meters), it is the highest point in Oregon and one of the most climbed glaciated peaks in the world. Despite its popularity, Mount Hood is notorious for its unpredictable weather, rapidly changing conditions, and technical challenges that can turn a routine climb into a life-threatening ordeal.

The mountain is an active stratovolcano, meaning it was formed by layers of hardened lava, tephra, and volcanic ash. While its last significant eruption occurred in the 1790s, the potential for future volcanic activity adds an additional layer of risk to those who climb it. The ascent of Mount Hood typically involves traversing glaciers, steep snowfields, and crevasses, which require climbers to have a good level of technical skill, physical fitness, and experience in mountaineering. However, the biggest danger on Mount Hood often comes from the weather, which can change from calm to stormy in a matter of minutes, creating whiteout conditions, high winds, and sudden temperature drops that can disorient and imperil even the most seasoned climbers.

The Fateful Climb

The Miracle on Mount Hood refers to an incident that occurred in December 2006, involving a group of three experienced climbers: Kelly James, Brian Hall, and Jerry "Nikko" Cooke. The three men, all in their 30s and 40s, were experienced mountaineers who had previously climbed together and successfully summited many peaks across North America. On this occasion, they aimed to climb Mount Hood via the challenging North Face route, which is known for its steepness and technical difficulty.

The North Face route, also known as the "Black Spider" for its intimidating appearance, is a winter ascent that is far more difficult than the standard routes used by most climbers. It requires advanced technical skills, including ice climbing, and presents significant risks, especially during the winter months when the weather can be particularly harsh. The trio was well-prepared for the climb, carrying the necessary gear, including ice axes, crampons, ropes, and enough food and supplies for a multi-day expedition.

The climb began on December 7, 2006. The group's plan was to reach the summit and then descend via the easier South Side route, which would allow for a safer and faster descent. However, the weather conditions began to deteriorate rapidly as the climbers made their ascent. By December 9, the mountain was engulfed in a severe winter storm, with high winds, heavy snowfall, and sub-zero temperatures. The storm, which was one of the worst to hit the region in years, created whiteout conditions, reducing visibility to near zero and making navigation almost impossible.

As the storm intensified, the climbers became separated. Kelly James, an experienced climber who had summited several major peaks, was the first to realize the severity of their situation. He managed to dig a snow cave near the summit, which provided some protection from the storm. From inside his makeshift shelter, he used his cell phone to make a brief call to his family on December 10, informing them that he was trapped near the summit, injured, and unable to move. It was the last communication anyone would have with the climbers.

The Search and Rescue Operation

The distress call triggered a massive search and rescue operation, one of the largest in Oregon's history. Given the extreme weather conditions and the high altitude, the rescue mission was a race against time. Rescue teams from across Oregon, as well as specialized units from neighboring states, were mobilized. The search involved helicopters, snowmobiles, and ground teams equipped with specialized gear for high-altitude rescues. However, the storm that had trapped the climbers also severely hampered rescue efforts. Helicopters were grounded due to high winds, and ground teams faced treacherous conditions, with visibility often reduced to just a few feet.

The search focused on both the North Face, where the climbers were believed to have been trapped, and the South Side, where they might have attempted to descend. Rescue teams had to contend with deep snow, hidden crevasses, and avalanche danger. Despite these challenges, the rescuers remained determined, driven by the hope that the climbers could still be alive, taking shelter in a snow cave or using their survival skills to withstand the storm.

On December 12, rescuers found the body of Kelly James inside his snow cave at an altitude of about 10,300 feet. James had succumbed to hypothermia, a result of prolonged exposure to the extreme cold.

His position near the summit suggested that he had been unable to descend due to his injuries, likely sustained in a fall or from the harsh conditions. The discovery of James's body marked a somber moment in the search, but it also provided crucial information about the possible locations of the other two climbers.

Despite the heartbreaking discovery, the search for Hall and Cooke continued with renewed urgency. The rescue teams combed the mountain, looking for any signs of the two missing climbers. However, the storm continued to batter the mountain, and the window for survival was closing rapidly. After several days of intensive searching, the rescue teams found no further signs of the missing climbers. On December 17, the official search was called off, though volunteers continued to search the mountain for weeks afterward, hoping against hope to find Hall and Cooke alive.

The Miracle of Survival and the Legacy of the Climb

The Miracle on Mount Hood, as it came to be known, is a testament to the extraordinary efforts of the search and rescue teams, the resilience of the climbers, and the brutal realities of high-altitude mountaineering. While the story ended in tragedy for Kelly James, Brian Hall, and Jerry Cooke, their plight highlighted the dangers inherent in mountaineering and the unpredictable nature of the mountains.

The incident also had a profound impact on the mountaineering community and the general public. It served as a stark reminder of the importance of preparation, the risks of climbing in winter conditions, and the critical role of search and rescue operations. The climbers' experience underscored the need for climbers to be fully aware of the challenges they face and the potential consequences of pushing the limits of their abilities, particularly in environments as unforgiving as Mount Hood.

In the aftermath of the tragedy, the families of the climbers established the Kelly James Memorial Foundation, dedicated to supporting search and rescue operations and promoting safety in mountaineering. The foundation has worked to raise awareness about the dangers of high-altitude climbing and to provide resources for rescuers who risk their lives to save others. The foundation's work has contributed to improving rescue operations on Mount Hood and other mountains across the United States.

The story of the Miracle on Mount Hood also resonated with many people beyond the mountaineering community. It became a symbol of the human spirit's capacity for hope, even in the face of overwhelming odds. The climbers' determination to survive, their skill in the mountains, and the dedication of the rescuers who searched tirelessly for them left a lasting legacy that continues to inspire and educate climbers and adventurers around the world.

Lessons Learned

The Miracle on Mount Hood offers several important lessons for mountaineers, rescuers, and anyone who ventures into the wilderness. One of the key takeaways from the incident is the importance of understanding the risks associated with winter climbing. The climbers were experienced and well-prepared, but they were ultimately caught in a situation where the weather conditions exceeded their ability to survive. This highlights the unpredictable nature of the mountains and the need for climbers to respect the power of nature.

Another lesson is the importance of communication and preparation. Kelly James's ability to make a phone call from his snow cave provided crucial information that guided the search and rescue efforts. It underscores the value of carrying communication devices, such as satellite phones or emergency beacons, especially in remote or high-risk areas. Additionally, the climbers' decision to dig a snow cave likely extended their lives, even if only by a few days. Knowing how to create emergency shelters and conserve energy in survival situations can make the difference between life and death.

The role of search and rescue teams in the Miracle on Mount Hood cannot be overstated. These highly trained professionals and volunteers risked their lives in the treacherous conditions of Mount Hood to try to save the climbers. Their efforts demonstrate the critical importance of having well-coordinated and well-equipped rescue operations in mountainous regions. The incident also led to discussions about the need for better funding and resources for search and rescue teams, as well as the development of more effective strategies for locating and rescuing climbers in difficult conditions.

Impact on the Mountaineering Community

The Miracle on Mount Hood had a significant impact on the mountaineering community, particularly in the Pacific Northwest. The incident prompted many climbers to re-evaluate their approach to winter ascents, leading to increased emphasis on safety, preparation, and respect for the mountains' power. Climbing organizations and guides began to offer more specialized training for winter conditions, focusing on avalanche awareness, weather forecasting, and emergency survival techniques.

The tragedy also brought attention to the psychological challenges of mountaineering. The emotional toll on the climbers' families, the rescuers, and the broader community was profound. It highlighted the need for support systems for those involved in mountaineering, including counseling and mental health resources for climbers, rescuers, and their loved ones. The incident also sparked conversations about the ethical considerations of high-risk climbing and the responsibility climbers have to themselves, their families, and the rescue teams that may be called upon to save them.

In the years following the Miracle on Mount Hood, the story has continued to be a point of reflection and learning for the climbing community. It has been the subject of numerous articles, documentaries, and discussions, all aimed at understanding what went wrong and how similar tragedies can be prevented in the future. The incident has also served as a powerful reminder of the respect and humility that climbers must have for the mountains and the importance of making informed decisions based on the conditions they face.

Conclusion

The Miracle on Mount Hood is a story that will be remembered for its profound impact on the mountaineering community and its lessons in survival, resilience, and the unpredictability of nature. The climbers involved in the incident were skilled and experienced, yet they were caught in a situation where the forces of nature proved overwhelming. Their story serves as a reminder of the dangers of high-altitude mountaineering, especially in winter conditions, and the need for thorough preparation, respect for the mountains, and the critical role of search and rescue operations.

The legacy of the Miracle on Mount Hood lives on in the continued efforts to improve safety in mountaineering, the ongoing support for search and rescue teams, and the inspiration it provides to those who face challenges in the wilderness. The story is a testament to the strength of the human spirit, the power of nature, and the importance of community in times of crisis. It is a reminder that, while the mountains can be unforgiving, they also bring out the best in those who seek to explore and understand them.

Chapter 17: The Survival of Bethany Hamilton

The survival story of Bethany Hamilton is one of the most inspiring and well-known tales of resilience, courage, and determination in the face of life-altering adversity. Bethany Hamilton's journey from a young, promising surfer to a global symbol of strength after a devastating shark attack is a testament to the human spirit's ability to overcome the most daunting challenges. Her story has captivated millions around the world, not only because of the dramatic nature of her experience but also because of the way she turned tragedy into triumph, continuing to pursue her passion for surfing and becoming an inspiration to countless individuals facing their own struggles.

Early Life and Love for Surfing

Bethany Meilani Hamilton was born on February 8, 1990, in Lihue, Hawaii, to Tom and Cheri Hamilton. Raised on the island of Kauai, she grew up in a family deeply connected to the ocean. Both of her parents were avid surfers, and they introduced Bethany and her two older brothers, Noah and Timmy, to the sport at an early age. The ocean was a central part of the Hamilton family's life, and Bethany quickly developed a love for surfing that would become her defining passion.

By the age of eight, Bethany was already competing in local surfing contests, showing exceptional talent and a natural affinity for the sport. She was known for her fearless approach to surfing, tackling waves with confidence and skill far beyond her years. Her dedication to the sport was evident, as she spent countless hours in the water, honing her technique and dreaming of becoming a professional surfer.

Bethany's determination and hard work began to pay off as she started to achieve success in competitive surfing. At just nine years old, she won her first major competition, the Rell Sun Menehune event on Oahu, a prestigious contest for young surfers. This victory marked the beginning of a promising career in surfing, and by the time she was 13, Bethany was already making a name for herself in the junior surfing circuit. She had her sights set on becoming a professional surfer, and it seemed that nothing could stand in her way.

The Shark Attack

On the morning of October 31, 2003, Bethany Hamilton's life changed forever. It was a typical day for the 13-year-old, who had gone out for an early morning surf session at Tunnels Beach on the north shore of Kauai. She was accompanied by her best friend Alana Blanchard, along with Alana's father, Holt, and brother, Byron. The waves were calm and the water was clear—a perfect day for surfing.

As Bethany lay on her surfboard, her left arm dangling in the water, a 14-foot tiger shark suddenly attacked her without warning. The shark bit into her left arm, severing it just below the shoulder in a single, powerful bite. The attack happened so quickly and silently that Bethany didn't initially realize the extent of her injury. It wasn't until she felt the water around her turning red with blood that she understood what had happened.

Despite the severity of the attack, Bethany remained remarkably calm. She immediately began paddling toward shore using her remaining arm, with Alana and her family rushing to her aid. They quickly helped Bethany out of the water and onto the beach, where they fashioned a tourniquet from a surfboard leash to stem the bleeding. Holt Blanchard then placed Bethany in his truck and drove her to the nearest hospital, all while keeping her conscious by talking to her and encouraging her to stay awake.

Bethany lost over 60% of her blood before reaching the hospital, and her survival was nothing short of a miracle. Once she arrived at Wilcox Memorial Hospital in Lihue, she was immediately taken into surgery. The doctors worked tirelessly to stabilize her condition, and against all odds, Bethany survived the traumatic ordeal. However, the attack resulted in the loss of her left arm, and the doctors advised her to get used to living with only one arm.

Recovery and Determination to Surf Again

For most people, the loss of an arm, especially under such traumatic circumstances, would have marked the end of a surfing career. But for Bethany Hamilton, it was only the beginning of a new chapter. Even while still in the hospital, Bethany was determined to return to the sport she loved. She made a promise to herself that she would surf again, no matter how difficult the journey might be.

Bethany's recovery was challenging, both physically and emotionally. She had to relearn how to perform everyday tasks with only one arm, and the process was often frustrating and painful. However, Bethany's strong faith, family support, and positive outlook played crucial roles in her recovery. Her parents and brothers provided unwavering support, helping her adapt to her new circumstances and encouraging her to stay focused on her goals.

Within just one month of the attack, Bethany was back in the water. On November 26, 2003, less than four weeks after losing her arm, she paddled out on her surfboard and caught her first wave since the attack. It was a moment of triumph and validation for Bethany, proving to herself and to the world that she was not going to let the shark attack define her or take away her passion for surfing.

Returning to the water was only the first step in Bethany's journey. She faced numerous challenges as she worked to regain her surfing abilities. Learning to balance on the board and catch waves with only one arm required her to adapt her technique significantly. She also had to rebuild her strength and endurance, as the loss of her arm had a profound impact on her physical abilities. Despite these challenges, Bethany approached her recovery with the same determination and resilience that had defined her early surfing career.

Return to Competitive Surfing

Bethany's return to competitive surfing was nothing short of extraordinary. Just over a year after the attack, in January 2004, she entered her first major competition, the National Scholastic Surfing Association (NSSA) Nationals in California. Bethany's performance was a testament to her skill and determination—she placed fifth in her division, competing against surfers with two arms. Her success at the NSSA Nationals marked her return to the competitive surfing world and demonstrated that she was not just surviving, but thriving.

In 2005, Bethany achieved one of her most significant victories since the attack, winning first place in the Explorer Women's division at the NSSA National Championships. This win was particularly meaningful for Bethany, as it solidified her place among the top young surfers in the country and proved that she could compete at the highest levels of the sport despite her physical challenges.

Bethany's competitive success continued in the years that followed. She went on to achieve numerous victories in both amateur and professional surfing competitions. Her remarkable achievements on the waves earned her widespread recognition and respect within the surfing community, as well as admiration from people around the world who were inspired by her story.

Bethany's Story Becomes a Global Inspiration

Bethany Hamilton's story of survival and resilience quickly gained international attention. Her experience resonated with people from all walks of life, many of whom saw her as a symbol of hope and perseverance in the face of adversity. Media outlets from around the world covered her story, and she appeared on numerous television shows, including "The Oprah Winfrey Show," "Good Morning America," and "The Ellen DeGeneres Show." Her positive attitude and unwavering determination captured the hearts of millions, and she became a role model for people facing their own challenges.

In 2004, Bethany published her autobiography, "Soul Surfer: A True Story of Faith, Family, and Fighting to Get Back on the Board." The book chronicles her life before and after the shark attack, detailing her journey of recovery and her unwavering faith in God, which she credits as the source of her strength. "Soul Surfer" became a best-seller and further cemented Bethany's status as an inspirational figure.

The impact of Bethany's story extended beyond the surfing community and the world of sports. She began to receive letters and messages from people all over the world who were inspired by her courage and determination. Many shared their own stories of overcoming adversity, and Bethany became an advocate for others facing challenges, encouraging them to persevere and pursue their passions despite the obstacles in their way.

The Film Adaptation: "Soul Surfer"

Bethany's story was brought to the big screen in 2011 with the release of the feature film "Soul Surfer," based on her autobiography. The film stars AnnaSophia Robb as Bethany and features a strong supporting cast, including Dennis Quaid, Helen Hunt, and Carrie

Underwood. "Soul Surfer" tells the story of Bethany's life, focusing on the shark attack, her recovery, and her return to competitive surfing.

The film was well-received by audiences and critics alike, praised for its inspirational message and the performances of its cast. "Soul Surfer" helped introduce Bethany's story to an even wider audience, and it became a source of motivation for people around the world. The film highlighted the importance of faith, family, and perseverance, themes that resonated deeply with viewers.

Bethany was closely involved in the making of the film, working with the filmmakers to ensure that her story was portrayed accurately and authentically. She even performed many of the surfing scenes herself, showcasing her incredible skills on the waves. The release of "Soul Surfer" further solidified Bethany's status as a global icon of resilience and strength.

Bethany's Continued Success and Advocacy

In the years following the release of "Soul Surfer," Bethany Hamilton continued to achieve success in both her surfing career and her personal life. She competed in numerous surfing competitions, consistently performing at a high level and earning respect from her peers. Her competitive spirit and determination remained as strong as ever, and she continued to push the boundaries of what was possible for an adaptive athlete.

Beyond her accomplishments on the waves, Bethany also became a dedicated advocate for a variety of causes. She used her platform to raise awareness about issues such as limb difference, disability inclusion, and ocean conservation. Bethany became a role model for people with disabilities, showing that it is possible to pursue one's passions and achieve greatness, regardless of physical limitations.

Bethany's advocacy work also extended to her faith. As a devout Christian, she often spoke about the role her faith played in her recovery and in her life as a whole. She shared her message of hope and perseverance through speaking engagements, books, and media appearances, reaching audiences around the world. Her story inspired countless individuals to find strength in their own faith and to face life's challenges with courage and determination.

Personal Life and Family

In addition to her professional achievements and advocacy work, Bethany Hamilton also found happiness in her personal life. In 2013, she married Adam Dirks, a youth minister, in a beautiful ceremony in Hawaii. The couple's shared faith and love for the ocean created a strong bond, and they quickly became a beloved couple within the public eye. Bethany and Adam's relationship was a source of joy and stability for Bethany, and they were soon blessed with children.

Bethany and Adam welcomed their first son, Tobias, in 2015, followed by their second son, Wesley, in 2018, and a third child in 2021. Bethany embraced motherhood with the same passion and dedication that she brought to her surfing career. She often shared her experiences as a mother on social media, offering insight into how she balanced her roles as a professional surfer, advocate, and parent. Her ability to navigate these different aspects of her life with grace and positivity endeared her to fans and followers around the world.

Bethany Hamilton's Legacy

Bethany Hamilton's legacy is one of courage, resilience, and unwavering determination. Her survival story is not just about overcoming a shark attack; it is about overcoming the fear, doubt, and physical limitations that followed the attack. Bethany's journey from that fateful day in 2003 to her continued success as a professional surfer and advocate is a testament to the power of the human spirit to overcome adversity.

Bethany's impact goes far beyond the world of surfing. She has inspired millions of people to face their challenges head-on, to never give up on their dreams, and to find strength in their faith and their communities. Her story has been a beacon of hope for those facing physical and emotional challenges, showing that with determination, support, and a positive attitude, anything is possible.

As Bethany continues to surf, advocate, and raise her family, she remains a symbol of resilience and positivity. Her story serves as a reminder that life's challenges, no matter how daunting, can be overcome with the right mindset and support. Bethany Hamilton's journey is a powerful example of what it means to turn tragedy into triumph, and her legacy will continue to inspire and uplift people for generations to come.

Chapter 18: The Sinking of the Titanic

The sinking of the RMS Titanic is one of the most infamous and tragic maritime disasters in history. This event has captured the imagination of millions and has been the subject of countless books, films, and studies. The story of the Titanic's maiden voyage, its collision with an iceberg, and the subsequent loss of over 1,500 lives is a tale of hubris, human error, technological innovation, and heartbreaking loss. The disaster not only revealed the vulnerabilities of human engineering but also prompted significant changes in maritime safety regulations that continue to influence the shipping industry to this day.

The Creation of the Titanic: A Marvel of Engineering

In the early 20th century, the competition among shipping lines for the transatlantic passenger trade was fierce. The White Star Line, a British shipping company, sought to dominate this market by constructing a trio of the largest and most luxurious ocean liners ever built: the Olympic, the Titanic, and the Britannic. The Titanic, the second of these ships, was designed to be the largest and most luxurious vessel afloat, a symbol of human achievement and technological prowess.

Construction of the Titanic began on March 31, 1909, at the Harland and Wolff shipyard in Belfast, Ireland. The ship was designed by J. Bruce Ismay, chairman of the White Star Line, and the renowned shipbuilder Thomas Andrews. The Titanic was an engineering marvel of its time, measuring 882 feet and 9 inches long, with a gross tonnage of 46,328 tons. It was equipped with the latest in maritime technology, including a double bottom and 16 watertight compartments that were designed to keep the ship afloat even if the hull was breached.

The ship's opulence was unparalleled, featuring a grand staircase, luxurious cabins, a swimming pool, a gymnasium, and multiple dining rooms. The first-class accommodations were particularly lavish, catering to some of the wealthiest and most influential people of the time. The Titanic was not just a mode of transportation; it was a floating palace, designed to offer its passengers the height of luxury and comfort during their journey across the Atlantic.

The ship's launch on May 31, 1911, was a significant event, drawing a crowd of over 100,000 spectators. The Titanic was hailed as "unsinkable," a claim that would later prove tragically ironic. The ship was equipped with the latest safety features, including a system of watertight doors that could be closed remotely in the event of an emergency. However, the Titanic was only equipped with enough lifeboats to accommodate about half of the passengers and crew, a decision based on outdated maritime safety regulations that did not take into account the ship's size and the number of people on board.

The Maiden Voyage: A Journey of Promise

The Titanic's maiden voyage was scheduled to depart from Southampton, England, on April 10, 1912, with stops in Cherbourg, France, and Queenstown (now Cobh), Ireland, before heading to New York City. The ship's departure was a momentous occasion, attended by thousands of people who came to witness the launch of the largest and most luxurious ship in the world.

The Titanic's passenger list was a reflection of the ship's grandeur, with some of the wealthiest and most famous individuals of the time on board. Among the first-class passengers were American millionaire John Jacob Astor IV, industrialist Benjamin Guggenheim, and Isidor Straus, co-owner of Macy's department store, along with his wife, Ida. The ship also carried many immigrants from Europe seeking a new life in America, traveling in third-class accommodations.

The Titanic's captain, Edward John Smith, was one of the most experienced and respected sea captains of the time. This was to be his final voyage before retirement, and he was chosen to command the Titanic due to his exemplary record and experience with large vessels. Captain Smith was well aware of the challenges of navigating the North Atlantic, especially during the spring, when icebergs were a common hazard.

As the Titanic set sail from Southampton, the mood on board was one of excitement and optimism. Passengers marveled at the ship's size, luxury, and modern amenities. The weather was clear, and the sea was calm, contributing to the sense of security and confidence that permeated the ship. For many on board, the Titanic's maiden voyage was a once-in-a-lifetime experience, an opportunity to travel in unprecedented luxury on a ship that was widely believed to be unsinkable.

The Iceberg Warning: A Catastrophic Oversight

As the Titanic made its way across the Atlantic, it received multiple warnings from other ships about the presence of icebergs in the area. On April 14, 1912, the day of the disaster, the ship received at least six ice warnings from various vessels. Despite these warnings, the Titanic maintained its speed of approximately 22 knots, just a few knots short of its maximum speed. The decision to continue at high speed was influenced by several factors, including the desire to make a fast crossing and the belief that the ship's size and modern construction would allow it to withstand any potential collision.

The Titanic's officers were aware of the ice warnings, but the ship's route was not altered significantly. The lookouts were instructed to keep a close watch for ice, but they were not provided with binoculars, which could have aided in spotting icebergs at a greater distance. Additionally, the moonless night and calm seas made it difficult to detect icebergs, as the lack of waves meant that the icebergs did not produce the telltale whitecaps that might have made them more visible.

At 11:40 PM on April 14, 1912, the lookouts in the crow's nest spotted an iceberg directly in the Titanic's path. They immediately rang the ship's bell and telephoned the bridge to alert the officers. First Officer William Murdoch, who was in command at the time, ordered the ship to turn hard to port and the engines to be reversed. However, the iceberg was too close, and the ship's momentum made it impossible to avoid a collision.

The iceberg struck the Titanic on its starboard side, creating a series of gashes below the waterline. The impact caused the hull plates to buckle, allowing water to flood into the first five watertight compartments. Although the Titanic was designed to stay afloat with up to four compartments breached, the flooding of the fifth compartment was catastrophic. The ship's bow began to sink, causing the stern to rise out of the water, placing immense stress on the vessel's structure.

The Sinking: Chaos and Heroism

As water poured into the Titanic's lower decks, it quickly became clear that the ship was doomed. Thomas Andrews, the ship's designer, conducted an inspection of the damage and reported to Captain Smith that the Titanic would sink within an hour and a half to two hours. Despite the initial disbelief, it was now a race against time to save as many lives as possible.

The Titanic was equipped with 20 lifeboats, which could accommodate a total of 1,178 people—far fewer than the 2,224 passengers and crew on board. The decision to carry fewer lifeboats was made to preserve the ship's aesthetic appeal and based on the assumption that the lifeboats would primarily be used to ferry passengers to a nearby rescue ship, not to evacuate the entire vessel. This tragic miscalculation would result in the loss of over 1,500 lives.

Captain Smith ordered the lifeboats to be uncovered and prepared for launching, but the evacuation process was chaotic and disorganized. Many passengers were initially reluctant to leave the perceived safety of the Titanic for the small, open lifeboats, especially since the ship still appeared stable. Additionally, there was confusion about the "women and children first" protocol, leading to lifeboats being launched partially filled, with some carrying as few as 12 people despite having a capacity of 65.

As the situation grew increasingly dire, passengers and crew began to realize the full gravity of the disaster. The ship's band, led by Wallace Hartley, famously continued to play music on the deck to calm passengers and maintain order. Their final song is widely believed to have been the hymn "Nearer, My God, to Thee," a poignant and tragic choice that has become synonymous with the sinking.

The Titanic's wireless operators, Jack Phillips and Harold Bride, worked tirelessly to send distress signals using the ship's Marconi wireless system. Their efforts were crucial in alerting nearby ships to the disaster, although the closest ship, the RMS Carpathia, was over 50 miles away and would not arrive in time to prevent the loss of life. The Californian, another ship in the area, was much closer but did not respond to the Titanic's distress signals, a failure that has been the subject of much controversy and speculation.

As the lifeboats were launched, the situation on board the Titanic grew increasingly desperate. The ship's forward motion had slowed, but the flooding continued unabated. Passengers in the lower decks, particularly those in third class, faced significant challenges in reaching the boat deck due to the ship's complex layout and the lack of clear instructions from the crew. Many third-class passengers were trapped below deck as the water rose, leading to a disproportionate loss of life among this group.

As the bow of the Titanic sank deeper into the water, the ship's stern began to rise, creating a steep incline that made it difficult for passengers and crew to move about the deck. At around 2:15 AM, the ship's lights flickered and then went out, plunging the Titanic into darkness. Moments later, the ship broke in two, with the stern remaining afloat for a brief period before it, too, sank beneath the icy waters of the North Atlantic.

The sinking of the Titanic was a terrifying and chaotic event, with passengers and crew struggling to find safety in the frigid waters. Many of those who had not made it into lifeboats were left clinging to debris or struggling to stay afloat in the freezing water, which was just 28°F (-2°C). Hypothermia set in quickly, and most of those in the water perished within minutes.

The Aftermath: Rescue and Reflection

The RMS Carpathia, commanded by Captain Arthur Rostron, arrived at the scene of the disaster at around 4:00 AM, approximately two hours after the Titanic had sunk. The Carpathia's crew worked tirelessly to rescue survivors from the lifeboats, pulling 705 people from the icy waters. The Carpathia's passengers, many of whom were awakened in the middle of the night to assist with the rescue efforts, provided blankets, clothing, and medical care to the survivors.

The rescue operation was a somber and emotional experience for all involved. Many of the survivors were in a state of shock, having lost friends, family members, and loved ones in the disaster. The Carpathia's passengers and crew did their best to comfort and care for the survivors, but the magnitude of the tragedy was overwhelming.

As the Carpathia made its way to New York, news of the Titanic's sinking began to spread, sending shockwaves around the world. The disaster dominated headlines, and people everywhere were horrified by the scale of the loss of life. The sinking of the Titanic was a stark reminder of the dangers of maritime travel and the limits of human engineering.

Upon arriving in New York on April 18, 1912, the Carpathia was met by a crowd of anxious relatives, friends, and reporters. The survivors were taken to hospitals, hotels, and other locations where they could receive care and begin the process of reuniting with their loved ones. The arrival of the Carpathia marked the end of the immediate crisis, but the impact of the Titanic's sinking would be felt for years to come.

The Legacy of the Titanic: Lessons Learned and Lasting Impact

The sinking of the Titanic had a profound impact on maritime safety regulations and practices. In the aftermath of the disaster, there was a widespread recognition that significant changes were needed to prevent such a tragedy from occurring again. The International Convention for the Safety of Life at Sea (SOLAS) was convened in 1914, resulting in a series of new safety regulations that remain in effect to this day.

One of the most significant changes was the requirement for all ships to carry enough lifeboats for every passenger and crew member on board, regardless of the ship's size or perceived safety. The practice of conducting regular lifeboat drills and ensuring that crew members were properly trained in emergency procedures also became mandatory. Additionally, the establishment of the International Ice Patrol, which monitors iceberg activity in the North Atlantic, was a direct response to the Titanic disaster.

The sinking of the Titanic also had a lasting impact on public consciousness. The story of the "unsinkable" ship that met a tragic end has become a symbol of human hubris and the dangers of overconfidence in technology. The Titanic's story has been retold countless times in books, films, documentaries, and exhibitions, each exploring different aspects of the disaster and its legacy.

Perhaps the most famous retelling of the Titanic's story is the 1997 film "Titanic," directed by James Cameron. The film, which became one of the highest-grossing movies of all time, brought the story of the Titanic to a new generation and rekindled interest in the disaster. The film's portrayal of the sinking, with its mix of historical accuracy and fictional elements, has become deeply ingrained in popular culture.

The Titanic has also been the subject of numerous expeditions and scientific studies. The wreck of the Titanic, discovered in 1985 by oceanographer Robert Ballard, lies at a depth of approximately 12,500 feet (3,800 meters) on the floor of the North Atlantic. The discovery of the wreck provided valuable insights into the final moments of the Titanic and the condition of the ship after more than 70 years underwater. The wreck has since become a site of historical and scientific significance, with ongoing efforts to preserve and study it.

Human Stories: Remembering the Lives Lost and Saved

While the Titanic is often remembered for its technological achievements and the scale of the disaster, it is important to remember that it was a human tragedy. The sinking claimed the lives of over 1,500 people, each with their own story, hopes, and dreams. The passengers and crew represented a cross-section of society, from the wealthy and powerful to the poor and vulnerable, all brought together by the promise of a new life or the adventure of a transatlantic journey.

The stories of those who survived and those who perished have been preserved through accounts, letters, and oral histories. Some of the most poignant stories include those of the families who were separated during the evacuation, the acts of bravery by crew members and passengers, and the heartbreak of those who waited in vain for news of their loved ones.

One of the most famous stories is that of the Straus family. Isidor Straus, the co-owner of Macy's department store, and his wife, Ida, were first-class passengers on the Titanic. When it came time to evacuate, Ida refused to leave her husband, stating that they had been together for many years and would not be separated now. The couple was last seen sitting together on the deck, holding hands as the ship went down.

Another story of bravery and selflessness is that of the ship's band, led by Wallace Hartley. The band continued to play music on the deck as the ship sank, providing comfort and solace to the passengers in their final moments. The band's actions have become legendary, symbolizing the courage and dignity displayed by many during the disaster.

The Titanic in Modern Culture: A Continuing Fascination

The story of the Titanic continues to captivate people around the world, more than a century after the disaster. The ship's name has become synonymous with both luxury and tragedy, and the events of April 14-15, 1912, have left an indelible mark on history.

The Titanic has inspired a vast body of literature, from historical accounts to fictionalized retellings. It has been the subject of countless documentaries, exhibitions, and even musical compositions. The ship's legacy is also preserved through the work of Titanic enthusiasts and historians who continue to study and share the story of the ill-fated voyage.

In recent years, there has been growing interest in the Titanic as an archaeological site. The wreck, lying at the bottom of the North Atlantic, has been the focus of numerous expeditions aimed at documenting and preserving the remains of the ship. The challenges of exploring and preserving the Titanic's wreck are immense, given the extreme depth, the corrosive environment, and the ethical considerations surrounding the site as a grave.

The Titanic also serves as a powerful reminder of the limits of human ambition and the need for humility in the face of nature's forces. The disaster prompted significant changes in maritime safety, but it also highlighted the need for ongoing vigilance and respect for the unpredictable power of the sea.

Conclusion: The Enduring Legacy of the Titanic

The sinking of the Titanic is a story of innovation, tragedy, and human resilience. It is a reminder of the fragility of life and the importance of preparedness, humility, and compassion. The disaster not only changed the course of maritime history but also left a lasting impact on the collective consciousness of people around the world.

As we reflect on the Titanic's legacy, it is essential to remember the human cost of the disaster and to honor the memories of those who were lost. The Titanic's story continues to resonate with us today, offering lessons in both the triumphs and the failures of human endeavor. It is a story that will continue to be told for generations to come, as a symbol of both the heights of human achievement and the depths of human tragedy.

Chapter 19: Hugh Glass' Journey

Hugh Glass' journey is one of the most legendary survival stories in American history, a tale of remarkable endurance, resilience, and sheer determination. The story of Hugh Glass has been immortalized in books, movies, and folklore, capturing the imagination of generations. Set against the backdrop of the American frontier in the early 19th century, Glass' journey is a testament to the human spirit's ability to overcome unimaginable odds.

Early Life and the American Frontier

Hugh Glass was born around 1783 in Pennsylvania to Irish immigrant parents. Little is known about his early life, but like many men of his time, Glass was drawn to the vast, untamed wilderness of the American frontier. The early 19th century was a period of westward expansion in the United States, with trappers, traders, and explorers venturing into the Rocky Mountains and beyond in search of furs, riches, and adventure.

The frontier was a harsh and dangerous place, inhabited by Native American tribes, wild animals, and unforgiving landscapes. Men like Glass were part of a hardy breed known as mountain men, who lived off the land, trapping beaver and other animals for their valuable pelts. These trappers often spent months or even years in the wilderness, facing extreme weather, isolation, and the constant threat of attack from both animals and humans.

Before his fateful journey, Glass had already experienced a life of danger and adventure. According to some accounts, he was captured by pirates in the Gulf of Mexico and forced to join their crew. After escaping, he made his way to the Texas coast, where he was reportedly captured by the Pawnee tribe. Unlike many captives, Glass managed to gain the trust of the Pawnee and lived among them for several years, learning their language and customs. These experiences would serve him well in the years to come, as they instilled in him the skills and knowledge needed to survive in the wild.

The Expedition with General William Henry Ashley

In 1822, Hugh Glass joined an expedition led by General William Henry Ashley, a prominent fur trader and businessman. Ashley's expedition was part of the larger fur trade enterprise known as the Rocky Mountain Fur Company, which sought to exploit the vast fur resources of the American West. The expedition was composed of trappers, traders, and explorers, all eager to make their fortunes in the wilderness.

The journey took Glass and his fellow trappers deep into the uncharted territories of the Missouri River and the Rocky Mountains. The men faced numerous challenges, including difficult terrain, unpredictable weather, and the ever-present threat of conflict with Native American tribes. Despite these dangers, the expedition pressed on, driven by the promise of lucrative fur trading opportunities.

Glass quickly earned a reputation as a skilled and resourceful trapper, known for his ability to navigate the wilderness and his deep understanding of the land. His experience living among the Pawnee gave him a unique perspective on survival, allowing him to thrive in the harsh conditions of the frontier. However, it was during this expedition that Glass would face the greatest challenge of his life.

The Grizzly Bear Attack

In the summer of 1823, while scouting ahead of the main party along the Grand River in present-day South Dakota, Hugh Glass encountered a mother grizzly bear with her two cubs. The bear, feeling threatened by Glass's presence, charged at him with incredible speed and ferocity. Glass had little time to react as the massive animal pounced on him, knocking him to the ground.

The grizzly bear inflicted horrific injuries on Glass, tearing at his flesh with its powerful claws and teeth. Despite the severity of his wounds, Glass managed to fight back, using his knife to stab the bear repeatedly. The struggle was fierce and brutal, with Glass sustaining multiple deep lacerations, a broken leg, and a nearly scalped head. Miraculously, he managed to kill the bear, but he was left severely injured and barely clinging to life.

When members of the expedition found Glass, they were shocked by the extent of his injuries. His wounds were so severe that it was clear he would not survive without immediate medical attention, which was impossible in the remote wilderness. The expedition leader, Andrew Henry, made the difficult decision to leave Glass behind, believing that he was beyond saving.

Two men, John Fitzgerald and a young Jim Bridger, were assigned to stay with Glass until he died and then bury him. However, after several days, when Glass did not succumb to his injuries, Fitzgerald and Bridger grew increasingly anxious. Fearing attacks from Native American tribes and impatient to rejoin the main party, the two men decided to abandon Glass, taking his rifle, knife, and other supplies with them. They left him to die alone in the wilderness, assuming that his death was inevitable.

The Journey of Survival

But Hugh Glass did not die. Despite his life-threatening injuries, he was determined to survive. Left with nothing but his will to live, Glass began one of the most remarkable journeys in the annals of survival history. He was over 200 miles from the nearest American settlement at Fort Kiowa, with no weapons, supplies, or companions, and facing a landscape filled with dangers.

Unable to walk due to his broken leg, Glass initially crawled, dragging himself through the wilderness inch by inch. His wounds were festering, and he was in constant agony, but he refused to give up. Glass knew that his only hope of survival was to reach the Cheyenne River, where he could find water and potentially fashion a crude raft to carry him downstream.

Glass's knowledge of the land and his survival skills were crucial during this time. He foraged for food, eating wild berries, roots, and small animals that he could catch. At one point, Glass reportedly fended off a pack of wolves to scavenge meat from a bison carcass, risking his life to stave off starvation. He also relied on his understanding of Native American medicine, using traditional remedies to treat his wounds and prevent infection.

As Glass continued his journey, he faced constant threats from the environment. The weather was harsh, with cold nights and scorching days. The terrain was unforgiving, with rugged mountains, dense forests, and treacherous rivers. Despite these challenges, Glass pressed on, driven by a combination of sheer determination and a desire for revenge against the men who had abandoned him.

After several weeks of crawling and eventually limping, Glass reached the Cheyenne River. Here, he was able to build a crude raft and float downstream toward Fort Kiowa. The journey on the river was perilous, with the constant risk of drowning or being attacked by hostile Native American tribes. However, Glass's luck held, and he eventually reached the safety of Fort Kiowa.

The Quest for Revenge

Upon reaching Fort Kiowa, Glass's first priority was to recover from his injuries. The fort's residents were astonished by his survival and helped nurse him back to health. However, Glass was not content to simply survive; he was consumed by a desire for revenge against John Fitzgerald and Jim Bridger, the men who had abandoned him to die.

Once he had recovered sufficiently, Glass set out to track down the two men. His journey took him through the wilderness and to various outposts and trading posts, where he gathered information about their whereabouts. Glass eventually found Bridger at a fur trading post. The young man, barely out of his teens, was terrified and remorseful. Glass, perhaps recognizing Bridger's youth and fear, decided to spare his life, instead giving him a stern warning.

Glass continued his quest for Fitzgerald, eventually tracking him down to Fort Atkinson, where Fitzgerald had enlisted in the U.S. Army. Enraged, Glass confronted Fitzgerald, but he was unable to exact his revenge due to Fitzgerald's status as a soldier. Killing a U.S. soldier would have resulted in severe consequences for Glass, so he reluctantly let Fitzgerald go, though not without reclaiming his stolen rifle.

Legacy and Impact

Hugh Glass's journey is one of the most extraordinary tales of survival and endurance in American history. His story has become a symbol of the indomitable human spirit, illustrating what can be achieved through sheer willpower and determination. Glass's survival was not just a physical feat; it was a triumph of the human spirit over adversity.

Glass returned to the life of a trapper and mountain man, continuing to live and work in the wilderness for many years. He eventually met his end in 1833, reportedly killed in an attack by the Arikara tribe near the Yellowstone River. However, his legend lived on, passed down through oral tradition, books, and later, popular media.

One of the most famous retellings of Glass's story is Michael Punke's novel *The Revenant*, which was later adapted into an Oscar-winning film starring Leonardo DiCaprio as Hugh Glass. The film brought Glass's story to a global audience, dramatizing his incredible journey of survival and revenge.

Glass's story has also been the subject of numerous historical studies, documentaries, and articles. Historians and writers have explored various aspects of his journey, from the accuracy of the accounts to the cultural significance of his survival. While some details of Glass's story have undoubtedly been embellished over time, the core of his journey—his struggle to survive against all odds—remains an inspiring and compelling narrative.

Cultural Significance and Mythology

Hugh Glass's journey has become more than just a story of survival; it has entered the realm of American mythology. Like other legendary figures of the American frontier, such as Daniel Boone and Davy Crockett, Glass represents the rugged individualism and pioneering spirit that characterized the early years of the United States. His story is a reflection of the challenges faced by those who ventured into the unknown, risking their lives in pursuit of fortune, freedom, or simply the thrill of adventure.

The mythologizing of Hugh Glass has also led to his story being interpreted in various ways. Some see Glass as a symbol of revenge and justice, a man who overcame insurmountable odds to seek retribution for the wrongs done to him. Others view him as a figure of endurance and resilience, embodying the qualities needed to survive in a hostile and unforgiving world.

In a broader sense, Hugh Glass's story is a reminder of the human capacity for survival. It speaks to the primal instincts that drive us to keep going, even when the odds are stacked against us. Glass's journey is a testament to the power of the human will, the ability to push through pain, fear, and despair in the pursuit of life.

Conclusion: The Enduring Legend of Hugh Glass

The legend of Hugh Glass continues to captivate and inspire people more than two centuries after his incredible journey. His story is a reminder of the harsh realities of life on the American frontier, a time and place where survival was often a matter of life and death. Glass's journey is a tale of courage, determination, and the relentless pursuit of life in the face of overwhelming adversity.

As we remember Hugh Glass, we honor not just the man, but the spirit of survival that he represents. His story is a beacon of hope for those who face their own struggles, a reminder that even in the darkest of times, the human spirit can prevail. Hugh Glass's journey is not just a story from the past; it is a timeless narrative that will continue to resonate with people for generations to come.

Chapter 20: Chris McCandless' Alaskan Odyssey

Chris McCandless' Alaskan odyssey is one of the most enigmatic and poignant stories of modern American exploration and adventure. His journey, which ultimately ended in tragedy, has captivated the imaginations of countless people around the world, inspiring books, documentaries, and films that seek to understand the motivations, dreams, and the ultimate demise of a young man who sought to live a life of uncompromising freedom and connection with nature.

Early Life and Influences

Christopher Johnson McCandless was born on February 12, 1968, in El Segundo, California, to Walt and Billie McCandless. From an early age, Chris exhibited a fierce independence and a desire to chart his own course in life. He was intelligent, introspective, and deeply passionate about literature, particularly the works of authors like Jack London, Henry David Thoreau, and Leo Tolstoy. These literary influences, which celebrated self-reliance, the beauty of the natural world, and the rejection of materialism, would play a significant role in shaping McCandless' worldview and the path he ultimately chose to follow.

Chris grew up in a middle-class family and had a relatively privileged upbringing. His father was a successful aerospace engineer, and his mother worked as a secretary before becoming involved in her husband's business. However, beneath the surface of this seemingly idyllic family life, there were tensions and conflicts that deeply affected Chris. He struggled with the hypocrisy and materialism he perceived in his parents, who he believed were more concerned with appearances and social status than with living authentically and meaningfully. This disillusionment with his family, combined with his growing admiration for the ideals of transcendentalism and the rugged individualism portrayed in the literature he loved, fueled Chris's desire to break away from conventional society and seek a more meaningful existence.

The Decision to Embark on a Journey

After graduating with honors from Emory University in Atlanta, Georgia, in 1990, Chris McCandless made a radical decision: he would abandon his comfortable life and embark on a journey of self-discovery across the United States. He donated his entire savings of $24,000 to Oxfam, a charity focused on alleviating global poverty, and set out on the road with little more than the clothes on his back, a few books, and a sense of purpose that few could understand.

Chris adopted the name "Alexander Supertramp" as he began his odyssey, a symbolic gesture that reflected his desire to leave behind his old life and identity. The name "Supertramp" itself was a nod to the idea of the wandering, free-spirited traveler, unburdened by societal expectations and constraints. He viewed his journey as a quest for truth and authenticity, an escape from the superficiality of modern life, and a return to a more primal and meaningful way of living.

Over the next two years, Chris traveled extensively across the United States, often hitchhiking, walking, or paddling his way from one place to another. He explored the deserts of the Southwest, the plains of the Midwest, and the forests of the Pacific Northwest. Along the way, he met a diverse cast of characters, many of whom were drawn to his charisma, idealism, and intensity. Despite his often solitary nature, Chris formed meaningful connections with several people during his travels, including an elderly man named Ron Franz, who was deeply affected by their friendship.

Chris's journey was marked by a deep sense of purpose and an unwavering commitment to living according to his principles. He sought to shed the trappings of modern society, including money, possessions, and relationships that he believed were inauthentic or superficial. Instead, he focused on cultivating self-reliance, simplicity, and a profound connection with nature. His journal entries and letters from this period reveal a young man who was both exhilarated and challenged by the freedom he had embraced, as well as someone who was constantly questioning the meaning of life and his place in the world.

The Alaskan Dream

For Chris McCandless, Alaska represented the ultimate test of his ideals and the culmination of his journey. The vast, unspoiled wilderness of the Alaskan interior was the perfect setting for him to live out his dream of self-sufficiency and communion with nature. He envisioned himself surviving alone in the wild, living off the land, and proving that he could endure the challenges that such a life would entail. Alaska, in his mind, was a place where he could escape the constraints of civilization and experience true freedom.

In April 1992, Chris made his way to Fairbanks, Alaska, after traveling through the western United States. He arrived in Fairbanks with minimal supplies, including a .22 caliber rifle, a bag of rice, some books, and a small collection of gear. His plan was to hike deep into the wilderness, far from any roads or towns, and live off the land for an extended period of time.

Before setting out on his journey, Chris received a ride from Jim Gallien, a local electrician, who dropped him off near the Stampede Trail, a remote and rugged path that led into the Alaskan interior. Gallien was concerned about Chris's lack of preparation and tried to persuade him to reconsider his plans, offering him food and better gear, but Chris was resolute. He believed that he could survive with what he had and was eager to begin his adventure.

On April 28, 1992, Chris McCandless, now fully embracing his identity as Alexander Supertramp, began his trek into the wilderness. He crossed the Teklanika River, which was relatively low at the time, and headed deeper into the wild. After several days of hiking, he stumbled upon an old, abandoned bus, known as "Bus 142," which had been left behind by a construction company in the 1960s. The bus, situated in a clearing surrounded by dense forest, offered shelter from the elements, and Chris decided to make it his base of operations.

Life in the Wild

For the next several months, Chris McCandless lived in and around the bus, attempting to fulfill his dream of self-sufficiency in the wild. He hunted small game, such as squirrels and birds, and foraged for edible plants, relying on his knowledge of the wilderness and the information he had gleaned from books. He also kept a journal, documenting his experiences, thoughts, and feelings as he adapted to life in the wild.

Initially, Chris appeared to thrive in the Alaskan wilderness. His journal entries from this period reflect a sense of accomplishment and contentment, as he successfully hunted and foraged for food, enjoyed the solitude of the wilderness, and reveled in the beauty of his surroundings. He wrote about the peace he found in nature, the satisfaction of living simply, and the joy of being free from the constraints of society.

However, as the weeks turned into months, the challenges of living in the wild began to take their toll. Chris's supplies began to dwindle, and he found it increasingly difficult to find enough food to sustain himself. His journal entries from this period reveal a growing sense of desperation as he struggled to cope with hunger, loneliness, and the harsh realities of the wilderness. Despite his initial optimism, it became clear that Chris was not as prepared for life in the wild as he had believed.

One of the most significant challenges Chris faced was his lack of knowledge about the local flora. While he had some understanding of edible plants, he made a critical mistake that would ultimately contribute to his downfall. In July 1992, Chris consumed seeds from a plant known as wild potato (Hedysarum alpinum), which he mistakenly believed were safe to eat. However, these seeds contain a toxic alkaloid that can cause paralysis and, in high enough doses, death. The exact cause of Chris's death remains a subject of debate, but many believe that his ingestion of the toxic seeds severely weakened him, making it impossible for him to gather food or hike out of the wilderness.

As Chris's condition deteriorated, he became increasingly isolated and desperate. His final journal entries, written in a shaky hand, reveal a young man who was aware that he was dying but who still clung to hope. He wrote about his longing to return to society, his regret for the pain he had caused his family, and his realization that happiness is only real when shared with others. In his final days, Chris scrawled a note that read, "I have had a happy life and thank the Lord. Goodbye and may God bless all!"

On September 6, 1992, Chris McCandless's body was discovered by a group of moose hunters who stumbled upon Bus 142. He had died of starvation, his body weighing just 67 pounds. The hunters notified authorities, and soon after, the story of Chris McCandless began to spread, capturing the attention of the public and the media.

The Aftermath and Public Reaction

The discovery of Chris McCandless's body sparked a wide range of reactions from the public and the media. Some people saw him as a hero, a modern-day Thoreau who had the courage to pursue his ideals and live life on his own terms. They admired his rejection of materialism, his love of nature, and his quest for spiritual and personal fulfillment. To these admirers, Chris's journey represented the ultimate expression of individualism and freedom, a noble if tragic, pursuit of a life unburdened by societal expectations.

Others, however, viewed Chris's odyssey as the folly of a naive and reckless young man who had been woefully unprepared for the harsh realities of the Alaskan wilderness. Critics argued that Chris's idealism had blinded him to the dangers of the wild and that his lack of preparation, experience, and respect for nature had ultimately led to his death. Some Alaskans, in particular, were critical of Chris, seeing him as an outsider who had romanticized the wilderness without understanding the skills and knowledge needed to survive in such a harsh environment.

The story of Chris McCandless was brought to a wider audience with the publication of Jon Krakauer's book *Into the Wild* in 1996. Krakauer, a journalist and mountaineer, became fascinated by Chris's story after writing a magazine article about him. In *Into the Wild*, Krakauer explores Chris's life, motivations, and the events that led to his death. The book delves into Chris's family background, his philosophical influences, and the people he met during his travels. Krakauer also draws parallels between Chris's journey and his own experiences as a young man, including his near-fatal climb of the Devil's Thumb in Alaska.

Into the Wild was both a commercial and critical success, and it sparked renewed interest in Chris McCandless's story. The book was later adapted into a film directed by Sean Penn, which further popularized the story and introduced it to a global audience. The film, like the book, presents a sympathetic portrayal of Chris, emphasizing his ideals, his love of nature, and his desire to live authentically. However, it also acknowledges the tragic nature of his journey and the mistakes that ultimately led to his death.

Legacy and Cultural Impact

The legacy of Chris McCandless is complex and multifaceted. His story has become a touchstone for discussions about the meaning of freedom, the allure of the wilderness, and the dangers of idealism. For some, Chris is a symbol of the human desire to break free from societal constraints and live a life of purpose and authenticity. His journey resonates with those who feel disillusioned with modern life and who long for a deeper connection with nature and themselves.

For others, Chris's story serves as a cautionary tale about the dangers of romanticizing the wilderness and underestimating the challenges it presents. His death is a reminder that while nature can be beautiful and inspiring, it is also unforgiving and indifferent to human aspirations. The wilderness demands respect, knowledge, and preparation, and those who venture into it without these things do so at their peril.

The bus where Chris McCandless spent his final days became a pilgrimage site for those who were inspired by his story. Over the years, hundreds of people made the difficult journey to visit the bus, leaving behind notes, mementos, and tributes to Chris. However, the increasing number of visitors, some of whom required rescue due to the dangerous conditions, prompted the authorities to remove the bus in 2020. The bus was relocated to the University of Alaska Museum of the North in Fairbanks, where it is now part of an exhibit dedicated to Chris's story.

Chris McCandless's story continues to provoke debate and discussion. His life and death raise important questions about the pursuit of freedom, the role of nature in our lives, and the balance between idealism and reality. His journey has inspired many to reflect on their own lives, their relationship with nature, and the choices they make in the pursuit of happiness and fulfillment.

Conclusion: The Enduring Mystery of Chris McCandless

Chris McCandless's Alaskan odyssey is a story that defies easy interpretation. It is a tale of adventure and tragedy, of ideals and mistakes, of a young man who sought something more from life and paid the ultimate price for his quest. His journey into the wild was driven by a desire to find truth, meaning, and freedom, but it ended in isolation, starvation, and death.

Yet, despite its tragic ending, Chris's story has continued to resonate with people around the world. His life and death have become a symbol of the human yearning for a life of purpose, authenticity, and connection with the natural world. While some may view his journey as a cautionary tale, others see it as an inspiring example of the lengths to which a person will go in the pursuit of their dreams.

In the end, Chris McCandless's story is a reminder of the complexities of the human spirit, the allure of the wild, and the dangers of uncompromising idealism. It is a story that challenges us to think about our own lives, our relationship with nature, and the choices we make in the pursuit of happiness. And it is a story that, despite its tragic conclusion, continues to inspire, provoke, and move those who hear it.

Chapter 21: The Survival of Steve Backshall

Steve Backshall's survival story is a compelling narrative of resilience, determination, and an unyielding passion for wildlife and adventure. Known for his work as a naturalist, explorer, and television presenter, Backshall has faced numerous life-threatening situations throughout his career, each of which has tested his limits and showcased his extraordinary ability to survive in some of the most challenging environments on Earth. His survival is not just about overcoming physical dangers but also about his psychological fortitude, his deep connection with nature, and his unwavering commitment to conservation.

Early Life and Formative Years

Born on April 21, 1973, in Bagshot, Surrey, England, Stephen James Backshall was raised in a rural environment that nurtured his love for the natural world. His parents were both deeply interested in nature, and they encouraged Steve's curiosity from a young age. He spent much of his childhood exploring the woods and fields near his home, developing a keen interest in wildlife. These formative experiences would lay the foundation for his future career as an adventurer and naturalist.

Backshall's early life was also marked by his fascination with books and stories about exploration and wildlife. He was particularly inspired by the works of naturalists like Gerald Durrell and Sir David Attenborough, whose documentaries and books opened up new worlds of discovery and adventure for the young Steve. This inspiration fueled his desire to pursue a life dedicated to understanding and protecting the natural world.

After completing his education, Backshall attended the University of Exeter, where he studied English and theater studies. However, his passion for the natural world continued to grow, leading him to pursue further studies in biology. He later attended the University of Canterbury in New Zealand, where he earned a diploma in wildlife filmmaking. This academic background, combined with his love for adventure, would set the stage for his remarkable career in wildlife exploration and television.

The Path to Adventure and Exploration

Steve Backshall's career as an adventurer and naturalist took off in the late 1990s when he began working as a travel writer and expedition leader. His work took him to some of the most remote and dangerous places on Earth, where he encountered a wide variety of wildlife and natural hazards. During this period, Backshall honed his survival skills, learning to navigate treacherous landscapes, avoid dangerous animals, and cope with the physical and psychological challenges of life in the wild.

One of Backshall's early adventures involved traveling through the rainforests of Southeast Asia, where he faced numerous dangers, including venomous snakes, predatory animals, and treacherous terrain. These experiences not only tested his physical endurance but also deepened his understanding of the natural world and its many complexities. He learned to read the signs of the jungle, to anticipate the behavior of animals, and to respect the power of nature.

In the early 2000s, Backshall's career took a significant leap forward when he joined the BBC as a presenter for the popular wildlife series "The Really Wild Show." This program, which was aimed at young audiences, allowed Backshall to share his passion for wildlife with a broader audience and to inspire a new generation of nature enthusiasts. His enthusiasm, knowledge, and adventurous spirit made him a natural fit for the show, and he quickly became one of its most popular presenters.

However, it was Backshall's work on the television series "Deadly 60" that truly established him as a global figure in wildlife exploration and conservation. In "Deadly 60," Backshall traveled the world in search of the planet's most dangerous animals, showcasing their incredible adaptations and behaviors while also highlighting the importance of their conservation. The series was a massive success, earning Backshall numerous awards and a dedicated fan base.

The Thrill of Adventure and the Risks Involved

Steve Backshall's adventures have taken him to some of the most extreme and remote environments on the planet, where he has faced numerous life-threatening situations. These experiences have tested his survival skills and pushed him to the limits of his physical and mental endurance.

One of the most harrowing experiences of Backshall's career occurred during an expedition to the Arctic, where he and his team were filming a documentary about polar bears. The Arctic is one of the most unforgiving environments on Earth, with temperatures that can plummet to -50 degrees Celsius, blinding snowstorms, and the constant threat of polar bear attacks. Despite these challenges, Backshall was determined to capture footage of these magnificent animals in their natural habitat.

During the expedition, Backshall and his team encountered a polar bear that began to approach their camp. Polar bears are among the most dangerous predators in the world, and they are known to attack humans when food is scarce. As the bear drew closer, the team had to make a quick decision: either stay in the camp and hope the bear would move on or try to scare it away. Backshall, understanding the gravity of the situation, took the lead and used a flare gun to deter the bear. The tactic worked, and the bear eventually retreated, but the experience left the team shaken and acutely aware of the dangers they faced in the Arctic wilderness.

Another perilous situation occurred during an expedition to the jungles of South America, where Backshall and his team were filming a documentary about venomous snakes. The jungle is a place of constant danger, with venomous creatures, deadly diseases, and unpredictable weather posing significant risks. During this expedition, Backshall came dangerously close to being bitten by a highly venomous bushmaster snake, one of the deadliest snakes in the world. The snake struck at Backshall, missing him by mere inches. Had the snake's bite connected, it could have been fatal, as the venom of a bushmaster can cause rapid organ failure and death within hours.

Despite the close call, Backshall remained calm and composed, demonstrating his deep understanding of animal behavior and his ability to stay focused under pressure. His knowledge of first aid and snake venom also played a crucial role in his survival, as he was prepared to administer emergency treatment if needed. This incident highlighted the importance of preparation, knowledge, and composure when working in dangerous environments.

In addition to his encounters with dangerous animals, Backshall has also faced significant physical challenges during his expeditions. One of the most grueling experiences of his career was his attempt to climb an unclimbed peak in the remote jungles of Papua New Guinea. The expedition required Backshall and his team to navigate dense, uncharted jungle, endure extreme humidity and heat, and climb treacherous cliffs. The physical demands of the climb were immense, pushing Backshall to the brink of exhaustion.

The team faced numerous obstacles during the climb, including torrential rain, dangerous wildlife, and the constant threat of landslides. At one point, Backshall slipped while climbing a steep, muddy slope and nearly fell to his death. Fortunately, he managed to grab hold of a tree root and pull himself to safety. The experience underscored the risks involved in exploration and the importance of physical fitness, mental toughness, and teamwork in overcoming such challenges.

Psychological Resilience and the Will to Survive

While physical endurance and survival skills are crucial in extreme environments, psychological resilience is equally important. Steve Backshall's ability to maintain his composure, focus, and determination in the face of danger has been a key factor in his survival. His experiences in the wild have taught him the importance of mental toughness, adaptability, and a positive mindset.

One of the most challenging aspects of Backshall's work is the isolation and loneliness that often comes with exploring remote areas. Whether he is deep in the jungle, high in the mountains, or out on the open ocean, Backshall often finds himself far from the comforts of civilization and human companionship. The psychological strain of such isolation can be immense, leading to feelings of loneliness, anxiety, and even despair.

To cope with these challenges, Backshall has developed a deep sense of purpose and connection with the natural world. His love for wildlife and his commitment to conservation provide him with the motivation to endure the hardships of life in the wild. He has also learned to embrace the solitude, using it as an opportunity for reflection, meditation, and a deeper connection with nature.

Another psychological challenge that Backshall has faced is the fear that comes with encountering dangerous animals and navigating treacherous landscapes. Fear is a natural response to danger, and it can be both a help and a hindrance in survival situations. For Backshall, managing fear has been a crucial aspect of his survival strategy. He has learned to harness fear as a source of energy and focus, allowing it to sharpen his senses and enhance his decision-making abilities.

Backshall's approach to managing fear is rooted in his deep understanding of the natural world and his belief in his own abilities. He relies on his knowledge of animal behavior, his survival skills, and his experience to assess risks and make informed decisions. This confidence, combined with his respect for the power of nature, enables him to stay calm and composed even in the most dangerous situations.

The Role of Preparation and Training

Preparation and training have been essential components of Steve Backshall's survival strategy. Before embarking on any expedition, Backshall spends months, if not years, preparing for the challenges he is likely to face. This preparation includes physical training, research into the local environment and wildlife, and the acquisition of necessary skills and equipment.

Physical fitness is a critical aspect of Backshall's preparation. His expeditions often require him to hike long distances, climb mountains, paddle through rough waters, and carry heavy loads. To maintain the physical stamina needed for such activities, Backshall follows a rigorous training regimen that includes strength training, cardiovascular exercise, and endurance workouts. This physical preparation not only enhances his ability to navigate difficult terrain but also reduces the risk of injury and exhaustion.

In addition to physical training, Backshall invests significant time in researching the environments he will be exploring. This research includes studying maps, weather patterns, and local wildlife, as well as learning about the culture and customs of the people who live in the area. Understanding the behavior of the animals he may encounter is particularly important, as it allows him to anticipate potential dangers and respond appropriately.

Backshall also places a strong emphasis on acquiring and maintaining the necessary survival skills. These skills include first aid, navigation, fire-starting, shelter-building, and the ability to find and purify water. In some cases, he has sought out specialized training, such as learning how to handle venomous snakes or survive in extreme cold. This commitment to continuous learning and skill development has been a key factor in his ability to survive in a wide range of environments.

Conservation and Education: A Life Dedicated to Nature

Beyond his survival stories, Steve Backshall's life and career are deeply intertwined with his passion for conservation and education. His experiences in the wild have given him a profound appreciation for the fragility of the natural world and the importance of protecting it for future generations. Throughout his career, Backshall has used his platform to raise awareness about environmental issues and to inspire others to take action in support of conservation.

One of Backshall's primary goals is to educate people, especially young audiences, about the wonders of the natural world and the importance of preserving it. Through his television programs, books, and public speaking engagements, he has reached millions of people around the world, sharing his knowledge and enthusiasm for wildlife. He believes that education is the key to fostering a greater understanding of nature and motivating people to protect it.

Backshall's commitment to conservation is evident in his involvement with various environmental organizations and initiatives. He has worked with groups such as the World Wildlife Fund (WWF), the Royal Geographical Society, and the Zoological Society of London to support conservation efforts around the globe. Whether it is protecting endangered species, preserving natural habitats, or advocating for sustainable practices, Backshall is dedicated to making a positive impact on the environment.

Conclusion: A Legacy of Adventure and Conservation

The survival of Steve Backshall is not just a story of physical endurance and overcoming danger; it is a testament to the power of passion, knowledge, and resilience. Throughout his life, Backshall has faced some of the most challenging environments on Earth, encountering deadly animals, harsh weather, and treacherous landscapes. Yet, through it all, he has remained committed to his mission of exploring and protecting the natural world.

Backshall's legacy extends beyond his survival stories. He has inspired countless people to appreciate the beauty and complexity of the natural world and to take action to preserve it. His work as an educator, conservationist, and adventurer has left a lasting impact on the way we understand and interact with nature.

In the end, Steve Backshall's story is one of courage, determination, and a deep love for the natural world. It is a story that reminds us of the importance of respecting nature, embracing adventure, and dedicating ourselves to the preservation of the planet we call home.

Chapter 22: The Survival of Anna Bågenholm

Anna Bågenholm's survival story is one of the most extraordinary tales of human resilience, medical innovation, and sheer determination in the face of insurmountable odds. Her experience, often referred to as one of the most remarkable medical recoveries in history, is a testament to the power of the human body and mind, as well as the incredible advancements in medical science. This story is not just about surviving against all odds; it is about the interplay between fate, the human will to live, and the cutting-edge medical techniques that ultimately saved her life.

The Background and Early Life of Anna Bågenholm

Anna Bågenholm was born on June 29, 1970, in the town of Vänersborg, Sweden. Growing up in a country known for its cold winters and rugged natural landscapes, she developed a love for the outdoors from a young age. Her childhood was filled with activities such as skiing, hiking, and exploring the wilderness, which instilled in her a deep appreciation for nature and a strong sense of adventure. This adventurous spirit would later play a crucial role in her life, both in terms of her career and her eventual survival story.

Bågenholm pursued a career in medicine, driven by her desire to help others and her fascination with the complexities of the human body. She became a radiologist, a profession that allowed her to combine her scientific interests with her commitment to patient care. As a young doctor, she was known for her dedication, her calm demeanor, and her ability to remain composed under pressure—traits that would become critically important during the events that would unfold in May 1999.

The Fateful Day: May 20, 1999

On May 20, 1999, Anna Bågenholm, who was 29 years old at the time, set out on what seemed like a routine ski trip in the mountains near Narvik, Norway. She was accompanied by two of her colleagues, both of whom were also doctors. The trio were experienced skiers, well-versed in the challenges of skiing in rugged and icy conditions. They were confident in their abilities and eager to enjoy the beautiful Norwegian landscape.

The group had chosen a challenging route, descending a steep mountain slope in the Kåfjord region, which is known for its stunning but treacherous terrain. The weather was typical for that time of year—cold, with a light snow cover—but nothing that would have raised significant concerns for the seasoned skiers.

As they made their way down the mountain, Bågenholm lost control of her skis while navigating a particularly steep section. She veered off course and found herself heading towards a frozen stream. Despite her best efforts to regain control, she crashed into the ice, breaking through the thin surface and becoming trapped underneath. This was the beginning of an ordeal that would push her to the brink of death and beyond.

The Struggle Under the Ice

The stream was fed by glacial meltwater, making it extremely cold, with temperatures just above freezing. As Bågenholm broke through the ice, she found herself submerged in the freezing water, unable to move or escape. The icy water rapidly sapped her body heat, and within minutes, she began to experience the initial stages of hypothermia.

Hypothermia is a condition where the body loses heat faster than it can produce it, leading to a dangerous drop in core body temperature. As her body temperature fell, Bågenholm's physiological responses began to slow down. Her heart rate decreased, her breathing became shallow, and her mental state started to deteriorate. Despite the dire situation, Bågenholm managed to find a small air pocket under the ice, which allowed her to keep her head above water and continue breathing, albeit with great difficulty.

Her colleagues, who witnessed the accident, immediately realized the severity of the situation. They rushed to her aid, but their attempts to pull her out of the water were unsuccessful. The ice was thick, and Bågenholm was trapped beneath it, unable to move or communicate effectively. As the minutes ticked by, her situation became increasingly dire.

Recognizing that they needed professional help, Bågenholm's colleagues made a desperate call to emergency services, explaining the situation and requesting immediate assistance. They also tried to keep Bågenholm calm, encouraging her to hold on as they waited for rescue. Despite their best efforts, however, Bågenholm's condition continued to deteriorate as the cold water took its toll on her body.

The Arrival of the Rescue Team

It took over 40 minutes for the rescue team to arrive at the scene. By this time, Bågenholm had been submerged in the freezing water for an extended period, and her chances of survival appeared slim. The rescue team, which included paramedics, firefighters, and mountain rescue specialists, immediately set to work trying to free her from the icy grip of the stream.

Using a variety of tools, including ice axes and chainsaws, the rescue team painstakingly cut through the ice to reach Bågenholm. It was a race against time, as they knew that every minute spent in the freezing water would reduce her chances of survival. After nearly an hour of intense effort, they finally managed to pull her from the water.

By the time Bågenholm was freed, she had been submerged in the ice-cold water for over 80 minutes. Her body temperature had plummeted to an astonishing 13.7 degrees Celsius (56.7 degrees Fahrenheit), the lowest body temperature ever recorded in a human who survived. She was unconscious, unresponsive, and, by all conventional medical standards, clinically dead.

The Fight for Life: Resuscitation and Medical Intervention

Despite her condition, the rescue team refused to give up on Bågenholm. They immediately began resuscitation efforts, performing CPR and attempting to restore her vital signs. However, her body was so cold that normal resuscitation techniques were ineffective. The decision was made to airlift her to the nearest hospital, the Tromsø University Hospital, which had the specialized equipment needed to treat such a severe case of hypothermia.

During the helicopter flight, the medical team continued their efforts to revive Bågenholm. They used defibrillators to try to restart her heart, but the extreme cold had slowed her metabolism to the point where her body was in a state of suspended animation. Her heart was barely beating, and her brain activity was minimal. However, the cold that had brought her so close to death was also the factor that could potentially save her life.

Upon arrival at the hospital, Bågenholm was immediately placed in the care of Dr. Mads Gilbert, a specialist in emergency medicine who was well-versed in the treatment of severe hypothermia. Dr. Gilbert and his team understood that Bågenholm's only chance of survival lay in gradually warming her body and restoring her normal physiological functions.

They began by administering warm intravenous fluids and using a heart-lung machine to slowly raise her body temperature. This machine, known as extracorporeal membrane oxygenation (ECMO), is used to oxygenate the blood outside the body and then pump it back into the patient, allowing the heart and lungs to rest while the body is warmed. The process was slow and delicate, as raising her temperature too quickly could lead to dangerous complications, such as cardiac arrhythmias.

For hours, the medical team worked tirelessly to stabilize Bågenholm's condition. Her heart eventually began to beat on its own, albeit weakly, and her body temperature slowly started to rise. However, the doctors knew that the most significant challenge lay ahead—assessing the extent of the damage caused by her prolonged exposure to the cold and her extended period without adequate oxygen.

The Road to Recovery

Against all odds, Anna Bågenholm began to show signs of recovery. Her heart rate stabilized, and her body temperature returned to normal. However, she remained in a coma, and the medical team was unsure whether she would ever regain consciousness. The primary concern was the potential for severe brain damage, as her brain had been deprived of oxygen for an extended period.

For ten days, Bågenholm remained in a coma, her condition closely monitored by the medical staff. The team feared that even if she survived, she might suffer from significant cognitive impairments or physical disabilities. But, in what can only be described as a medical miracle, Bågenholm defied all expectations.

Slowly but surely, she began to regain consciousness. As she woke from the coma, it became clear that her brain function had been preserved far better than anyone had anticipated. She was able to recognize her family and communicate with the medical staff, indicating that her cognitive abilities were largely intact. Over the following weeks, Bågenholm continued to make remarkable progress. She regained the ability to speak, move, and perform basic tasks. Her recovery was nothing short of miraculous, and it astounded the medical community.

As she gradually regained her strength, Bågenholm was transferred from the intensive care unit to a rehabilitation center, where she underwent extensive physical and occupational therapy. The focus was on rebuilding her muscle strength, improving her coordination, and helping her relearn everyday skills. The road to recovery was long and challenging, but Bågenholm faced it with the same determination and resilience that had kept her alive in the icy waters.

The Science Behind Her Survival

Anna Bågenholm's survival is not only a testament to her extraordinary resilience but also a significant case study in the science of hypothermia and resuscitation. Her case provided valuable insights into how the human body can survive extreme conditions and how modern medical techniques can push the boundaries of life and death.

One of the key factors in Bågenholm's survival was the concept of "suspended animation," a state in which the body's metabolic processes are slowed to the point where they require minimal oxygen. When Bågenholm's body temperature dropped to 13.7 degrees Celsius, her metabolism slowed dramatically, reducing the amount of oxygen her brain and other vital organs needed to function. This slowing of metabolic processes is what allowed her to survive for so long without adequate oxygen.

Another critical factor was the use of ECMO, which allowed the medical team to oxygenate her blood and gradually raise her body temperature while her heart and lungs were supported. This technique is now a standard treatment for severe hypothermia, and Bågenholm's case helped to establish its effectiveness.

Bågenholm's survival also highlighted the importance of prompt and continuous resuscitation efforts. Despite being clinically dead for over two hours, the rescue team and medical staff never gave up on her, continuing their efforts to revive her even when the situation seemed hopeless. Their persistence, combined with the advanced medical techniques used, ultimately saved her life.

Life After Survival: Anna Bågenholm Today

After her miraculous recovery, Anna Bågenholm returned to her life with a new perspective. While she had some lingering physical effects from her ordeal, including occasional weakness in her hands, she was able to resume her work as a radiologist. Her experience had given her a deeper appreciation for life and a renewed sense of purpose in her medical career.

Bågenholm's story has inspired countless people around the world. Her survival is often cited as one of the most remarkable examples of human resilience and the power of modern medicine. She has shared her story in interviews, documentaries, and medical conferences, helping to raise awareness about the dangers of hypothermia and the potential for recovery even in the most extreme cases.

Her case has also had a lasting impact on the medical community, contributing to advancements in the treatment of hypothermia and influencing protocols for resuscitation and critical care. Bågenholm's survival has shown that with the right combination of medical knowledge, technology, and human determination, it is possible to bring someone back from the brink of death.

Conclusion: A Tale of Miraculous Survival

The survival of Anna Bågenholm is a story that transcends the boundaries of medicine, science, and human endurance. It is a story that challenges our understanding of life and death and pushes the limits of what we believe is possible. Bågenholm's ordeal in the icy waters of Norway is a testament to the strength of the human spirit, the power of medical innovation, and the enduring will to live.

Her survival is not just a medical miracle; it is a profound reminder of the fragility of life and the extraordinary capacity of the human body and mind to overcome the most extreme challenges. Anna Bågenholm's story continues to inspire, educate, and remind us that even in the face of overwhelming odds, there is always hope.

Chapter 23: The Miracle of the Sichuan Earthquake

The Sichuan Earthquake, often referred to as the 2008 Wenchuan Earthquake, is one of the most devastating natural disasters in recent history. Striking the Sichuan province of China on May 12, 2008, this massive earthquake measured 7.9 on the Richter scale and resulted in widespread destruction, leaving behind a tragic loss of life and a massive humanitarian crisis. Despite the overwhelming devastation, stories of survival and resilience emerged from the rubble, leading many to describe the event as a "miracle." The Sichuan Earthquake is not just a tale of destruction and loss, but also one of hope, heroism, and the indomitable human spirit.

The Earthquake: A Catastrophic Event

The earthquake struck at 2:28 PM local time, with its epicenter located in Wenchuan County, about 80 kilometers northwest of Chengdu, the capital of Sichuan province. The seismic event was caused by the collision of the Indian and Eurasian tectonic plates, a process that has been ongoing for millions of years and is responsible for the formation of the Himalayan Mountain range.

The magnitude of the earthquake was immense, and its impact was felt over a vast area, with tremors being reported as far away as Beijing and Shanghai. The quake released an enormous amount of energy, equivalent to the detonation of hundreds of atomic bombs, causing the ground to shake violently and leading to widespread structural failures.

The Sichuan province, known for its rugged terrain, was particularly vulnerable to the earthquake's effects. The steep mountains and deep valleys of the region amplified the seismic waves, causing landslides and collapsing buildings. The earthquake's shallow depth of just 19 kilometers further exacerbated the damage, as the seismic energy was concentrated near the surface, leading to more intense shaking.

The Devastation: Human and Material Losses

The immediate aftermath of the earthquake was catastrophic. Entire towns and villages were reduced to rubble, with many buildings collapsing in seconds. Schools, hospitals, and residential buildings were among the hardest hit, leading to a significant loss of life. In some areas, the destruction was so complete that little remained standing.

The human toll was staggering. Official reports estimate that approximately 87,000 people lost their lives, including nearly 5,000 children who were trapped in the ruins of their schools. In addition to the fatalities, over 370,000 people were injured, many of them seriously. More than 18,000 people were reported missing, and millions were left homeless, forced to live in makeshift shelters in the days and weeks following the quake.

The material losses were equally severe. The earthquake destroyed or severely damaged nearly 7 million buildings, including critical infrastructure such as roads, bridges, and dams. The economic impact was estimated to be in the hundreds of billions of dollars, as the region's economy, which relied heavily on agriculture, industry, and tourism, was devastated.

The scale of the disaster overwhelmed local and national authorities, leading to a massive humanitarian crisis. Rescue and relief efforts were hampered by the destruction of transportation networks, as landslides and collapsed bridges made many areas inaccessible. The situation was further complicated by aftershocks, some of which were powerful enough to cause additional damage and loss of life.

The Response: National and International Efforts

In the wake of the earthquake, the Chinese government launched one of the largest emergency response efforts in its history. The People's Liberation Army (PLA) was mobilized, with tens of thousands of soldiers and paramilitary personnel dispatched to the affected areas to assist with rescue and relief operations. The government also called for volunteers and appealed to the international community for assistance.

The response was swift and overwhelming. Within hours of the earthquake, rescue teams began arriving in the affected areas, working tirelessly to search for survivors and provide medical care to the injured. The scale of the destruction made the task daunting, but the rescuers were undeterred. Using everything from heavy machinery to their bare hands, they dug through the rubble in search of life.

One of the most heart-wrenching aspects of the disaster was the collapse of numerous schools, which led to the deaths of thousands of children. In many cases, these schools had been poorly constructed, a fact that became a source of outrage and grief for parents and communities. The government's response included a pledge to investigate the causes of the school collapses and to hold those responsible accountable.

International aid poured in from around the world. Dozens of countries and international organizations provided financial assistance, medical supplies, and rescue teams. The United Nations, the Red Cross, and numerous non-governmental organizations (NGOs) played a crucial role in coordinating the global response. The international community's support was instrumental in alleviating the immediate suffering of the survivors and in beginning the long process of rebuilding.

Miracles Amidst the Rubble: Stories of Survival

Amidst the overwhelming devastation, stories of survival began to emerge, providing glimmers of hope in an otherwise bleak landscape. These stories, often referred to as "miracles," highlighted the incredible resilience of the human spirit and the determination of both survivors and rescuers.

One of the most famous stories is that of a three-year-old girl named Song Xinyi, who was rescued after being buried under the rubble of her home for over 70 hours. When rescuers finally reached her, they found that she had been protected by her grandmother, who had shielded her with her own body. Tragically, the grandmother did not survive, but her selfless act saved Song's life. The image of the little girl, her face caked with dust but alive, became a symbol of hope and resilience.

Another remarkable story is that of a schoolteacher named Fan Meizhong, who became known as the "running teacher" after he famously fled his classroom during the earthquake, leaving his students behind. Although initially criticized for his actions, Fan later explained that he had acted on instinct and was overwhelmed by fear. Despite his own survival, he was haunted by guilt and remorse, becoming a controversial figure in the aftermath of the disaster.

In another miraculous case, a woman named Tang Xiong was rescued after being trapped in the rubble of her office building for 146 hours. Tang, who worked as a secretary, survived on rainwater that seeped through the debris and used her limited strength to call out for help whenever she heard rescuers nearby. Her eventual rescue was a testament to her incredible will to live and the determination of the rescue teams who refused to give up on her.

One of the most extraordinary survival stories is that of a man named Peng Qinghai, who was trapped under the rubble of his home for 266 hours—more than 11 days—before being rescued. Peng survived by drinking water that had collected in a pool near him and rationing the small amount of food he had with him. His survival defied all expectations, as experts had believed that anyone trapped for more than a week would likely not make it.

These and many other stories of survival captivated the world, offering a glimpse of hope and humanity in the midst of an overwhelming tragedy. The survivors became symbols of resilience, their stories serving as a reminder of the strength of the human spirit and the importance of never giving up, even in the face of seemingly insurmountable odds.

The Emotional and Psychological Impact

While the physical destruction caused by the Sichuan Earthquake was immense, the emotional and psychological toll on survivors and rescuers was equally profound. The sudden and violent nature of the disaster left deep scars on those who experienced it, leading to widespread trauma and grief.

For many survivors, the loss of loved ones was the most difficult aspect of the earthquake to come to terms with. The collapse of schools, in particular, led to the deaths of thousands of children, leaving parents and communities devastated. The grief was compounded by the knowledge that many of the school buildings had been poorly constructed, leading to accusations of negligence and corruption.

The psychological impact of the earthquake was felt across all age groups, but children were particularly vulnerable. Many young survivors experienced nightmares, anxiety, and difficulty concentrating in the aftermath of the disaster. Schools that were able to reopen faced the challenge of helping students cope with their trauma, often with limited resources and support.

The emotional toll was not limited to survivors. Rescuers, too, were deeply affected by what they witnessed. The sight of so many lives lost, particularly those of children, left a lasting impact on many of the rescuers, leading to feelings of helplessness, guilt, and depression. In the months and years following the earthquake, there was a growing recognition of the need for psychological support for both survivors and rescuers, leading to the establishment of counseling services and mental health programs.

Rebuilding Sichuan: The Long Road to Recovery

In the aftermath of the earthquake, the Chinese government and international community faced the enormous task of rebuilding the devastated region. The scale of the destruction meant that the recovery process would be long and complex, requiring not only the reconstruction of physical infrastructure but also the healing of communities and the restoration of livelihoods.

The Chinese government committed to a massive reconstruction effort, pledging billions of dollars in aid and resources to rebuild the affected areas. The focus was on constructing earthquake-resistant buildings, restoring infrastructure, and revitalizing the economy. In addition to government efforts, private companies, NGOs, and international organizations played a crucial role in the recovery process.

One of the most significant challenges was the relocation of survivors who had lost their homes. The earthquake left millions of people homeless, many of whom were forced to live in temporary shelters for months or even years. The government implemented a large-scale resettlement program, building new homes and communities for those displaced by the disaster. While the program provided much-needed relief, it also faced challenges, including ensuring that the new housing was safe and that communities were adequately supported.

Another critical aspect of the recovery was the reconstruction of schools and hospitals. The collapse of so many schools during the earthquake had highlighted the need for better building standards and greater oversight. In the rebuilding process, the government implemented stricter regulations to ensure that new schools were constructed to withstand future earthquakes. The goal was not only to rebuild but to build back better, creating safer and more resilient communities.

The economic recovery of the region was also a priority. The earthquake had devastated the local economy, with many businesses destroyed and livelihoods lost. The government provided financial assistance to help businesses get back on their feet and invested in infrastructure projects to stimulate economic growth. Tourism, which had been an important part of the region's economy, was also promoted as a way to attract visitors and boost local incomes.

Lessons Learned: The Legacy of the Sichuan Earthquake

The Sichuan Earthquake was a tragedy of immense proportions, but it also provided important lessons for China and the world. The disaster highlighted the importance of disaster preparedness and the need for better building standards, particularly in earthquake-prone regions. In the years following the earthquake, the Chinese government implemented a range of measures to improve disaster response and reduce the risk of future earthquakes.

One of the key lessons was the importance of early warning systems and public education. While the earthquake itself could not have been prevented, better preparedness could have reduced the loss of life. In response, China invested in improving its earthquake monitoring and early warning systems, as well as launching public education campaigns to raise awareness about earthquake safety.

The earthquake also underscored the importance of international cooperation in disaster response. The global outpouring of support for China in the aftermath of the earthquake demonstrated the value of solidarity and collaboration in times of crisis. The experience of the Sichuan Earthquake has informed disaster response efforts in other parts of the world, contributing to a greater understanding of how to respond effectively to large-scale natural disasters.

The legacy of the Sichuan Earthquake is also one of resilience and hope. Despite the immense loss and suffering, the people of Sichuan demonstrated incredible strength and determination in rebuilding their lives and communities. Their stories of survival and recovery continue to inspire others, serving as a reminder of the power of the human spirit to overcome even the greatest challenges.

Conclusion: A Story of Tragedy and Triumph

The Miracle of the Sichuan Earthquake is a story that encapsulates the duality of human experience: the profound suffering and loss caused by a natural disaster, and the remarkable resilience and hope that emerge in its aftermath. It is a story of a community and a nation coming together in the face of overwhelming adversity, of individuals who refused to give up, and of a world that responded with compassion and solidarity.

The earthquake left an indelible mark on the region and on the lives of those who experienced it. But it also left behind a legacy of lessons learned and a testament to the strength of the human spirit. The survivors of the Sichuan Earthquake, and the countless heroes who worked to save lives and rebuild communities, will forever be remembered as symbols of hope and resilience in the face of unimaginable tragedy.

Chapter 24: Shackleton's Endurance Expedition

Shackleton's Endurance Expedition is one of the most extraordinary tales of survival, leadership, and human endurance in the annals of exploration. Led by Sir Ernest Shackleton, a seasoned polar explorer, the expedition was intended to be the first to cross the Antarctic continent from sea to sea via the South Pole. However, the journey quickly turned into a harrowing struggle for survival when the expedition's ship, the Endurance, became trapped and eventually crushed by the relentless pack ice of the Weddell Sea. Over the next two years, Shackleton and his men faced some of the most extreme conditions on Earth as they battled to stay alive and find a way back to civilization.

Background: The Age of Antarctic Exploration

The early 20th century was known as the Heroic Age of Antarctic Exploration, a period marked by numerous expeditions to the southernmost continent. Explorers like Robert Falcon Scott, Roald Amundsen, and Ernest Shackleton had ventured into the icy unknown, driven by a combination of scientific curiosity, national pride, and the desire for glory. The race to reach the South Pole culminated in December 1911 when Norwegian explorer Roald Amundsen became the first to achieve this feat, narrowly beating Scott, whose expedition ended in tragedy.

Ernest Shackleton, who had previously led the British Antarctic Expedition of 1907-1909, during which he and his team came within 97 miles of the South Pole, was determined to make his mark on Antarctic exploration. Though Amundsen had already claimed the prize of reaching the Pole, Shackleton set his sights on an even more ambitious goal: the first trans-Antarctic crossing. His plan was to land on the Weddell Sea coast, cross the continent via the South Pole, and emerge on the Ross Sea coast.

To accomplish this, Shackleton organized what he called the Imperial Trans-Antarctic Expedition. He secured financial backing, assembled a crew of seasoned sailors, scientists, and adventurers, and acquired a ship capable of navigating the treacherous Antarctic waters. This ship, the Endurance, would become the central character in one of the greatest survival stories of all time.

The Endurance: A Ship Built for Ice

The Endurance, originally named the Polaris, was a three-masted barquentine built in Norway specifically for polar conditions. Launched in 1912, the ship was 144 feet long, with a beam of 25 feet and a displacement of 350 tons. Her hull was constructed of oak and Norwegian fir, reinforced with greenheart, an extremely hard wood, to withstand the pressures of the polar ice. The ship was further strengthened with steel plates along the bow and keel, making her one of the strongest wooden vessels of her time.

The Endurance was also equipped with a 350-horsepower coal-fired steam engine, which could drive the ship at a speed of up to 10 knots. Despite these formidable specifications, Shackleton knew that the Antarctic ice would be a formidable adversary. The ship's name, Endurance, was inspired by Shackleton's family motto: "By endurance we conquer," a fitting emblem for the challenges that lay ahead.

The Journey Begins: Departure and Early Challenges

The Endurance set sail from Plymouth, England, on August 8, 1914, just as Europe was being plunged into the chaos of World War I. Shackleton had offered to postpone the expedition and put his ship at the disposal of the British Admiralty, but he was told that his mission was of national importance, and so the voyage continued. The ship made stops in Buenos Aires, Argentina, and Grytviken, South Georgia, an island in the southern Atlantic Ocean, where Shackleton received final updates on the ice conditions in the Weddell Sea.

On December 5, 1914, the Endurance left South Georgia and headed south into the Weddell Sea, aiming to reach the coast of Antarctica. Almost immediately, the ship encountered heavy pack ice, which made progress slow and hazardous. The Endurance was forced to navigate through narrow leads (openings in the ice) and frequently became trapped, requiring the crew to laboriously free the ship by cutting through the ice with saws and using ice anchors.

Despite these difficulties, Shackleton remained optimistic, urging his men to press on. However, the pack ice gradually closed in around the Endurance, and by January 18, 1915, the ship was completely immobilized. She was held fast in the ice, drifting slowly with the floes as the Antarctic winter approached. Shackleton and his crew were now prisoners of the Weddell Sea, with no way to free the ship or reach their intended landing point on the Antarctic continent.

Trapped in the Ice: The Long Antarctic Winter

As the days grew shorter and the temperature plummeted, the crew of the Endurance settled into an uneasy routine. Shackleton, aware that morale would be crucial to their survival, took great pains to keep his men occupied and optimistic. He instituted a daily schedule of duties and recreation, including physical exercises, card games, and even a midwinter's day celebration complete with homemade costumes and a special meal.

The ship was well-provisioned, with enough food to last for more than a year, and the crew made use of the Endurance's warm, well-insulated quarters to stay as comfortable as possible. However, the isolation and uncertainty of their situation weighed heavily on the men. Shackleton's leadership was tested as he worked to maintain order and keep his crew focused on the tasks at hand, even as the ship's position remained at the mercy of the drifting ice.

As the Antarctic winter deepened, the ice around the Endurance thickened and tightened its grip on the ship. The pressure of the ice was immense, and the wooden hull began to creak and groan under the strain. Shackleton and his men could only watch helplessly as the ice slowly crushed the ship, causing the hull to buckle and water to seep into the lower decks.

On October 27, 1915, after months of enduring the relentless pressure, Shackleton gave the order to abandon ship. The Endurance was mortally wounded, her hull breached and her timbers shattered. The crew hastily salvaged what supplies and equipment they could, setting up camp on the ice floe next to the dying ship. Shackleton named this temporary refuge "Ocean Camp," and the men braced themselves for the next phase of their ordeal.

Life on the Ice: A Struggle for Survival

With the Endurance gone, Shackleton and his men faced the grim reality of their situation. They were stranded on a drifting ice floe, hundreds of miles from the nearest land, with no means of communication and no hope of rescue. The nearest inhabited outpost was the whaling station on South Georgia Island, over 800 miles to the northeast, across the treacherous Southern Ocean.

Shackleton knew that their survival depended on staying together and maintaining discipline. He imposed a strict routine, with daily chores, regular meals, and physical activity to keep the men fit and focused. He also made sure that everyone had a role to play, even if it was as simple as keeping watch for changes in the ice or tending to the sled dogs that had accompanied them on the expedition.

The crew lived in makeshift tents made from the sails of the Endurance, using their sledges and boats as windbreaks. They slept on the ice, huddled together for warmth, and ate a diet of canned food, biscuits, and, eventually, the meat of the sled dogs, which were sacrificed as their situation grew more desperate. The cold was relentless, with temperatures often plunging below -20 degrees Fahrenheit, and the constant wind and snow made every task a challenge.

Despite these hardships, Shackleton remained determined to lead his men to safety. He knew that their only hope of survival lay in reaching solid land, where they could find a way to signal for help or be discovered by a passing ship. However, the drifting ice floe on which they were camped was moving slowly northward, away from the Antarctic continent and toward the open sea. Shackleton realized that they would eventually have to abandon the ice and take to the water in their lifeboats.

The Open Boat Journey: A Desperate Gamble

By April 1916, after more than five months on the ice, the floe on which the men were camped began to break up. Shackleton decided that the time had come to launch the lifeboats and attempt to reach land. The three boats—named the James Caird, the Dudley Docker, and the Stancomb Wills—were small, open vessels, each about 22 feet long, designed for short trips, not extended voyages across the Southern Ocean.

On April 9, 1916, the men loaded the boats with their remaining supplies and launched them into the icy waters. What followed was a week-long ordeal as they navigated through the labyrinth of ice floes, battling freezing temperatures, high winds, and rough seas. The boats were constantly at risk of being crushed by the shifting ice or swamped by waves, and the men were soaked through, shivering with cold and exhaustion.

Shackleton's leadership was once again crucial during this phase of the journey. He divided the crew among the three boats, taking the helm of the James Caird himself and assigning his most trusted officers to command the other two. He set a course for Elephant Island, a remote, uninhabited outcrop of rock and ice about 100 miles north of their position, which he hoped would provide a temporary refuge until they could plan their next move.

After seven days of relentless rowing and sailing, during which the men endured near-constant exposure to the elements and the constant threat of capsizing, the boats finally reached the desolate shores of Elephant Island on April 15, 1916. The men were physically and mentally exhausted, but they were alive, and for the first time in more than a year, they were on solid ground.

Elephant Island: A Temporary Refuge

Elephant Island was a bleak and inhospitable place, but to Shackleton's men, it represented a glimmer of hope. They were now on land, but they were still far from safety. The island was isolated and far from any shipping routes, and the chances of being spotted by a passing ship were slim. Shackleton knew that they could not remain there indefinitely and that their only hope of rescue was to reach the whaling stations on South Georgia Island, over 800 miles away.

Shackleton decided to make a desperate gamble. He would take the strongest of the three lifeboats, the James Caird, and sail with a small crew to South Georgia, leaving the rest of the men on Elephant

Island to await rescue. It was a perilous plan, as the James Caird was not designed for such a long and hazardous voyage, and the Southern Ocean was one of the most treacherous stretches of water on Earth.

On April 24, 1916, Shackleton and five of his men—Frank Worsley, Tom Crean, Timothy McCarthy, Harry McNish, and John Vincent—set out in the James Caird on what would become one of the most remarkable small-boat journeys in history. The boat had been modified with a makeshift deck and extra reinforcement to withstand the rough seas, but it was still a tiny vessel, vulnerable to the towering waves and gale-force winds of the Southern Ocean.

The Voyage of the James Caird: A Feat of Seamanship

The journey from Elephant Island to South Georgia is one of the greatest feats of navigation and seamanship ever recorded. Over the course of 16 days, Shackleton and his men battled through some of the most dangerous waters on the planet, enduring constant cold, wet, and exhaustion. The James Caird was buffeted by waves that threatened to capsize the boat at any moment, and the men were soaked to the bone, their clothes frozen stiff by the icy spray.

Frank Worsley, the expedition's navigator, performed near-miracles with his sextant, taking sightings of the sun whenever it briefly broke through the clouds to calculate their position. Despite the overwhelming odds, Worsley's calculations proved astonishingly accurate, guiding the James Caird toward its destination with remarkable precision.

On May 8, 1916, after more than two weeks at sea, the men sighted the rocky cliffs of South Georgia. However, their ordeal was not yet over. The winds and currents were against them, and it took several more days of grueling effort to reach the island. Finally, on May 10, the James Caird made landfall on the uninhabited southern coast of South Georgia, at a place called King Haakon Bay.

Crossing South Georgia: The Final Trial

Though they had reached South Georgia, Shackleton and his men were not yet safe. The whaling stations were on the opposite side of the island, separated by a range of jagged, snow-covered mountains that had never been crossed before. The men were exhausted, frostbitten, and half-starved, but there was no time to lose. Shackleton decided to take Worsley and Crean with him to make the crossing, while the other three men remained behind with the James Caird.

On May 19, 1916, Shackleton, Worsley, and Crean set out on foot across the mountains of South Georgia. They had no proper climbing equipment, only a length of rope and a carpenter's adze, and they were dressed in the same clothes they had worn during their boat journey. The terrain was treacherous, with steep slopes, deep snow, and hidden crevasses, but the men pressed on, driven by the knowledge that their comrades' lives depended on their success.

After 36 hours of continuous climbing and hiking, during which they covered nearly 30 miles of rugged terrain, Shackleton and his companions reached the whaling station at Stromness on the northern coast of South Georgia. Their arrival was met with astonishment by the whalers, who had given them up for dead. Shackleton immediately arranged for a ship to rescue the men they had left behind on the southern coast and then began organizing a rescue mission for the rest of the crew stranded on Elephant Island.

The Rescue: Return to Elephant Island

It took several attempts to reach Elephant Island, as the ice and weather conditions made navigation treacherous. Shackleton's first three rescue attempts were thwarted by ice, but he refused to give up. Finally, on August 30, 1916, Shackleton, aboard the Chilean ship Yelcho, reached Elephant Island. Remarkably, all 22 men who had been left behind were still alive. After more than four months of waiting, they were finally rescued.

The men on Elephant Island had endured extreme cold, hunger, and isolation, but they had managed to survive, thanks in large part to the leadership of Frank Wild, Shackleton's second-in-command, who had kept them organized and hopeful during Shackleton's absence.

Aftermath: The Legacy of the Endurance Expedition

The return of Shackleton and his men was met with great relief and admiration, but their story was somewhat overshadowed by the ongoing carnage of World War I. Nevertheless, the Endurance expedition became a legendary tale of survival, leadership, and the indomitable human spirit.

Shackleton's decision to prioritize the safety of his men over the success of the expedition, his ability to maintain morale under the direst circumstances, and his extraordinary journey in the James Caird have all become benchmarks of exceptional leadership. The story of the Endurance has been recounted in countless books, documentaries, and films, and Shackleton himself is often cited as a model of effective leadership in the face of adversity.

In the years following the expedition, Shackleton continued his polar explorations, though he never achieved the same level of success as he had with the Endurance. He died of a heart attack in 1922 while preparing for another Antarctic expedition. He was buried on South Georgia, the island that had played such a crucial role in his most famous journey.

The Endurance expedition remains one of the greatest survival stories of all time, a testament to the power of human resilience and the extraordinary capabilities of those who refuse to give up in the face of overwhelming odds.

Chapter 25: Juliane Koepcke's Plane Crash

Juliane Koepcke's survival story is one of the most remarkable and harrowing tales of human endurance in the face of overwhelming odds. On December 24, 1971, at the age of 17, Juliane was the sole survivor of a plane crash in the Peruvian Amazon. The flight, LANSA Flight 508, was struck by lightning during a severe thunderstorm, causing it to break apart in mid-air. Juliane plummeted more than two miles to the ground, still strapped into her seat, and miraculously survived. What followed was an incredible 11-day journey through the dense, dangerous jungle, where she battled injuries, infections, and the elements before finally being rescued. Her story is a powerful testament to the resilience of the human spirit and the will to survive.

Background: The Koepcke Family and the Christmas Eve Flight

Juliane Koepcke was born on October 10, 1954, in Lima, Peru, to German parents Hans-Wilhelm and Maria Koepcke. Her father was a biologist, and her mother was an ornithologist. The Koepcke family was deeply connected to the natural world, and Juliane grew up surrounded by the wonders of the Amazon rainforest. Her parents worked at the biological research station called Panguana, located in the remote rainforest of Peru, where they studied the flora and fauna of the region. Juliane spent much of her childhood in this environment, gaining a deep appreciation and understanding of the jungle.

By 1971, Juliane was a high school student in Lima, and her mother was working at the Natural History Museum in the city. With Christmas approaching, Juliane and her mother decided to fly from Lima to Pucallpa, a city near Panguana, to reunite with her father for the holidays. They booked tickets on LANSA Flight 508, a Lockheed L-188 Electra turboprop airliner operated by Líneas Aéreas Nacionales S.A. (LANSA), a Peruvian airline.

LANSA had a checkered safety record, with previous crashes that had resulted in significant loss of life. Despite these concerns, the Koepckes decided to take the flight, which was scheduled to depart from Lima's Jorge Chávez International Airport on the morning of December 24, 1971. The flight was meant to be a short, hour-long journey over the Andes and into the Amazon basin, but it would turn into a nightmare that Juliane could never have imagined.

The Flight: Tragedy Strikes in the Sky

LANSA Flight 508 took off from Lima with 92 passengers and crew on board, including Juliane and her mother, Maria. The flight initially proceeded without incident as it climbed to its cruising altitude. However, as the plane approached the Andes, it encountered severe weather. The region was notorious for its unpredictable and violent thunderstorms, which could develop rapidly and pose significant dangers to aircraft.

As the plane flew into the storm, turbulence intensified, and the passengers began to feel the full force of the storm's power. Lightning flashed around the aircraft, and the plane was buffeted by strong winds. The crew tried to navigate through the storm, but conditions worsened. At approximately 12,000 feet, the plane was struck by a bolt of lightning, which caused a catastrophic failure.

The lightning strike ignited a fuel tank, leading to an explosion that tore the plane apart in mid-air. Juliane, still strapped into her seat, was suddenly in freefall. The plane disintegrated around her, and she plummeted toward the jungle below, surrounded by the wreckage of the aircraft. It was a terrifying descent, and Juliane later recalled that

the only sounds she could hear were the howling wind and the roar
of the engines as they fell with her.

The Fall: A Miracle in the Midst of Tragedy

Juliane's fall from the sky is nothing short of miraculous. The odds of
surviving such a plunge are astronomical, yet somehow, Juliane did.
Still strapped into her seat, she fell approximately 10,000 feet—more
than two miles—into the dense Amazon rainforest. The thick
canopy of trees likely helped to cushion her fall, slowing her descent
and reducing the impact. The seat also played a crucial role in
absorbing some of the shock when she hit the ground.

When Juliane regained consciousness, she found herself lying on the
forest floor, still strapped to the seat, surrounded by the wreckage of
the plane. She had suffered a concussion, a broken collarbone, deep
cuts on her legs, and a swollen eye. Despite these injuries, she was
alive, and she was alone. The impact had knocked her unconscious,
and she had no idea how long she had been out. All she knew was
that she had survived the crash, but she was now stranded in one of
the most inhospitable environments on Earth.

Survival Instincts: Alone in the Amazon Jungle

The Amazon rainforest is one of the most biodiverse regions in the
world, but it is also one of the most dangerous. It is home to
venomous snakes, jaguars, and other predators, as well as countless
insects that carry diseases. The dense foliage, oppressive humidity,
and constant threat of rain made it a challenging environment for
even the most seasoned survivalists. For a 17-year-old girl with no
supplies, no proper clothing, and serious injuries, the situation was
dire.

Juliane's first challenge was to assess her injuries and figure out her
next steps. Her survival instincts kicked in, likely honed by her

upbringing in the rainforest. She knew that she needed to find water and keep moving if she had any hope of being rescued. She had no food, but she remembered her father's advice: that if she could find a stream and follow it, it would eventually lead to a larger river and, hopefully, to civilization.

Juliane's injuries made it difficult to move, but she managed to free herself from the seat and stand up. She realized that her right eye was swollen shut, and her vision in the other eye was blurred. Her collarbone was broken, making it painful to use her right arm. Despite these obstacles, she began to search the area around the crash site for other survivors, calling out for her mother. Sadly, there was no response, and she found no signs of life among the wreckage.

With no other options, Juliane decided to follow the advice her father had given her and set out to find a stream. She knew that water was essential for survival and that rivers often lead to human settlements. She began to walk, stumbling through the dense underbrush, her body aching with every step. The jungle was a disorienting maze of trees, vines, and undergrowth, and Juliane had no compass or map to guide her. All she had was her determination to survive.

Eleven Days in the Jungle: A Battle Against the Elements

For the next 11 days, Juliane fought to survive in the Amazon jungle. Her journey was a grueling test of endurance, as she battled hunger, thirst, injury, and the relentless dangers of the rainforest. Each day brought new challenges, and each night was a struggle to find shelter from the rain and the countless insects that swarmed around her.

Juliane's primary concern was finding water. Dehydration would be deadly in the humid jungle, and she was constantly on the lookout for streams or pools of water. On the second day of her ordeal, she found a small creek, which she began to follow. The water was her lifeline, providing not only hydration but also a sense of direction. She knew that the creek would eventually lead to a larger river, and rivers were the best chance of finding help.

The jungle was teeming with life, but it was also full of dangers. Juliane encountered venomous snakes, including the deadly bushmaster, but she managed to avoid being bitten. She also had to deal with the constant threat of insects, particularly mosquitoes and flies. Her wounds became infected, and she was plagued by maggots that burrowed into her flesh. Despite the pain and discomfort, Juliane pressed on, driven by the hope that she would eventually find help.

Food was another major concern. Juliane had no supplies, and the jungle offered little in the way of sustenance. She occasionally found fruit on the forest floor, but it was often rotten or infested with insects. At one point, she discovered a bag of candy in the wreckage of the plane, which provided a brief but much-needed source of energy. However, for the most part, she had to rely on her wits and instincts to survive.

The physical challenges were immense, but the psychological toll was equally severe. Juliane was alone in the vast, unforgiving jungle, with no way of knowing if she would ever be found. The days seemed to stretch on endlessly, and the nights were filled with the sounds of the jungle—howling monkeys, chirping insects, and the occasional roar of a distant predator. Despite the fear and uncertainty, Juliane remained focused on her goal: to find help and survive.

Rescue: A Miraculous Discovery

After 10 days of struggling through the jungle, Juliane's situation was becoming increasingly desperate. Her injuries were worsening, and she was growing weaker by the day. She continued to follow the creek, which had now grown into a larger river. On the eleventh day, she finally spotted something that filled her with hope: a small boat moored on the riverbank. The sight of the boat was a sign that she was close to civilization.

Juliane called out for help, but there was no response. She was too weak to climb into the boat, so she decided to rest nearby, hoping that someone would come. The following day, a group of local fishermen discovered her. They were astonished to find a lone girl, badly injured and emaciated, in the middle of the jungle. They took her back to their village, where she received basic medical care.

From there, Juliane was transported by canoe to a more populated area, and eventually, she was flown to a hospital in Pucallpa. The news of her survival quickly spread, and she was reunited with her father, who had feared the worst. Juliane was the sole survivor of the crash—everyone else on the plane had perished, including her mother, whose body was later found still strapped into her seat.

Aftermath: A Life Marked by Survival

Juliane's survival story made headlines around the world, and she was hailed as a modern-day miracle. However, the experience left deep scars, both physical and emotional. The loss of her mother was a devastating blow, and Juliane struggled with survivor's guilt. She later wrote about her ordeal in her memoir, "When I Fell From the Sky," where she detailed her journey and the impact it had on her life.

After recovering from her injuries, Juliane followed in her parents' footsteps, pursuing a career in biology. She earned a PhD in zoology and became a respected researcher, focusing on the wildlife of the Amazon. Her work brought her back to the rainforest many times, and she eventually took over the management of the Panguana research station, where she continues to contribute to the conservation of the region's biodiversity.

Juliane's story has been the subject of numerous documentaries, books, and interviews, and it remains one of the most extraordinary survival stories in history. Her experience is a powerful reminder of the resilience of the human spirit and the will to survive against all odds.

Chapter 26: The Essex Whaling Ship Disaster

The story of the Essex whaling ship disaster is one of the most harrowing and tragic tales of survival at sea. The Essex, a Nantucket-based whaling ship, set sail in 1819 on what was intended to be a routine whaling expedition but ended in unimaginable horror. The ship was attacked and sunk by a massive sperm whale in the middle of the Pacific Ocean, leaving the crew stranded thousands of miles from land. The ensuing ordeal, marked by starvation, dehydration, and cannibalism, inspired Herman Melville's famous novel *Moby-Dick*. The Essex disaster is not just a story of survival; it is a profound exploration of human endurance, desperation, and the often brutal realities of life at sea.

Background: The Whaling Industry in the Early 19th Century

In the early 19th century, Nantucket, an island off the coast of Massachusetts, was the epicenter of the American whaling industry. Whale oil was a valuable commodity, used primarily for lighting lamps and as a lubricant in the growing industrial economy. Whaling was a dangerous and grueling profession, but it was also highly profitable, attracting men willing to endure long voyages and harsh conditions in pursuit of fortune.

Whaling ships, like the Essex, were often at sea for two to three years at a time, traveling to distant oceans in search of whales. The crew of these ships was typically made up of hardened sailors, many of whom were young men from Nantucket or other coastal communities. The work was physically demanding and perilous, involving the hunting and processing of massive sperm whales, which could weigh up to 60 tons.

The Essex was a relatively small whaling ship, measuring 87 feet in length and weighing about 238 tons. Despite its modest size, it had completed several successful whaling voyages and was considered a sturdy vessel. Its captain, George Pollard Jr., was just 28 years old but came from a long line of whalers. The first mate, Owen Chase, was an experienced and capable sailor, known for his skill in harpooning whales.

In August 1819, the Essex set sail from Nantucket on what was expected to be a routine whaling expedition in the South Pacific. The ship's crew of 21 men included a mix of seasoned whalers and young greenhands, who were on their first voyage. The mood was optimistic as the Essex left port, but the men had no idea that they were embarking on a journey that would end in tragedy and leave a lasting scar on maritime history.

The Fateful Voyage: Initial Challenges and Misfortunes

The Essex's journey began like any other whaling expedition, with the ship sailing southward along the Atlantic coast of South America, rounding Cape Horn, and entering the Pacific Ocean. The crew encountered their first whale off the coast of Chile and quickly set to work hunting it. However, this early success was marred by a series of misfortunes that foreshadowed the disaster to come.

First, the Essex was caught in a violent storm, known as a squall, which nearly capsized the ship. The storm severely damaged the ship's topmasts, reducing its speed and maneuverability. Although the crew managed to repair the damage, the incident was a bad omen, shaking the men's confidence in their voyage.

As the Essex continued its journey, the crew struggled to find enough whales to meet their quota. Whaling was a labor-intensive process, requiring the men to row small whaleboats close to the massive animals, harpoon them, and then endure hours-long struggles to kill the whales and tow them back to the ship. Once aboard, the whales were processed for their valuable oil, which was stored in barrels in the ship's hold. Each whale could yield several barrels of oil, but the process was dangerous and exhausting.

Despite their efforts, the crew of the Essex found themselves increasingly frustrated by the scarcity of whales. This led Captain Pollard to make a fateful decision: he would take the ship into uncharted waters farther west, where it was rumored that large pods of sperm whales could be found. This decision would take the Essex far from known whaling grounds and deep into the heart of the Pacific Ocean, where help would be virtually impossible to find in the event of an emergency.

The Whale Attack: A Terrifying Encounter

On November 20, 1820, after months of sailing and struggling to find whales, the Essex finally encountered a pod of sperm whales about 2,000 miles west of the coast of South America. The crew launched three whaleboats and set out to hunt the whales, eager to secure a valuable catch. The hunt initially went as planned, with the men managing to harpoon several whales. However, the situation quickly took a dramatic turn.

While the crew was occupied with the hunt, the lookout aboard the Essex spotted an enormous sperm whale, estimated to be about 85 feet long, approaching the ship. The whale was acting strangely, swimming erratically and making loud splashing noises. Then, to the crew's horror, the whale turned and charged directly at the Essex. The whale rammed the ship's bow with tremendous force, causing it to shudder violently.

The impact of the whale's attack was devastating. The Essex's bow was badly damaged, and the ship began to take on water. But the worst was yet to come. The whale swam a short distance away, then turned and charged the ship a second time, striking it with even greater force. This second attack caused the Essex to keel over on its side, and the ship began to sink rapidly.

The crew of the Essex was in shock. A whale attacking a ship was an almost unheard-of event, and the sheer power of the whale's assault left them stunned and terrified. Captain Pollard and First Mate Chase quickly realized that the ship was doomed. They had no choice but to abandon the Essex and take to the whaleboats, hoping to survive in the vast and unforgiving Pacific Ocean.

The Struggle for Survival: Adrift in the Pacific

With the Essex sinking, the crew scrambled to gather whatever supplies they could salvage. They managed to retrieve a few navigational instruments, some bread, and fresh water, but their provisions were woefully inadequate for the ordeal ahead. The 20 men divided themselves among three whaleboats, small open vessels designed for hunting whales but not for long-term survival at sea.

The men were now adrift in one of the most remote parts of the Pacific Ocean, thousands of miles from the nearest land. The South Pacific is a vast expanse of open water, dotted with tiny islands, many of which were uncharted at the time. The crew faced an agonizing decision: should they try to reach the South American coast, more than 2,000 miles to the east, or head for the Marquesas Islands, about 1,200 miles to the west?

Captain Pollard initially favored heading for the Marquesas, but the crew, fearful of encountering cannibals rumored to inhabit the islands, persuaded him to attempt the longer journey to South

America. This decision would have dire consequences, as it would prolong their time at sea and push them closer to the limits of human endurance.

The days turned into weeks as the men struggled to survive in their small whaleboats. They faced searing heat during the day, freezing temperatures at night, and relentless exposure to the sun and saltwater. Their meager rations quickly dwindled, and they were forced to ration their food and water to the barest minimum. The lack of fresh water was particularly devastating, as dehydration set in and the men grew weaker by the day.

As the situation grew increasingly desperate, the crew's mental and physical health began to deteriorate. The vastness of the ocean, with no land in sight, took a toll on their morale, and despair began to set in. The men were tormented by hunger and thirst, and the knowledge that rescue was unlikely to come weighed heavily on them.

Desperation and Cannibalism: The Ultimate Horror

As the weeks passed, the crew's condition became more and more dire. The men were starving, and their bodies were wasting away. By early January 1821, the situation had become so desperate that they were faced with an unthinkable choice: resort to cannibalism or face certain death from starvation.

The first death occurred on January 10, when a young sailor named Thomas Nickerson died of hunger and exposure. The crew, driven by sheer desperation, made the grim decision to consume his body in order to survive. It was a horrific act, but one that the men felt was necessary if they were to have any hope of survival. The remains were carefully rationed among the crew, providing them with a small but vital source of sustenance.

The cannibalism continued as more men succumbed to starvation. By mid-January, the crew had lost several members, and the survivors were barely clinging to life. The whaleboats, battered by storms and relentless waves, were falling apart, and the men had little energy left to repair them. The psychological toll of their situation was immense, and the men were haunted by the memory of their fallen comrades.

The ultimate horror came when the crew realized that their dwindling numbers meant that they would soon have no more bodies to consume. Faced with this grim reality, they made the agonizing decision to draw lots to determine who would be sacrificed next. The first lot fell to a young sailor named Owen Coffin, who was Captain Pollard's cousin. Despite Pollard's protests, Coffin accepted his fate, and the crew carried out the execution with heavy hearts.

The horror of this act weighed heavily on the survivors, but it provided them with a few more days of life. The cannibalism and the decision to draw lots have been the most notorious aspects of the Essex disaster, capturing the public's imagination and leaving a lasting mark on the story's legacy.

Rescue and Aftermath: The Survivors' Return

By late January 1821, after more than two months adrift at sea, the survivors of the Essex were on the brink of death. Their ordeal finally came to an end when they were rescued by two passing ships. The first, the British vessel *Indian*, found the boat containing Captain Pollard and two other survivors on February 23, 1821. The second, the American ship *Dauphin*, rescued Owen Chase and two other men a week later.

In total, only eight of the original 20 crew members survived the ordeal. They were skeletal, barely recognizable as human, and deeply traumatized by their experience. The survivors were taken to Valparaiso, Chile, where they received medical treatment and began to recover from their physical injuries. However, the psychological scars would remain with them for the rest of their lives.

The story of the Essex quickly spread, both in America and abroad, shocking the public with its tale of horror and survival. The survivors, particularly Owen Chase and Thomas Nickerson, later wrote detailed accounts of the disaster, which provided the basis for much of what is known about the event today.

Captain Pollard, despite his leadership during the ordeal, was haunted by guilt over the loss of his cousin and the men under his command. He returned to Nantucket, where he faced a mixed reception. While some viewed him with sympathy, others saw him as a failure. Pollard would go on to captain another whaling ship, the *Two Brothers*, but it too met a tragic end when it was wrecked on a coral reef in 1823. Pollard never went to sea again, spending the rest of his life in obscurity.

Owen Chase, on the other hand, continued his whaling career, though he was deeply affected by the experience. He suffered from nightmares and mental health issues for the rest of his life, and his account of the Essex disaster became one of the most famous survival stories of the 19th century.

Legacy: The Essex in Popular Culture

The Essex disaster has left a lasting legacy in both history and literature. Herman Melville, who met Owen Chase's son years later, was deeply inspired by the story and used it as the basis for his novel *Moby-Dick*, published in 1851. In *Moby-Dick*, the white whale becomes a symbol of nature's uncontrollable power and the human obsession with conquering it. The novel, initially a commercial failure, is now considered one of the greatest works of American literature.

The Essex's story has also been the subject of numerous books, documentaries, and films. In 2015, the disaster was dramatized in the movie *In the Heart of the Sea*, based on Nathaniel Philbrick's book of the same name. The film brought the story to a new generation, highlighting the tragic and heroic aspects of the Essex's voyage.

The Essex disaster remains a powerful example of human endurance in the face of unimaginable adversity. It is a reminder of the dangers of the sea, the fragility of life, and the extreme measures to which people will go in order to survive. The men of the Essex faced a situation that tested the limits of their humanity, and their story continues to resonate with audiences today as a testament to the strength of the human spirit in the direst of circumstances.

Chapter 27: John McCain's POW Experience

John Sidney McCain III was a U.S. Navy pilot, a decorated war hero, and a senator who endured one of the most harrowing experiences imaginable during the Vietnam War. His time as a prisoner of war (POW) in North Vietnam is a testament to his resilience, courage, and the indomitable human spirit. McCain's experience not only shaped his personal character but also had a lasting impact on American politics and military history.

The Downing of John McCain's Aircraft

On October 26, 1967, during a bombing mission over Hanoi as part of Operation Rolling Thunder, John McCain's A-4E Skyhawk was struck by a surface-to-air missile. The missile hit his aircraft, causing severe damage. Despite the critical situation, McCain managed to eject from the plane, but his troubles were far from over. As he ejected, he broke both arms and one leg, injuries that would plague him throughout his captivity. McCain parachuted into Truc Bach Lake in Hanoi, where he was immediately surrounded by North Vietnamese soldiers and civilians. His injuries were severe, and upon being captured, he was brutally beaten by the crowd before being taken to Hoa Lo Prison, infamously known as the "Hanoi Hilton."

The "Hanoi Hilton"

Hoa Lo Prison, nicknamed the "Hanoi Hilton" by American POWs, was notorious for its brutal treatment of prisoners. The conditions were harsh, with prisoners enduring solitary confinement, poor nutrition, inadequate medical care, and relentless torture. McCain, already severely injured, was given minimal medical attention. His captors discovered that he was the son of Admiral John S. McCain

Jr., commander of U.S. forces in the Pacific, which they believed could be leveraged for propaganda purposes.

Refusal of Early Release

McCain's status as the son of a high-ranking admiral prompted the North Vietnamese to offer him an early release. This offer was not out of kindness but as a calculated move to demoralize other POWs and use McCain as a propaganda tool. Despite the immense physical and psychological toll of his injuries and imprisonment, McCain refused the offer. He adhered to the military code of conduct, which stipulated that prisoners should be released in the order of their capture. Accepting early release would have violated this code and left his fellow prisoners in a vulnerable position. McCain's refusal to accept special treatment exemplified his deep sense of honor and duty.

Endurance Under Torture

The refusal of early release subjected McCain to even more brutal treatment. The North Vietnamese guards intensified their torture, aiming to break his spirit. He was frequently subjected to beatings, starvation, and periods of solitary confinement. The physical abuse was designed to extract military information or false confessions that could be used in propaganda. McCain was often tied in painful positions, beaten until he lost consciousness, and denied medical treatment for his injuries. His arms, already broken during the ejection, were re-injured multiple times during torture sessions, causing him unimaginable pain. Yet, through all of this, McCain remained steadfast, resisting his captors' efforts to break him mentally and emotionally.

The Conditions Inside the Hanoi Hilton

Life inside the Hanoi Hilton was a constant struggle for survival. The prison cells were small, damp, and infested with vermin. The prisoners were often denied basic necessities, such as sufficient food and clean water. They lived in squalid conditions, with little protection from the elements, and were regularly subjected to malnutrition and disease. Communication between prisoners was restricted, but they developed ingenious methods to maintain morale and share information, such as using a tap code. This camaraderie and mutual support among POWs were crucial to their survival. Despite the oppressive environment, the prisoners maintained a sense of solidarity, resisting the psychological tactics employed by their captors.

The Psychological Toll

The psychological toll of McCain's imprisonment was immense. The isolation, constant fear of torture, and uncertainty about his fate weighed heavily on him. He faced moments of despair and hopelessness, questioning whether he would ever see his family or his country again. However, McCain's resolve remained unbroken. He drew strength from his fellow prisoners, his commitment to his country, and his determination to maintain his honor. His resilience in the face of such adversity became a defining aspect of his character, shaping his future career and personal life.

Release and Return to the United States

After five and a half years of captivity, John McCain was finally released on March 14, 1973, as part of Operation Homecoming, a series of negotiated prisoner releases following the Paris Peace Accords. McCain's return to the United States was marked by widespread admiration for his courage and resilience. Despite the physical and emotional scars of his imprisonment, McCain resumed his military career, underwent numerous surgeries to repair his injuries, and eventually entered politics.

Legacy of McCain's POW Experience

John McCain's experience as a POW left an indelible mark on his life and legacy. It shaped his views on military service, patriotism, and the responsibilities of leadership. McCain became a vocal advocate for veterans' rights, military preparedness, and the ethical treatment of prisoners of war. His time in the Hanoi Hilton also influenced his views on foreign policy and human rights, making him a staunch defender of American values on the global stage.

Conclusion

John McCain's POW experience is a story of extraordinary courage, resilience, and unwavering commitment to his country. His ordeal in the Hanoi Hilton stands as a testament to the strength of the human spirit and the enduring power of honor and duty. McCain's legacy, shaped by his experiences in Vietnam, continues to inspire generations of Americans and serves as a powerful reminder of the sacrifices made by those who serve in the armed forces.

Chapter 28: The Miracle of Hurricane Katrina

Hurricane Katrina, one of the deadliest and most destructive storms in U.S. history, struck the Gulf Coast in August 2005. The hurricane, which reached Category 5 strength at its peak, caused catastrophic damage, particularly in New Orleans, Louisiana. With over 1,800 lives lost and tens of thousands displaced, the storm left an indelible mark on the region. Amid the devastation, there were numerous tales of extraordinary survival—stories that have come to be known as the "Miracle of Hurricane Katrina." These accounts highlight the resilience of the human spirit and the ability to endure and overcome seemingly insurmountable challenges.

The Storm's Approach and Impact

In late August 2005, meteorologists began tracking a tropical depression that quickly intensified into a powerful hurricane. By August 28, Hurricane Katrina had reached Category 5 status, with sustained winds of up to 175 miles per hour. The National Weather Service issued dire warnings, predicting catastrophic damage and urging residents in the storm's path to evacuate. Despite these warnings, many people in New Orleans and the surrounding areas were unable to leave due to financial constraints, health issues, or lack of transportation. Others chose to stay, either underestimating the storm's severity or believing they could weather it as they had previous hurricanes.

On August 29, Katrina made landfall on the Gulf Coast, first in southeastern Louisiana and then in Mississippi. The storm surge, combined with heavy rainfall, overwhelmed the levee system in New Orleans, causing widespread flooding. The lower Ninth Ward, St. Bernard Parish, and other low-lying areas were inundated with water.

In some places, the water reached depths of 15 feet or more, trapping thousands of residents in their homes, attics, or on rooftops. The wind and floodwaters caused extensive damage to buildings, infrastructure, and vehicles, leaving much of the city in ruins.

Survival in the Face of Catastrophe

As the waters rose and the levees failed, those who had stayed behind found themselves in life-threatening situations. With no power, communication, or access to emergency services, many were left to fend for themselves. Yet, in the midst of this chaos, remarkable stories of survival emerged.

One of the most harrowing accounts is that of a family in the Lower Ninth Ward who were trapped in their attic as the floodwaters surged into their home. With no way to escape and the water rising rapidly, the family faced the grim reality of drowning in their own home. Desperate, they used a hammer to break through the roof, creating a small opening through which they could climb onto the roof. From there, they signaled for help, hoping against hope that someone would come to their rescue. After several hours, a makeshift flotilla of neighbors, using whatever they could find—pieces of wood, plastic containers, and even an old canoe—arrived and helped the family to safety. This act of community solidarity and resourcefulness exemplified the miracles of survival that occurred throughout the city.

In another part of New Orleans, an elderly woman, who had lived alone for years, found herself trapped on the second floor of her home as the floodwaters filled the lower level. With no food, water, or medication, and unable to move due to a pre-existing condition, she was certain she would not survive. However, days later, a group of teenagers, navigating the flooded streets in a small boat they had found, heard her cries for help. They broke into her house, carried her down to their boat, and took her to higher ground. For this woman, the arrival of those teenagers was nothing short of miraculous, and it was a reminder that in times of crisis, humanity often rises to its greatest heights.

The Superdome and Convention Center: Scenes of Desperation

While many of the survival stories during Hurricane Katrina took place in individual homes and neighborhoods, some of the most dramatic and widely reported tales occurred at the Louisiana Superdome and the Ernest N. Morial Convention Center. These locations had been designated as "shelters of last resort" for those who could not evacuate the city. However, neither facility was prepared for the sheer number of people who sought refuge there.

At the Superdome, tens of thousands of people crowded into the stadium, many with little more than the clothes on their backs. Conditions quickly deteriorated as the storm battered the building, tearing off parts of the roof and causing power outages. The lack of adequate food, water, and sanitation facilities turned the Superdome into a scene of desperation. Yet, even in these dire circumstances, stories of survival and solidarity emerged. Strangers banded together to share whatever resources they had, and makeshift medical stations were set up to care for the sick and injured. Amid the chaos, parents and children clung to each other, determined to survive.

The situation at the Convention Center was even more dire. With no official supplies or security, the thousands of people who had sought refuge there were left in squalid conditions. Days passed with little food, water, or medical care, and the situation seemed hopeless. Yet, even in this bleak environment, people found ways to survive. Groups of individuals took it upon themselves to organize food distribution, assist the elderly and disabled, and maintain order as best they could. These efforts, though often overlooked in the broader narrative of the disaster, were nothing short of miraculous for those who benefited from them.

The Role of Rescue Operations

As the full extent of the disaster became apparent, rescue operations were launched on an unprecedented scale. The U.S. Coast Guard, National Guard, and countless volunteers from across the country converged on New Orleans to rescue those trapped by the floodwaters. Helicopters plucked people from rooftops, and boats navigated the submerged streets to reach stranded residents. The sheer scale of the rescue effort was a testament to the determination and bravery of the responders, many of whom risked their lives to save others.

One of the most remarkable rescues involved a group of nursing home residents who had been left behind as the storm approached. The facility, located in a low-lying area, was quickly overwhelmed by floodwaters, leaving the residents trapped inside. With no electricity and rising water levels, their situation was dire. However, a group of volunteers, using a fleet of private boats, managed to reach the nursing home and evacuate the residents just as the building was beginning to collapse. For these elderly individuals, who had been all but forgotten, the arrival of their rescuers was nothing short of miraculous.

Another notable rescue occurred in the St. Bernard Parish, where a man had been stranded on his rooftop for several days. With no food, water, or means of communication, he had begun to lose hope. Just as he was about to give up, a helicopter appeared overhead, and rescuers descended to lift him to safety. His survival, against all odds, was a poignant reminder of the resilience of the human spirit in the face of overwhelming adversity.

The Aftermath and Lessons Learned

The aftermath of Hurricane Katrina was marked by a profound sense of loss and devastation. Entire neighborhoods were destroyed, and the city of New Orleans was forever changed. Yet, amid the rubble and heartache, the stories of survival—of individuals, families, and communities who endured the storm and its aftermath—stood as powerful testaments to the strength of the human spirit.

In the years since Katrina, these stories have been told and retold, serving as both inspiration and a reminder of the importance of preparation and resilience in the face of natural disasters. The lessons learned from Katrina have led to significant changes in emergency management and disaster response, with an emphasis on ensuring that vulnerable populations are not left behind.

Conclusion

The Miracle of Hurricane Katrina is not just one story, but a collection of countless individual tales of survival. These stories highlight the extraordinary capacity of people to endure, adapt, and overcome even the most harrowing circumstances. Whether trapped in an attic, stranded on a rooftop, or huddled in a makeshift shelter, those who survived Hurricane Katrina did so through a combination of resourcefulness, courage, and the help of others. Their experiences serve as a powerful reminder of the resilience of the human spirit and the importance of community in times of crisis. The legacy of these survivors continues to inspire and inform, ensuring that their stories are never forgotten.

Chapter 29: The Survival of Harrison Okene

Harrison Okene's survival story is one of the most extraordinary accounts of human endurance and resilience ever recorded. On May 26, 2013, Okene, a Nigerian cook, found himself in a situation that defied the odds—trapped 100 feet underwater in a capsized tugboat for nearly three days. His survival, against all expectations, became a symbol of hope and an incredible testament to the power of the human spirit.

The Incident: Capsizing of the Jascon-4 Tugboat

The Jascon-4, a tugboat operated by West African Ventures, was assigned to help stabilize a Chevron oil tanker off the coast of Nigeria. Harrison Okene, who worked as a cook on the vessel, had started his day as usual, preparing meals for the 11 other crew members on board. However, early that morning, the weather took a sudden turn for the worse. The Atlantic Ocean, which had been relatively calm, began to churn with increasing ferocity. The waves grew larger, and the winds picked up, creating treacherous conditions for the tugboat.

As the storm intensified, the Jascon-4 was hit by a massive wave that caused the vessel to capsize. The boat flipped over, and water began to flood the interior. The crew, most of whom were sleeping at the time, were caught completely off guard. In the chaos that ensued, the majority of the crew were trapped and drowned as the tugboat quickly sank to the seabed, settling at a depth of 100 feet. Harrison Okene, however, found himself in a small air pocket within the wreckage—a pocket of life in an otherwise deadly situation.

Trapped in the Depths: Harrison Okene's Struggle for Survival

When the tugboat capsized, Harrison Okene was in the bathroom, a position that likely saved his life. As the vessel flipped over, he was thrown around by the force of the water but managed to find his way out of the bathroom and into an adjoining room. In this room, he discovered an air pocket, a small space where the water had not completely filled the compartment, allowing him to breathe.

Okene was in complete darkness, surrounded by the cold waters of the Atlantic Ocean, with no food, fresh water, or means of communication. The temperature of the water was frigid, and he was wearing only his underwear, making hypothermia a constant threat. The air pocket was limited in size and would only last for so long before becoming depleted of oxygen. Moreover, the rising water level and the toxic buildup of carbon dioxide made his chances of survival slim.

Despite the overwhelming fear and isolation, Okene clung to life. He knew that the chances of rescue were minimal, but he refused to give in to despair. He spent the next 60 hours in complete darkness, listening to the sounds of the sea and the creaking of the wrecked tugboat. The knowledge that he was the only one alive on a vessel that had become a tomb for his fellow crew members weighed heavily on him.

Faith and Determination: Harrison Okene's Mental Fortitude

Throughout his ordeal, Okene drew strength from his faith and his determination to survive. He prayed continuously, reciting passages from the Bible that he remembered and asking God for a miracle. His faith provided him with a mental anchor, helping him to stay calm and focused despite the terrifying circumstances.

Okene also used his survival instincts to ration the limited resources available to him. He found a can of Coca-Cola and sipped it slowly to conserve the small amount of liquid. He also had to contend with the physical discomfort of his situation, as the cramped space made it difficult to move, and the cold water sapped his strength. Despite these challenges, Okene's resolve never wavered. He believed that he could survive, and that belief kept him going.

The Rescue: A Miraculous Discovery

Meanwhile, on the surface, rescue efforts were already underway. The oil company and Nigerian authorities had been alerted to the capsizing of the Jascon-4, but initial efforts were focused on recovering the bodies of the crew members, as survival seemed impossible given the circumstances. Divers from the Dutch company DCN Global were dispatched to the wreck to recover the bodies. They did not expect to find anyone alive.

On the morning of May 28, 2013, nearly three days after the tugboat had capsized, the divers began their recovery operation. Equipped with video cameras, they entered the wreck to search for bodies. As one of the divers explored the submerged sections of the boat, he was startled to see a human hand reach out in the murky water. Initially, he thought it was the hand of a deceased crew member, but when the hand grabbed his, he realized with shock that someone was still alive.

Harrison Okene had heard the divers and, with his last reserves of strength, reached out to them. The diver immediately alerted his colleagues, and the rescue operation quickly shifted focus. The team worked to bring Okene to the surface, but this was no simple task. Okene had been breathing compressed air in the small pocket, and bringing him up too quickly could result in decompression sickness, commonly known as "the bends." To prevent this, the rescue team had to place Okene in a diving bell and gradually bring him to the surface while carefully managing the pressure.

After what must have seemed like an eternity to Okene, he was finally brought to the surface, where he was immediately placed in a decompression chamber to safely normalize his body's pressure levels. The ordeal was not over, as he had to spend another 60 hours in the decompression chamber to avoid the life-threatening effects of rapid depressurization. But he had made it—against all odds, Harrison Okene had survived.

The Aftermath: Harrison Okene's Reflections on Survival

Harrison Okene's survival was nothing short of miraculous. His story captured the attention of the world, with many marveling at how he managed to endure such a harrowing experience. For Okene himself, the experience was life-altering. He attributed his survival to his faith, believing that it was a divine intervention that allowed him to live through the ordeal.

Physically, Okene had to recover from the effects of his time underwater. The cold, the stress, and the prolonged exposure to toxic air had taken their toll on his body. Mentally, the trauma of losing his crewmates and being trapped in the dark, cold water was profound. However, Okene emerged from the experience with a new perspective on life. He expressed deep gratitude for his survival and a renewed appreciation for the time he had been given.

Okene's story also had a significant impact on the diving and maritime industries. His survival prompted a review of safety protocols and emergency preparedness on vessels operating in dangerous waters. The incident highlighted the importance of training and equipping crews with the knowledge and tools needed to survive unexpected disasters.

The Broader Significance: A Testament to Human Resilience

Harrison Okene's story is not just a tale of personal survival; it is a powerful example of the resilience of the human spirit. Trapped in a situation that most would consider hopeless, Okene refused to give up. His faith, determination, and will to survive carried him through one of the most terrifying experiences imaginable.

The story also underscores the unpredictability of life and the importance of hope in the face of adversity. In situations where all seems lost, the human capacity to endure and overcome can lead to outcomes that defy logic and reason. Okene's survival serves as an inspiration to many, a reminder that even in the darkest of times, there is always a possibility for a miracle.

Conclusion

The survival of Harrison Okene is one of the most remarkable survival stories in modern history. Trapped underwater in a capsized tugboat for nearly three days, Okene's endurance, faith, and determination allowed him to beat overwhelming odds. His story has become a symbol of hope and the incredible power of the human will to survive. It is a story that continues to inspire and remind us of the resilience that lies within each of us, waiting to be called upon in times of great need.

Chapter 30: The Miracle of the Andaman Sea

The Andaman Sea, a body of water in the northeastern Indian Ocean, is known for its stunning beauty, with turquoise waters and picturesque islands. However, beneath this serene surface lies a sea that can turn treacherous in an instant. The region is prone to sudden storms, strong currents, and unpredictable weather patterns, making it a challenging environment for sailors, fishermen, and travelers. The Andaman Sea has seen its share of maritime disasters, but among these, one stands out as a remarkable tale of human endurance and survival—a story that has come to be known as "The Miracle of the Andaman Sea."

The Setting: A Voyage into Danger

In the early 21st century, a group of Thai fishermen set out on what they expected to be a routine fishing trip in the Andaman Sea. The crew, made up of experienced seafarers, had ventured into these waters countless times, navigating the sea's challenges with skill and confidence. They were well-versed in the sea's moods, aware that the tranquil waters could quickly give way to violent storms. However, nothing could have prepared them for the catastrophe they were about to face.

On this particular voyage, the weather had been forecasted as favorable. The skies were clear, and the sea was calm as the fishermen cast their nets, hoping for a bountiful catch. They had no reason to suspect that the situation would take a drastic turn. But the Andaman Sea is notorious for its unpredictable weather, and as the day progressed, the first signs of trouble began to appear.

The Storm: Nature's Fury Unleashed

Without warning, the clear skies began to darken, and the wind picked up speed. The fishermen, seasoned as they were, recognized the signs of an impending storm and began to take precautions. They secured their gear, battened down the hatches, and prepared to ride out the storm. But the storm that was brewing was unlike anything they had encountered before.

The wind rapidly intensified, howling with a ferocity that shook the boat. The waves, once gentle, grew into towering walls of water that crashed against the vessel with tremendous force. The fishermen fought to maintain control of their boat, but the sea was relentless. Within minutes, the storm had reached its full fury, with lightning flashing across the sky and rain pouring down in torrents.

The crew's situation grew more perilous by the second. The boat, now at the mercy of the storm, was tossed about like a toy in a bathtub. The fishermen clung to whatever they could find, struggling to stay aboard as the waves threatened to capsize the vessel. The roar of the wind and the crashing of the waves drowned out all other sounds, and the fishermen could only pray that the storm would pass quickly.

But the storm showed no signs of abating. For hours, the crew battled the elements, their strength and resolve tested to the limit. Despite their efforts, the storm proved too powerful. A massive wave struck the boat with such force that it capsized, throwing the fishermen into the churning sea. In an instant, they went from fighting to save their boat to fighting for their lives.

The Fight for Survival: Alone in the Andaman Sea

The fishermen, now scattered in the turbulent waters of the Andaman Sea, faced an unimaginable ordeal. Separated from each other and their boat, they were at the mercy of the storm and the sea's powerful currents. The waves continued to pummel them, and the rain reduced visibility to almost nothing. With no land in sight and no means of communication, their situation seemed hopeless.

Yet, in the face of such overwhelming odds, the fishermen refused to give up. Each man fought to stay afloat, using whatever debris from the boat they could find as makeshift flotation devices. Some clung to pieces of wood, while others managed to grab hold of life vests that had been thrown from the boat. The sea was cold, and the relentless battering of the waves sapped their strength, but they knew that their survival depended on their ability to stay afloat and maintain hope.

Hours turned into a day, and then another. The storm eventually passed, but the sea remained rough, and the fishermen were still adrift, miles from the nearest shore. The sun beat down on them during the day, while the nights were cold and unforgiving. They had no food, no fresh water, and no way of knowing if rescue was on the way. Yet, they clung to life, driven by the will to survive and the hope that they would be found.

The Rescue: A Beacon of Hope in the Distance

As the days passed, the fishermen's situation grew increasingly dire. Dehydration and exposure began to take their toll, and the men's strength was waning. Some began to lose hope, but others continued to encourage their comrades, urging them to hold on just a little longer. They knew that their only chance of survival was to be spotted by a passing ship or aircraft, but the vastness of the sea made this seem unlikely.

On the fourth day, when hope was beginning to fade, one of the fishermen spotted something on the horizon—a faint, distant shape that appeared to be moving. At first, it was difficult to tell if it was a ship or a trick of the light, but as the shape grew larger, the fishermen realized that it was indeed a ship. Their hearts leaped with hope, but they knew they had to attract the ship's attention.

Using the last of their strength, the fishermen waved their arms, shouted, and tried to make themselves as visible as possible. One of them managed to find a piece of reflective material, which they used to signal the ship. For what seemed like an eternity, they waited, praying that the ship would see them and change course.

To their immense relief, the ship began to turn in their direction. As it drew closer, the fishermen could see the crew on the deck, scanning the water. Moments later, a lifeboat was lowered, and the fishermen were finally pulled from the sea. Exhausted, dehydrated, and on the brink of collapse, they had survived one of the most harrowing ordeals of their lives.

The Aftermath: Reflections on the Miracle of Survival

The fishermen were taken aboard the ship, where they received medical attention, food, and water. Their ordeal in the Andaman Sea had lasted four days, during which they had faced some of the most challenging conditions imaginable. Their survival was hailed as a miracle, a testament to their resilience, determination, and the will to live.

In the aftermath of their rescue, the fishermen reflected on their experience. They spoke of the terror they felt as the storm overtook them, the loneliness of being adrift in the vast ocean, and the struggle to stay alive against all odds. They also spoke of the bonds that had formed between them during their ordeal, the camaraderie that had helped them to keep going even when hope seemed lost.

Their story became an inspiration to others, a reminder that even in the most desperate of situations, survival is possible if one holds onto hope and refuses to give up. The fishermen credited their survival to a combination of luck, faith, and the unbreakable human spirit. Their story, known as "The Miracle of the Andaman Sea," was shared widely, becoming a symbol of hope and resilience.

The Broader Impact: Lessons from the Andaman Sea

The Miracle of the Andaman Sea had a profound impact, not only on the fishermen who survived but also on the broader community. The story highlighted the dangers faced by those who work at sea and the importance of preparedness and safety measures. In the aftermath of the incident, there was a renewed emphasis on equipping fishing vessels with better safety gear, including more reliable life vests, emergency communication devices, and distress signals.

The incident also led to improvements in search and rescue operations in the region. The fact that the fishermen were eventually rescued, despite being adrift for days, underscored the importance of coordinated search efforts and the use of technology to locate survivors in remote areas. The story served as a catalyst for change, leading to enhanced safety protocols and greater awareness of the risks associated with maritime activities in the Andaman Sea.

Conclusion: The Enduring Legacy of Survival

The Miracle of the Andaman Sea is more than just a survival story; it is a powerful testament to the resilience of the human spirit. The fishermen who survived the storm and their days adrift in the sea faced unimaginable challenges, yet they never lost hope. Their story serves as a reminder that even in the face of nature's most terrifying forces, the will to survive can carry people through the darkest of times.

The legacy of the Miracle of the Andaman Sea lives on, inspiring others to persevere in the face of adversity and to never underestimate the power of hope. It is a story that will be told for generations, a symbol of the strength and courage that lies within us all. Whether facing the wrath of the sea or the trials of everyday life, the story of these fishermen reminds us that survival is always possible, as long as we hold onto hope and never give up.

Chapter 31: The Survival of Tami Oldham Ashcraft

Tami Oldham Ashcraft's survival story is one of the most harrowing and inspiring tales of human endurance ever recorded. In 1983, at the age of 23, Tami set out on what was supposed to be a dream journey—a sailing adventure across the Pacific Ocean with her fiancé, Richard Sharp. What began as an idyllic voyage turned into a nightmare when they encountered one of the most powerful hurricanes ever recorded in the Pacific. Tami's survival, alone on the open ocean for 41 days, is a remarkable testament to human resilience, the will to live, and the power of love.

The Beginning: A Love Born of Adventure

Tami Oldham was an adventurous young woman from San Diego, California. She had always been drawn to the sea and had a passion for sailing, a pursuit that led her to cross paths with Richard Sharp, a handsome and experienced British sailor. The two quickly fell in love, united by their shared love for the ocean and the thrill of adventure. Richard, a seasoned sailor who had already completed several transatlantic crossings, was captivated by Tami's spirit and zest for life.

In 1983, the couple was living in Tahiti, where they were presented with an opportunity to sail a luxury yacht, the Hazana, from Tahiti to San Diego. The owner of the yacht, a wealthy Californian, had hired Richard to deliver the vessel safely back to the United States. Richard and Tami eagerly accepted the offer, seeing it as a chance to embark on the adventure of a lifetime. The journey would take them across 4,000 miles of the Pacific Ocean, through some of the most remote and beautiful waters in the world.

The Journey Begins: A Voyage into the Unknown

The Hazana, a 44-foot luxury yacht, was well-equipped for the journey, with advanced navigation systems, plenty of provisions, and a sturdy build capable of handling rough seas. Richard and Tami set sail from Papeete, Tahiti, in September 1983, with high spirits and great anticipation. The first few weeks of the voyage were idyllic. The weather was perfect, with clear skies and calm seas, and the couple enjoyed their time on the open ocean, reveling in the beauty of their surroundings and the freedom of life at sea.

As they sailed further from the islands, they found themselves completely alone in the vast expanse of the Pacific. The isolation was both exhilarating and humbling, a reminder of the power and majesty of the ocean. They spent their days navigating the yacht, fishing, and enjoying each other's company. It was a time of pure joy and contentment, a voyage that seemed destined to end in triumph.

The Storm Approaches: A Sudden Change in the Weather

However, as they approached the halfway point of their journey, the weather began to change. The clear skies darkened, and the winds picked up speed. Richard, ever vigilant, began to monitor the weather reports more closely. It soon became clear that a major storm was brewing—a storm that would later be identified as Hurricane Raymond, a Category 4 hurricane with winds exceeding 140 miles per hour.

Richard and Tami knew they were in serious danger. The Hazana, though well-built, was no match for a hurricane of this magnitude. They tried to change course to avoid the storm, but the hurricane was moving too quickly, and they found themselves directly in its path. With no way to outrun the storm, Richard and Tami prepared the yacht as best they could, securing everything on deck, reefing the sails, and battening down the hatches. They knew they were in for the fight of their lives.

The Fury of the Storm: A Battle for Survival

As Hurricane Raymond bore down on them, the sea turned violent. The wind howled like a banshee, and the waves grew to monstrous heights, towering over the yacht. The Hazana was tossed about like a cork in a tempest, with each wave threatening to capsize the vessel. Tami and Richard were both terrified, but they kept their wits about them, doing everything they could to keep the yacht from being swamped by the waves.

For hours, they battled the storm, with Richard at the helm and Tami assisting wherever she could. But the hurricane was relentless. At the height of the storm, a massive wave—later estimated to be over 40 feet high—struck the yacht with devastating force. The impact was catastrophic. The Hazana was flipped, turning completely upside down before righting itself. The force of the wave threw Tami violently across the cabin, where she struck her head and was knocked unconscious. The last thing she remembered was the sound of Richard screaming her name.

Awakening to a Nightmare: The Aftermath of the Hurricane

When Tami regained consciousness, she found herself alone in the wreckage of the yacht. The interior of the cabin was a shambles, with water pouring in from the broken windows. Her head throbbed with pain from the injury she had sustained, and she felt disoriented and weak. As she struggled to her feet, the reality of the situation began to dawn on her. Richard was nowhere to be found.

In a state of shock, Tami searched the yacht, calling out for Richard. But there was no answer. The deck was a twisted mess of broken rigging and torn sails, and the lifeboat was gone. Tami was completely alone, adrift in the middle of the Pacific Ocean, with no way to navigate, no means of communication, and no idea how far she was from land.

Despite the overwhelming despair she felt at the loss of Richard, Tami knew she had to focus on survival. The yacht was badly damaged, but it was still afloat. She would have to make the best of the situation and find a way to stay alive until she could be rescued.

Survival Mode: Adapting to Life at Sea

Tami's first priority was to secure the yacht and prevent it from sinking. The cabin was partially flooded, and the broken mast and rigging made it impossible to sail. Using her limited resources, Tami managed to jury-rig a makeshift sail using a broken spinnaker pole and some canvas she found in the wreckage. She also bailed out the water from the cabin, patching the holes as best she could to keep the yacht afloat.

Next, she took stock of her provisions. The storm had washed away most of their supplies, but Tami managed to salvage some canned goods, a bag of rice, and a few gallons of water. She knew that rationing would be crucial to her survival, so she carefully calculated how long her supplies would last. She also rigged a solar still, a device that uses the sun's heat to distill seawater into drinkable water, to supplement her limited freshwater supply.

With the yacht barely seaworthy, Tami faced the daunting challenge of navigating her way to safety. The yacht's electronic navigation systems were destroyed, and she had no working compass or sextant. However, Tami had basic knowledge of celestial navigation, and she used the sun and stars to approximate her position. Based on her rough calculations, she estimated that she was somewhere near the equator, far from any major shipping lanes. Her only hope was to steer the yacht toward Hawaii, more than 1,500 miles away, in the faint hope of being spotted by a passing ship.

The Long Days at Sea: A Battle of Mind and Body

The next 41 days would test Tami's physical and mental endurance to the limit. The solitude was crushing, and the grief over losing Richard was almost unbearable. But Tami knew that if she allowed herself to succumb to despair, she would not survive. She kept herself busy with the daily tasks necessary to keep the yacht afloat and to navigate her course. She also took solace in the memories of Richard, using his love and the promise she had made to him to stay alive as her motivation.

The days blended into each other as Tami drifted across the vast, empty ocean. She faced numerous challenges, from repairing the constant leaks in the yacht's hull to dealing with the scorching sun and the bitter cold of the nights. Her physical condition deteriorated as she lost weight and grew weaker from the lack of sufficient food and the strain of her injuries. But through it all, she clung to life, driven by an unyielding will to survive.

Tami also had to contend with the psychological toll of her ordeal. The loneliness was profound, and she often found herself talking to Richard as if he were still there with her. She imagined his voice guiding her, encouraging her to keep going, and offering her comfort in her darkest moments. These conversations, though imaginary, provided her with the strength she needed to endure the isolation and the uncertainty of her situation.

A Glimmer of Hope: The Sighting of Land

After weeks adrift, with her supplies dwindling and her strength fading, Tami began to lose hope. She had no way of knowing how far she had traveled or if she was even on course for Hawaii. The endless expanse of water seemed to stretch on forever, with no sign of land or rescue in sight. But just as she was beginning to despair, Tami spotted something on the horizon—a faint, dark shape that looked like land.

At first, she thought it might be a mirage, a trick of the light after so many days at sea. But as the hours passed, the shape grew larger and more distinct. It was an island, the first land she had seen since the hurricane struck. Tami's heart soared with hope. She adjusted her makeshift sail, steering the yacht toward the island with every ounce of strength she had left.

As she drew closer, she recognized the island as one of the Hawaiian Islands. After 41 days adrift, she had managed to navigate her way to safety, against all odds. The sight of the lush, green land was a balm to her weary soul, a promise that her ordeal was finally over.

Rescue and Recovery: The End of the Nightmare

On October 12, 1983, Tami Oldham Ashcraft was finally rescued by the crew of a Japanese research vessel that had spotted her yacht off the coast of Hilo, Hawaii. She was weak, dehydrated, and emaciated, but she was alive. The crew brought her aboard, where she received medical attention, food, and water. Her 41-day ordeal was over.

In the days and weeks that followed, Tami began the slow process of physical and emotional recovery. The trauma of losing Richard and the experience of surviving alone on the open ocean left deep scars, but Tami's indomitable spirit helped her to heal. She returned to San Diego, where she was reunited with her family and friends, who had feared the worst after losing contact with her so many weeks before.

Reflections on Survival: The Lessons of the Sea

Tami Oldham Ashcraft's survival story is not just a tale of endurance; it is also a story of love, loss, and the power of the human spirit.

Throughout her ordeal, Tami was sustained by her love for Richard and the memory of the life they had shared. Her determination to survive was driven by the promise she had made to him, a promise to live and to carry on despite the overwhelming odds against her.

In the years that followed, Tami wrote a book about her experience, titled *Red Sky in Mourning: A True Story of Love, Loss, and Survival at Sea*. The book became a bestseller and was later adapted into a feature film titled *Adrift*, starring Shailene Woodley as Tami. Her story has inspired countless people around the world, a testament to the resilience of the human spirit and the capacity for hope even in the darkest of times.

Tami's experience also serves as a powerful reminder of the dangers of the sea and the importance of preparation, resilience, and mental fortitude in the face of adversity. Her survival was the result of a combination of factors—her sailing skills, her resourcefulness, and her unwavering will to live. But it was also a story of the profound connection between two people, a love that transcended life and death and provided the strength to endure the unimaginable.

Conclusion: The Enduring Legacy of Tami Oldham Ashcraft

Today, Tami Oldham Ashcraft continues to share her story with the world, speaking about her experiences and the lessons she learned from her time at sea. Her survival is a symbol of hope, a reminder that even in the face of overwhelming odds, the human spirit is capable of extraordinary resilience.

The story of Tami Oldham Ashcraft is more than just a tale of survival; it is a story of love, loss, and the unbreakable bond between two people. It is a story that will continue to inspire and move people for generations to come, a testament to the power of the human will and the enduring strength of the human spirit.

Chapter 32: The Donner Party

The story of the Donner Party stands as one of the most harrowing episodes in American history. Set against the backdrop of the 19th-century westward expansion, this tragic tale of ambition, misfortune, and survival is a stark reminder of the perils faced by pioneers who sought a better life in the uncharted territories of the American West. The Donner Party's journey, which began with hope and promise, ended in a nightmare of starvation, desperation, and unimaginable suffering. This narrative delves deep into the circumstances that led to the disaster, the trials endured by the emigrants, and the legacy of their ordeal.

The Call of the West: Manifest Destiny and the Promise of California

In the mid-1800s, the United States was gripped by the fever of Manifest Destiny, the belief that the nation was destined to expand its territory across the North American continent. This belief, coupled with the promise of fertile land, economic opportunity, and a fresh start, drove thousands of families to embark on the arduous journey westward. The discovery of gold in California, along with tales of its mild climate and abundant resources, further fueled the desire to move west.

Among those drawn to the promise of California were the Donner and Reed families. George Donner, a prosperous farmer from Illinois, and his brother Jacob, decided to head west in 1846, seeking new opportunities in the California territory. They were joined by James Reed, a successful businessman and close friend of the Donners. The combined Donner-Reed Party, consisting of several families and hired hands, began their journey in the spring of 1846, full of optimism and anticipation.

The Journey Begins: The Wagon Train Heads West

The Donner Party's journey began like many others of the time, with the families gathering in Independence, Missouri, the starting point for the Oregon and California Trails. They set out in May 1846, joining a larger wagon train led by William H. Russell, one of the many organized groups traveling west that year. The journey was expected to take four to six months, covering more than 2,000 miles of rugged terrain.

The wagon train made steady progress along the well-established trail, passing through the prairies of Kansas and the Platte River Valley in Nebraska. The travelers endured the usual hardships of the trail—long days of travel, rough terrain, limited water, and occasional skirmishes with Native American tribes. Despite these challenges, morale remained high, and the families bonded over shared experiences and the excitement of their journey.

As the Donner Party moved westward, they reached Fort Laramie, Wyoming, a key resupply point for emigrants. It was here that James Reed learned of a new route to California, known as the Hastings Cutoff, which promised to save time and shorten the journey by several hundred miles. The route was promoted by Lansford Hastings, an ambitious lawyer and explorer who sought to establish a faster, more direct path to California.

The Fatal Decision: The Hastings Cutoff

The decision to take the Hastings Cutoff would prove to be a fatal one for the Donner Party. Despite warnings from experienced mountain men and fellow travelers, Reed was convinced that the shortcut would give them an advantage over other wagon trains, allowing them to reach California before the onset of winter. He persuaded the Donners and several other families to follow him on the untested route.

In mid-July, the Donner Party split from the main wagon train and set off on the Hastings Cutoff, heading south from Fort Bridger, Wyoming, toward the Great Salt Lake Desert. The shortcut took them through the Wasatch Mountains, where they encountered dense forests, steep inclines, and narrow passes. The terrain was far more challenging than they had anticipated, and the wagons struggled to make progress. Days were lost as they hacked their way through the dense underbrush, and the travelers began to realize that the shortcut was anything but.

By the time they reached the Great Salt Lake Desert, the Donner Party was already weeks behind schedule. The desert crossing, which Hastings had claimed would take two days, stretched into five days of brutal heat, blinding salt flats, and scarce water. The oxen and livestock suffered greatly, many dying of exhaustion and thirst, while the emigrants themselves were weakened and demoralized. The desert crossing took a heavy toll, and the party emerged on the other side severely depleted in both resources and morale.

The Sierra Nevada: A Barrier Between Life and Death

By early October 1846, the Donner Party finally reached the eastern foothills of the Sierra Nevada, the last major obstacle before reaching California. However, their ordeal was far from over. The Sierra Nevada range, known for its towering peaks and treacherous passes, presented a formidable challenge, especially with winter fast approaching. The emigrants were exhausted, their supplies were running dangerously low, and their animals were too weakened to continue at a rapid pace.

In a final attempt to reach safety, the party decided to push on through the mountains, hoping to cross the range before the winter snows set in. Unfortunately, they were too late. On October 28, an early snowstorm descended upon the mountains, trapping the Donner Party in the high-altitude passes near what is now known as Donner Lake, just a few miles from the summit. The snow fell relentlessly, burying the trails and making it impossible for the wagons to move forward or retreat.

Trapped by Snow: The Struggle for Survival Begins

With the party trapped by snow and unable to continue, the families were forced to set up camp in the frigid wilderness. They built makeshift shelters out of their wagons and whatever materials they could find, including branches, logs, and animal hides. The conditions were harsh and unforgiving, with temperatures plummeting below freezing and snowdrifts reaching depths of 20 feet or more.

As the days turned into weeks, the emigrants' food supplies dwindled, and hunger became a constant, gnawing presence. They rationed their remaining provisions as best they could, but it was clear that they would not last the winter. In desperation, they began to slaughter their remaining oxen and horses, but the meat was quickly consumed. With no game to hunt and no way to reach civilization, the situation grew increasingly dire.

The psychological toll of the ordeal was immense. The emigrants were isolated in the frozen wilderness, cut off from the outside world, and facing the grim reality that they might not survive. The stress and fear began to take a toll on the group's cohesion, leading to arguments, mistrust, and, in some cases, violence. The Reed family, in particular, faced difficulties after James Reed killed another member of the party, John Snyder, in a dispute over the treatment of

the oxen. As a result, Reed was banished from the group and forced
to continue on alone, leaving his family behind.

The Forlorn Hope: A Desperate Bid for Rescue

As the situation grew more desperate, a group of 15 of the strongest
members of the party, later known as the "Forlorn Hope," decided
to attempt a rescue. They fashioned crude snowshoes from ox hide
and set out on foot across the snow-covered mountains in a bid to
reach the nearest settlement and bring back help. The journey was
grueling, with deep snow, freezing temperatures, and treacherous
terrain making progress slow and painful.

The Forlorn Hope faced unimaginable hardships on their journey.
They were inadequately equipped for the harsh conditions, with
little food, inadequate clothing, and no shelter from the elements. As
the days passed and their rations ran out, they were forced to resort
to cannibalism, consuming the bodies of those who had died from
exposure and starvation in order to stay alive. It was a horrific and
desperate act, but it was the only way they could hope to survive.

After 33 days of unimaginable suffering, seven members of the
Forlorn Hope finally reached a settlement in California. They were
exhausted, emaciated, and traumatized by their ordeal, but they had
succeeded in their mission. Upon hearing their story, local settlers
immediately organized rescue parties to bring aid to the remaining
members of the Donner Party still trapped in the mountains.

The Rescues: A Race Against Time

The first rescue party set out in late February 1847, more than three
months after the Donner Party had become trapped. They found the
survivors in a pitiful state, many of them on the brink of death from
starvation and exposure. The rescuers were shocked by the scene
that greeted them—emaciated figures huddled in their makeshift

shelters, surrounded by the remains of their livestock and, in some cases, human bones.

The rescuers managed to bring out 23 survivors in the first group, but many were too weak to travel, and the journey down the mountain was perilous. A second rescue party arrived in March, followed by a third in April, each finding the survivors in increasingly dire conditions. By the time the last rescue party arrived, only a few members of the Donner Party were still alive, having endured one of the most brutal winters on record.

In total, out of the 87 members of the Donner Party who set out on the journey, only 48 survived. The survivors were a mix of men, women, and children, all of whom had endured unimaginable hardships and witnessed horrors that would haunt them for the rest of their lives. The tragedy of the Donner Party became a national sensation, with newspapers across the country reporting on the ordeal and the survivors' accounts of cannibalism, starvation, and despair.

The Aftermath: A Legacy of Tragedy and Resilience

The Donner Party's story is one of the most infamous and tragic episodes in the history of the American West. The factors that led to their disaster were numerous and complex, including poor decision-making, the treacherous terrain of the Sierra Nevada, and the unforgiving nature of the winter climate. Yet, their ordeal also serves as a testament to the resilience and determination of the human spirit.

For the survivors, the experience left deep physical and psychological scars. Many struggled to come to terms with the horrors they had witnessed and the choices they had been forced to make in order to survive. Some became reclusive, while others sought to rebuild their lives and move forward. James Reed, who had been banished from the party, was one of the first to reach safety and was instrumental in organizing the rescue efforts that saved his family and others.

The Donner Party's ordeal also had a lasting impact on the development of the American West. Their tragic experience served as a cautionary tale for future emigrants, highlighting the dangers of taking untested shortcuts and the importance of careful planning and preparation. The incident led to increased awareness of the perils of the western trails and prompted improvements in the support systems for pioneers, including the establishment of more reliable supply routes and the creation of government-sponsored relief programs for stranded emigrants.

Conclusion: The Donner Party's Enduring Place in History

Today, the story of the Donner Party is remembered as one of the most tragic and compelling tales of survival in American history. It is a story that has been retold in countless books, documentaries, and films, each exploring different aspects of the ordeal and the people who lived through it. The site of the Donner Party's encampment near Donner Lake has been preserved as a historical landmark, a solemn reminder of the lives lost and the resilience of those who survived.

The Donner Party's legacy is a complex one, marked by both tragedy and triumph. It serves as a powerful reminder of the fragility of human life in the face of nature's overwhelming forces and the lengths to which people will go to survive. Their story is a testament to the dangers of overconfidence and poor decision-making, but also to the strength of the human spirit in the most desperate of circumstances.

The tale of the Donner Party continues to captivate and horrify, serving as both a historical lesson and a cautionary tale. It is a story that forces us to confront the darker aspects of human nature, as well as the incredible capacity for endurance and survival in the face of seemingly insurmountable odds.

Chapter 33: The Survival of Jessica Lynch

The story of Jessica Lynch's survival is one of the most widely known and controversial episodes from the Iraq War. Lynch, a U.S. Army supply clerk, became a symbol of American resilience after her capture and subsequent rescue during the early stages of the conflict. Her ordeal not only highlighted the perils faced by soldiers in combat but also sparked a national conversation about the nature of war, the role of the media, and the fine line between fact and fiction in the narrative of heroism.

In March 2003, the United States, along with coalition forces, launched an invasion of Iraq, marking the beginning of what would become a prolonged and contentious conflict. The invasion aimed to overthrow the regime of Saddam Hussein, who was accused of possessing weapons of mass destruction and supporting terrorism. As U.S. troops advanced into Iraq, they encountered sporadic resistance from Iraqi forces, leading to a series of intense and often chaotic engagements.

Jessica Lynch, a 19-year-old private first class from Palestine, West Virginia, was part of the 507th Maintenance Company, a unit tasked with transporting supplies and equipment to the front lines. Like many soldiers in her unit, Lynch was not a combat soldier but rather a support personnel responsible for logistical operations. Nevertheless, the unpredictable nature of the war meant that even non-combat units were at risk of encountering enemy forces.

On March 23, 2003, just days after the invasion began, Lynch's unit found itself in a perilous situation. As they navigated through the desert in southern Iraq, near the city of Nasiriyah, they became lost and strayed into an area controlled by Iraqi forces. The convoy was ambushed by Iraqi soldiers, who unleashed a barrage of gunfire, rocket-propelled grenades, and mortars on the unsuspecting Americans. The ambush quickly turned into a nightmare as vehicles were disabled, soldiers were wounded, and chaos erupted.

Capture and Imprisonment: Lynch's Ordeal Begins

During the ambush, Jessica Lynch's vehicle was hit by a rocket-propelled grenade, causing it to crash. The impact left Lynch severely injured, with multiple fractures to her legs, arm, and spine, as well as a head wound. Unable to move or defend herself, Lynch was captured by Iraqi forces along with several other members of her unit. Her injuries were so severe that she was initially believed to be dead by some of her comrades.

Lynch was taken to an Iraqi hospital in Nasiriyah, where she was held as a prisoner of war (POW). The conditions in the hospital were far from ideal, with limited medical supplies and facilities. Despite her injuries, Lynch received some medical treatment from the Iraqi staff, who reportedly made efforts to care for her as best they could under the circumstances. However, she was still a prisoner, and her fate remained uncertain as the war raged on around her.

Lynch's capture and imprisonment became a focal point of concern for the U.S. military and government. The Pentagon was determined to locate and rescue her, but the chaotic and fluid nature of the conflict made it difficult to gather accurate intelligence. As the days passed, Lynch's story began to garner attention in the United States, where the media and public became increasingly concerned about her well-being.

The Rescue Operation: A Daring Mission

The rescue of Jessica Lynch became a top priority for the U.S. military, which launched a series of operations to locate and retrieve her from enemy hands. After several days of intelligence gathering and reconnaissance, U.S. forces pinpointed her location at the hospital in Nasiriyah. The operation to rescue Lynch, codenamed "Operation Dawn," was set in motion on the night of April 1, 2003.

The rescue mission involved a combination of U.S. Special Forces, including Navy SEALs, Army Rangers, and Air Force Pararescuemen, who were tasked with infiltrating the hospital and extracting Lynch. The mission was fraught with danger, as the hospital was located in a hostile area with significant Iraqi military presence. The operation required precise coordination and execution to minimize the risk to both Lynch and the rescue team.

Under the cover of darkness, the U.S. forces launched a daring assault on the hospital, entering the building and securing the area with overwhelming force. The rescue team quickly located Lynch, who was lying in a hospital bed, weak and disoriented from her injuries and the ordeal she had endured. Despite the confusion and tension of the moment, the rescuers managed to safely extract Lynch from the hospital and evacuate her by helicopter to a nearby military base.

The successful rescue of Jessica Lynch was hailed as a triumph by the U.S. military and the media, who portrayed her as a symbol of American courage and resilience. The operation was the first successful rescue of an American POW in Iraq, and it provided a significant morale boost to U.S. forces and the American public. Lynch was flown to a military hospital in Germany, where she received advanced medical treatment before being transferred to Walter Reed Army Medical Center in Washington, D.C.

The Media Frenzy: Fact, Fiction, and Heroism

In the aftermath of her rescue, Jessica Lynch became a national sensation. The media coverage of her story was intense, with news outlets across the country reporting on her ordeal, rescue, and recovery. Lynch was portrayed as a heroic figure, a young woman who had endured unimaginable hardship and had been saved by the bravery and skill of U.S. forces.

However, as more details emerged, the narrative surrounding Lynch's capture and rescue became the subject of controversy. Early reports had suggested that Lynch had engaged in a fierce firefight with her captors, firing her weapon until she ran out of ammunition. These reports, later revealed to be inaccurate, painted a picture of Lynch as a valiant warrior who had fought to the last, embodying the ideal of the American soldier.

The Pentagon and the media played a significant role in shaping this narrative, with some accusing the military of exaggerating or fabricating details to boost public support for the war. The true nature of Lynch's capture and rescue was far more complex and less sensational than initially portrayed. It was eventually revealed that Lynch had not fired her weapon during the ambush, as her rifle had jammed, and that she had been unconscious for much of the ordeal due to her injuries.

Lynch herself later spoke out about the discrepancies in the media's portrayal of her story. In interviews and public appearances, she expressed frustration with the way her experience had been sensationalized and distorted. She emphasized that she was not a hero in the way she had been depicted, and that her survival was due to the efforts of others, including the Iraqi medical staff who had cared for her and the U.S. soldiers who had risked their lives to rescue her.

The Aftermath: Recovery and Reflection

Jessica Lynch's survival and rescue marked the beginning of a long and difficult recovery process. Her injuries were severe, requiring multiple surgeries and extensive rehabilitation. She faced months of physical therapy to regain mobility and strength, as well as the psychological challenges of coping with the trauma of her experience.

Despite the challenges, Lynch demonstrated remarkable resilience in her recovery. She eventually returned to her hometown of Palestine, West Virginia, where she was greeted as a local hero. The community rallied around her, offering support and encouragement as she worked to rebuild her life. Lynch's story continued to resonate with the American public, who followed her progress and celebrated her milestones.

In the years following her rescue, Lynch took steps to set the record straight about her experience. She co-authored a memoir titled *I Am a Soldier, Too: The Jessica Lynch Story*, which provided a more accurate account of her ordeal and addressed the misconceptions that had arisen in the media. The book, written with the help of journalist Rick Bragg, offered a candid and introspective look at the events that had shaped her life and the impact of the intense media scrutiny she had faced.

Lynch also became an advocate for veterans' rights and spoke out on issues related to the treatment of wounded soldiers, the challenges of reintegration into civilian life, and the importance of mental health care for those who had experienced trauma in combat. She used her platform to raise awareness about the realities of war and the need for comprehensive support systems for returning service members.

Legacy and Reflection: The Broader Implications of Lynch's Story

The story of Jessica Lynch's survival is not just a tale of individual resilience but also a reflection of the broader complexities of war, media, and heroism. Her experience highlights the often-blurred line between fact and fiction in the narratives that emerge from conflict, as well as the ways in which individuals can become symbols in the larger discourse of war.

Lynch's story also underscores the challenges faced by women in the military, who, despite not being assigned to combat roles at the time, often found themselves in the line of fire. Her ordeal brought attention to the contributions and sacrifices of female service members, who, like their male counterparts, faced the dangers and uncertainties of warfare.

The controversy surrounding the portrayal of Lynch's story also serves as a cautionary tale about the role of the media in shaping public perception. The initial narrative, which was driven by a combination of military statements, media sensationalism, and public desire for a heroic figure, ultimately obscured the more nuanced and complex reality of her experience. Lynch's efforts to correct the record highlight the importance of truth and accuracy in storytelling, particularly in the context of war.

Conclusion: The Enduring Impact of Jessica Lynch's Survival

Today, Jessica Lynch's survival story continues to resonate as a powerful example of the challenges and complexities of war. Her experience serves as a reminder of the resilience of the human spirit in the face of adversity, as well as the importance of honesty and integrity in the narratives we create and share.

Lynch's journey from a small-town girl in West Virginia to a national symbol of survival and then to an advocate for veterans' rights is a testament to her strength and determination. While the media may have initially cast her as a simplistic figure of heroism, Lynch's own words and actions have revealed a more authentic and inspiring story—one of a young woman who, despite being thrust into a situation beyond her control, faced her circumstances with courage, dignity, and grace.

The story of Jessica Lynch will likely continue to be remembered and studied for years to come, not only as a chapter in the history of the Iraq War but also as a reflection of the enduring human struggle to survive, to heal, and to seek the truth amidst the chaos of conflict.

Chapter 34: Apollo 13 Mission

The Apollo 13 mission, often referred to as NASA's "successful failure," is one of the most remarkable and dramatic episodes in the history of space exploration. The mission, which was intended to be the third manned landing on the Moon, became an extraordinary story of survival and ingenuity in the face of almost certain disaster. The events that unfolded during Apollo 13 captured the world's attention, showcasing the courage of the astronauts, the skill of the NASA team, and the resilience of human spirit in overcoming impossible odds.

The Apollo program, initiated by NASA in the early 1960s, was a bold and ambitious effort to land a man on the Moon and return him safely to Earth. The program was a direct response to the Cold War-era space race between the United States and the Soviet Union. After the successful landing of Apollo 11 in July 1969, followed by the smooth execution of Apollo 12 in November of the same year, the Apollo 13 mission was set to continue NASA's momentum, further advancing scientific exploration and demonstrating American technological prowess.

Scheduled for launch on April 11, 1970, Apollo 13's primary mission was to explore the Fra Mauro region of the Moon, a site of significant geological interest. The crew, consisting of Commander James A. Lovell Jr., Command Module Pilot John L. "Jack" Swigert Jr., and Lunar Module Pilot Fred W. Haise Jr., was well-prepared for the mission, with Lovell being a veteran astronaut who had already flown in space three times. Confidence was high, and the mission was expected to be another step forward in the exploration of the lunar surface.

However, Apollo 13 would become far more than just another Moon landing mission. It would become a story of how the combined efforts of astronauts and mission control could turn a near-fatal disaster into a tale of ingenuity, teamwork, and survival that would be remembered for generations.

The Calm Before the Storm: Launch and Early Troubles

Apollo 13 lifted off from Kennedy Space Center in Florida at 13:13 CST on April 11, 1970. The launch was nearly flawless, and the spacecraft quickly reached Earth orbit before executing the Trans-Lunar Injection (TLI) burn that would send it on its way to the Moon. For the first two days of the mission, everything proceeded smoothly, with the spacecraft performing as expected and the crew settling into their routine tasks.

However, the mission began to experience minor problems that, while not immediately alarming, hinted at the challenges that lay ahead. One of the first issues arose with the center engine of the Saturn V rocket, which shut down prematurely during the second stage of the launch. Although the other engines compensated for the loss, the incident was a sign that things were not going as smoothly as anticipated. Additionally, a few hours after launch, the crew noted an unusual oscillation in the spacecraft, which was later attributed to a misalignment of the platform that was used for navigation.

These early hiccups, while disconcerting, were not seen as major threats to the mission. The crew and mission control addressed each problem methodically, confident in their ability to overcome any technical issues that might arise. The true test, however, was yet to come.

The Explosion: A Routine Procedure Turns into Catastrophe

The pivotal moment of the Apollo 13 mission occurred on the evening of April 13, 1970, as the spacecraft was approximately 200,000 miles from Earth and nearing the point where the lunar landing phase of the mission would begin. The crew was conducting a routine procedure known as a "cryogenic stir" in the service module's oxygen tanks. The procedure involved turning on fans inside the tanks to stir the liquid oxygen, which prevented the contents from settling and stratifying.

At 55 hours and 54 minutes into the mission, as the crew executed the stir, a catastrophic explosion rocked the spacecraft. The explosion was caused by a damaged electrical wire inside Oxygen Tank 2, which had been damaged during manufacturing and testing. The spark ignited the oxygen, causing a massive rupture in the tank. The force of the explosion blew off a side panel of the service module, venting precious oxygen into space and severely damaging the spacecraft's power and propulsion systems.

The explosion was so powerful that it shook the entire spacecraft, and the crew immediately knew that something was terribly wrong. The first indication to the world that something was amiss came when Jack Swigert famously radioed back to mission control with the now-iconic words, "Houston, we've had a problem." Moments later, Jim Lovell looked out the window and saw gas venting into space—an unmistakable sign that the spacecraft was losing oxygen.

The Struggle for Survival: Dealing with Limited Resources

The explosion had transformed the mission from one of exploration to one of survival. The immediate priority was to assess the damage and determine the status of the spacecraft's systems. It quickly became apparent that the command module, Odyssey, had lost most of its oxygen supply, which also meant a loss of power, water, and the ability to remove carbon dioxide from the cabin air. The lunar module, Aquarius, which had been designed as a landing craft, suddenly became the crew's lifeboat.

Aquarius was equipped with its own life-support system, but it was only intended to sustain two astronauts for about two days during the lunar landing phase. Now, it would have to support three men for the four-day journey back to Earth. The lunar module's descent engine, which was designed to slow the craft during landing, would have to be used to perform course corrections and adjustments to ensure a safe return trajectory.

The crew faced a series of daunting challenges in their fight for survival. First, they had to shut down nearly all power systems in the command module to conserve energy for reentry into Earth's atmosphere. This left them without heat in the cabin, forcing the astronauts to endure temperatures that dropped to near freezing. They also had to carefully ration water and food, consuming as little as possible to stretch their limited supplies.

Another critical problem was the buildup of carbon dioxide in the cabin. The lunar module's carbon dioxide scrubbers were designed to handle the breathing of two astronauts for a limited time, and they quickly began to reach their capacity. Ingeniously, the team at mission control, led by Flight Director Gene Kranz, devised a solution to adapt the square filters from the command module to fit the round openings in the lunar module's system. Using only materials available on board, such as duct tape, plastic bags, and cardboard, the astronauts were able to construct an improvised filtration system that kept them alive.

As the spacecraft looped around the Moon, using its gravity to slingshot back toward Earth, the crew and mission control worked tirelessly to overcome each new obstacle. Every decision had to be carefully weighed, as even a small mistake could have dire consequences. The mission became a race against time, with the astronauts' lives hanging in the balance.

The Return to Earth: Navigating the Final Challenges

As Apollo 13 hurtled back toward Earth, the crew faced one final challenge: reentry into the Earth's atmosphere. The command module, which had been powered down to conserve energy, had to be reactivated in a precise sequence to ensure that it would function properly during the critical reentry phase. This process was complicated by the fact that the spacecraft's power and communication systems were severely compromised.

The command module's heat shield, which was essential for surviving the intense heat of reentry, had also been damaged in the explosion. There was concern that it might not be able to withstand the extreme temperatures, which could result in the spacecraft burning up upon reentry. Additionally, the spacecraft's guidance system, which had been deactivated to conserve power, had to be realigned with Earth to ensure a safe reentry trajectory.

Despite these challenges, the crew and mission control meticulously worked through the procedures, reactivating the command module and aligning it for reentry. The final burn of the lunar module's descent engine was executed perfectly, setting the spacecraft on a course that would bring it safely back to Earth.

As the command module reentered Earth's atmosphere on April 17, 1970, tension in mission control and around the world was palpable. The spacecraft disappeared behind a communications blackout as it passed through the intense heat of reentry, leaving everyone anxiously awaiting its reemergence. After several agonizing minutes, the command module, Odyssey, reestablished communication with mission control, signaling that the crew had survived reentry.

Moments later, the spacecraft's parachutes deployed, and Apollo 13 splashed down safely in the Pacific Ocean, where it was quickly recovered by the USS Iwo Jima. The astronauts—Jim Lovell, Jack Swigert, and Fred Haise—were hailed as heroes, having overcome incredible odds to return safely to Earth.

The Aftermath: A Triumph of Ingenuity and Teamwork

The successful return of Apollo 13 was celebrated around the world as a testament to human ingenuity, teamwork, and the indomitable spirit of exploration. The mission, which had started with such high hopes of landing on the Moon, had turned into a near-disaster that tested the limits of both the astronauts and the NASA team on the ground. Yet, through a combination of skill, resourcefulness, and determination, they had turned a potential tragedy into one of the most remarkable survival stories in history.

The mission also had a profound impact on NASA and the future of space exploration. The lessons learned from Apollo 13 led to significant changes in the design and operation of spacecraft, including improvements in safety protocols, redundancies in critical systems, and better training for astronauts and mission control personnel. The mission highlighted the importance of preparation, adaptability, and clear communication in the face of unforeseen challenges.

In the years that followed, the story of Apollo 13 became the subject of numerous books, documentaries, and films, most notably the 1995 movie "Apollo 13," directed by Ron Howard and starring Tom Hanks as Jim Lovell. The film, which closely followed the real events of the mission, brought the story to a new generation, further cementing its place in popular culture.

For the astronauts themselves, the experience of Apollo 13 was life-changing. Jim Lovell, who had previously flown on Gemini 7, Gemini 12, and Apollo 8, became a symbol of courage and leadership, often speaking about the mission and the lessons learned from it. Jack Swigert, who had joined the mission at the last minute after the original command module pilot, Ken Mattingly, was exposed to German measles, later entered politics, though he passed away before taking office. Fred Haise, who had suffered a serious urinary tract infection during the mission due to dehydration, went on to have a successful career as a test pilot and aerospace executive.

Conclusion: The Enduring Legacy of Apollo 13

The Apollo 13 mission stands as a powerful reminder of the challenges and risks inherent in space exploration. It is a story that transcends its time, capturing the essence of human perseverance in the face of overwhelming odds. The mission's legacy is one of hope, innovation, and the unyielding belief that, even in the direst circumstances, the human spirit can prevail.

As we continue to explore the cosmos, the story of Apollo 13 serves as both a cautionary tale and an inspiration. It reminds us that while space travel is fraught with dangers, it is also an endeavor that pushes the boundaries of what is possible. The survival of the Apollo 13 crew is a testament to the power of human ingenuity and the enduring quest to reach for the stars, no matter how difficult the journey may be.

Chapter 35: The Miracle of the Baby Jessica

On October 14, 1987, the world stood still as the heart-wrenching story of an 18-month-old toddler, Jessica McClure, unfolded in Midland, Texas. What began as a routine day for the McClure family quickly spiraled into a 58-hour-long ordeal that captured the attention of millions around the globe. Known as "Baby Jessica," the little girl's plight became a symbol of resilience, the power of community, and the strength of the human spirit in the face of overwhelming odds.

The incident began innocuously enough, with Jessica playing in her aunt's backyard. In a matter of moments, however, she disappeared from sight, having fallen into an abandoned well shaft that was only 8 inches in diameter but plunged 22 feet into the ground. The well was an old relic from an era when such shafts were common in oil-rich regions like Midland, and it had been left uncovered, a tragic oversight that would soon place Baby Jessica at the center of a dramatic rescue operation.

As news of the incident spread, the small town of Midland became the focus of a massive rescue effort, with teams of experts, volunteers, and media descending upon the site. The story of Baby Jessica became a real-time drama broadcast to millions of households across the United States and around the world. The rescue operation, fraught with challenges and setbacks, would ultimately become a defining moment in the history of emergency response, a testament to human ingenuity, and a landmark event in the evolution of media coverage.

The Fall: A Moment of Terror

On that fateful October day, Jessica McClure's mother, Reba McClure, was briefly distracted by a phone call when the toddler, playing with several other children in the backyard, wandered over to the well shaft. In an instant, Jessica slipped and fell into the narrow opening, her cries echoing up from the darkness below. Reba's initial disbelief turned to horror as she realized what had happened. Panicked and desperate, she called for help, and within minutes, neighbors and local authorities arrived on the scene.

The first responders quickly assessed the situation and realized the gravity of the challenge before them. Jessica was trapped deep underground in a space too narrow for rescuers to reach her directly. The shaft, a mere 8 inches wide, was too small for any adult to descend, and the depth made traditional rescue methods nearly impossible. Moreover, the well's walls were jagged and unstable, posing a constant threat of collapse. Any misstep could lead to further disaster, either by pushing Jessica deeper into the well or by causing the walls to cave in on her.

As news of the incident spread, the local fire department, police, and emergency medical services were soon joined by a team of experts, including drilling specialists, engineers, and geologists. The operation quickly grew in complexity, with each passing hour bringing new challenges and dangers. The goal was clear: to rescue Baby Jessica before her time ran out, but the path to achieving that goal was anything but straightforward.

The Rescue Operation: Innovation and Determination

The plan that eventually took shape involved drilling a parallel shaft next to the well where Jessica was trapped. This new shaft would be large enough for rescuers to descend and dig a horizontal tunnel to reach the toddler. However, the task was fraught with difficulties. The earth in the area was composed of hard rock layers interspersed with pockets of loose soil, making the drilling process slow and arduous. Additionally, the proximity of the new shaft to the well posed a constant risk of collapse, which could have catastrophic consequences.

Time was of the essence, but the rescuers also had to proceed with extreme caution. To make matters worse, Jessica's position within the well was precarious. Her right leg was pinned above her head, and she was wedged into a narrow section of the shaft, making any movement risky. The rescuers had to be mindful of her position as they worked to avoid causing further injury or dislodging her into a more dangerous position.

As the hours turned into days, the entire nation watched with bated breath. The media had descended upon Midland, transforming the rescue into a live, round-the-clock broadcast. News networks provided continuous coverage, with updates on the rescue effort, interviews with officials, and heart-wrenching images of the McClure family waiting anxiously for news of their daughter. The story of Baby Jessica became a symbol of hope, with millions of people across the country praying for her safe rescue.

The drilling of the parallel shaft was slow and laborious, taking far longer than initially anticipated. The rescuers encountered numerous setbacks, including equipment malfunctions, shifts in the earth, and the ever-present danger of a collapse. Despite these challenges, the team remained focused and determined, driven by the knowledge that a young life was at stake.

One of the key figures in the rescue operation was Robert O'Donnell, a paramedic who volunteered to be the one to descend into the newly drilled shaft and attempt the final, delicate task of freeing Jessica. O'Donnell's role was critical, as he would have to navigate the narrow space, carefully chip away at the rock and soil around Jessica, and pull her free without causing further harm. The physical and emotional toll on O'Donnell and the other rescuers was immense, as they worked under extreme pressure, knowing that any mistake could be fatal.

The Media's Role: A Global Audience in Real-Time

The rescue of Baby Jessica was one of the first major news events to be broadcast live in real-time to a global audience. The media's presence at the scene turned the operation into a spectacle, with millions of viewers tuning in to watch the drama unfold. The coverage was relentless, with news anchors providing minute-by-minute updates, interviews with rescuers, and emotional appeals from the McClure family. The story became a unifying moment for the nation, with people from all walks of life offering their prayers, support, and even donations to aid the rescue effort.

The extensive media coverage also had a profound impact on the rescue operation itself. The rescuers were acutely aware that their every move was being watched by millions, adding an additional layer of pressure to an already intense situation. The media's presence also helped to galvanize public support, with volunteers, donations, and resources pouring in from across the country. The story of Baby Jessica became a symbol of hope and resilience, with people drawing inspiration from the courage and determination of the rescuers and the strength of the little girl trapped deep underground.

The media's role in the Baby Jessica rescue also marked a turning point in the way news was covered and consumed. The event demonstrated the power of live broadcasting to capture the public's attention and to bring people together in moments of crisis. It also highlighted the influence of the media in shaping public perception and the importance of responsible journalism in reporting on sensitive and emotionally charged events.

The Moment of Rescue: A Miracle Unfolds

After 58 grueling hours, the moment of rescue finally arrived. On the morning of October 16, 1987, Robert O'Donnell descended into the narrow shaft for the final time. With painstaking care, he inched his way through the tunnel that had been dug to reach Jessica, using a chisel and his hands to remove the last bits of rock and soil that held her captive. The tension was palpable as the world watched, holding its collective breath.

At 8:30 AM, O'Donnell emerged from the shaft, cradling Baby Jessica in his arms. The sight of the little girl, alive and finally free from the well, brought a wave of relief and jubilation. The rescuers, exhausted but elated, erupted in cheers, while the McClure family was overcome with emotion. The moment was captured on live television, and the images of Baby Jessica's rescue became iconic, symbolizing the triumph of hope and human spirit over adversity.

Jessica was rushed to a nearby hospital, where she was treated for dehydration, hypothermia, and minor injuries. Remarkably, despite the ordeal, she suffered no permanent physical harm, though she bore a small scar on her forehead as a reminder of the experience. The doctors marveled at her resilience, dubbing her survival nothing short of a miracle.

The rescue of Baby Jessica was hailed as a triumph of human ingenuity, determination, and the power of community. It was a moment that brought people together, transcending boundaries of race, class, and geography. The story of her rescue became a symbol of hope and resilience, inspiring countless others facing their own challenges and adversities.

The Aftermath: A Lasting Legacy

In the years that followed, the story of Baby Jessica remained etched in the collective memory of the nation. Jessica McClure, who became known as "America's baby," grew up in the spotlight, though her parents made every effort to shield her from the public eye. The family received an outpouring of support from across the country, with donations pouring in to help cover Jessica's medical expenses and to provide for her future.

As she grew older, Jessica's life returned to a semblance of normalcy. She attended school, made friends, and pursued her interests like any other child. However, the events of October 1987 continued to cast a shadow over her life. The media attention, while initially a source of support, eventually became a burden, with the McClure family facing the challenges of maintaining privacy and protecting Jessica from the pressures of public scrutiny.

The rescue operation also had a lasting impact on the community of Midland and on the field of emergency response. The incident led to increased awareness of the dangers posed by abandoned wells and other hazards, prompting changes in regulations and safety standards. The lessons learned from the rescue of Baby Jessica also influenced the development of new techniques and technologies in search and rescue operations, with a greater emphasis on collaboration, innovation, and the use of media to galvanize public support.

For the rescuers who were involved in the operation, the experience left a deep and lasting impression. Robert O'Donnell, hailed as a hero for his role in saving Jessica, struggled with the emotional toll of the rescue, and his life took a tragic turn in the years that followed. Despite the accolades and recognition, O'Donnell faced personal challenges that ultimately led to his untimely death, a somber reminder of the immense pressures faced by those who risk their lives to save others.

Conclusion: A Story of Hope and Humanity

The story of Baby Jessica's rescue is one that continues to resonate, even decades after the event. It is a story of hope, resilience, and the power of community, a reminder that in moments of crisis, ordinary people can achieve extraordinary things. The rescue of Baby Jessica brought together a nation, united by the shared goal of saving a young life, and in doing so, it demonstrated the best of humanity.

The legacy of Baby Jessica's rescue lives on, not only in the memories of those who witnessed it but also in the lessons learned and the lives touched by her story. It serves as a powerful reminder of the importance of compassion, perseverance, and the unyielding belief that even in the darkest of times, miracles can and do happen.

Chapter 36: The Doolittle Raid

In the early months of 1942, the United States was reeling from the devastating attack on Pearl Harbor. The surprise assault by the Japanese had crippled the U.S. Pacific Fleet, leaving the nation vulnerable and shocked. In response, President Franklin D. Roosevelt sought a way to strike back at Japan, both to boost American morale and to send a message to the Japanese Empire that the United States would not be easily defeated. This desire to retaliate culminated in one of the most daring and audacious missions of World War II: the Doolittle Raid.

The brainchild of Lieutenant Colonel James H. Doolittle, the raid was a bold plan to launch a surprise air attack on Tokyo and other major Japanese cities. The mission, officially known as the Tokyo Raid, was designed not only as a retaliatory strike but also as a psychological blow to the Japanese, who believed their homeland was impervious to enemy attacks. The raid would involve 16 B-25 Mitchell bombers taking off from the USS Hornet, an aircraft carrier, flying over 600 miles to their targets in Japan, and then continuing on to land in China, where they would be aided by Chinese allies.

The Doolittle Raid was fraught with challenges from the outset. The B-25 bombers, while capable aircraft, had never before been launched from an aircraft carrier, and their range was barely sufficient to reach the Japanese mainland, let alone continue to China. The plan required the pilots to launch their bombers much closer to Japan than originally intended, as the USS Hornet was spotted by a Japanese picket boat, forcing the raid to be launched earlier than planned. This change in the mission's parameters would have far-reaching consequences for the raiders, turning what was already a perilous operation into a desperate struggle for survival.

The Preparation: Training for an Impossible Mission

In the months leading up to the raid, the selected airmen underwent rigorous training to prepare for the unique challenges of the mission. The pilots and crews had to learn how to take off from the limited deck space of an aircraft carrier, a maneuver that had never been attempted with B-25 bombers. The bombers had to be stripped of all non-essential equipment to reduce weight and make room for extra fuel tanks, as every drop of fuel would be crucial to reaching their targets and, hopefully, landing safely in China.

Doolittle, an experienced aviator and a pioneer in aviation, was chosen to lead the mission. His leadership and expertise were critical in overcoming the numerous obstacles that arose during the preparation phase. The airmen were aware of the dangers they faced, including the possibility that they might not have enough fuel to reach China or that they could be captured or killed if they crash-landed in Japanese-occupied territory. Despite these risks, the men remained committed to the mission, driven by a deep sense of duty and the desire to strike a blow against the enemy.

The training took place in secret, with the airmen practicing short takeoffs on runways marked to simulate the deck of the USS Hornet. They also rehearsed the bombing runs they would make over Tokyo and other cities, using maps and intelligence gathered by American spies and Chinese resistance fighters. The secrecy of the mission was paramount, as any leak could jeopardize the entire operation and endanger the lives of the men involved.

As the day of the raid approached, the tension among the airmen grew. They knew they were about to embark on a mission that could change the course of the war, but they also knew that the odds were stacked against them. The success of the raid would depend on their skill, courage, and a significant amount of luck.

The Raid: A Daring Attack on the Japanese Homeland

On the morning of April 18, 1942, the USS Hornet, accompanied by a task force of support ships, was steaming towards Japan in the North Pacific Ocean. The bombers, lined up on the carrier's deck, were ready for takeoff. However, the mission's timetable was suddenly accelerated when the task force was spotted by a Japanese patrol boat. Though the boat was quickly destroyed, it was feared that the Japanese had already been alerted to the presence of the American fleet. With no time to lose, Doolittle made the decision to launch the raid immediately, even though the Hornet was still 170 miles farther from Japan than originally planned.

The decision to launch early meant that the bombers would have to fly an additional distance to reach their targets and would likely run out of fuel before reaching the safety of Chinese territory. Nevertheless, the airmen accepted the risk and prepared for takeoff. One by one, the 16 bombers roared down the deck of the Hornet and lifted off into the gray skies, heading towards Japan.

As they approached the Japanese mainland, the crews were filled with a mixture of fear and determination. The sight of Tokyo coming into view was both awe-inspiring and terrifying. For many of the airmen, this was their first time in combat, and they knew that their mission was fraught with danger. The Japanese had formidable air defenses, and the bombers were vulnerable to attack from both anti-aircraft fire and enemy fighters.

The bombers flew in low over the city, dropping their payloads on military and industrial targets in Tokyo, Yokohama, Kobe, and

Nagoya. The bombs caused significant damage, though the physical destruction was less important than the psychological impact. The Japanese, who had believed their homeland was invulnerable, were stunned by the audacity of the attack. The raid shattered their sense of security and demonstrated that the United States was capable of striking back, even at great distances.

After completing their bombing runs, the bombers turned southwest, heading towards China. The crews knew that they were running dangerously low on fuel, and many of the planes would not make it to their intended landing sites. The raiders faced the daunting prospect of ditching their aircraft in the sea, crash-landing in enemy territory, or trying to find makeshift airstrips in the Chinese countryside.

The Aftermath: A Desperate Fight for Survival

As the bombers neared the Chinese coast, the situation became increasingly dire. Several of the planes ran out of fuel and were forced to crash-land in the sea or on the rugged terrain of eastern China. The crews who survived the crash landings found themselves in hostile territory, with Japanese forces scouring the countryside in search of the American raiders.

For many of the airmen, the days and weeks that followed were a harrowing test of their endurance and will to survive. Those who landed in Japanese-occupied areas faced the immediate threat of capture. Some were taken prisoner by the Japanese and subjected to brutal interrogations, while others evaded capture with the help of Chinese resistance fighters. The Japanese, enraged by the attack on their homeland, launched a massive retaliation against the Chinese, resulting in the deaths of an estimated 250,000 civilians in the regions where the raiders had landed.

Of the 80 airmen who participated in the Doolittle Raid, three were killed during the mission, and eight were captured by the Japanese. Of those captured, three were executed, and one died of starvation and mistreatment in a Japanese prison. The remaining four prisoners were eventually liberated at the end of the war, though they bore the physical and psychological scars of their captivity.

For the airmen who evaded capture, the journey to safety was long and perilous. Many of them were aided by Chinese civilians and resistance fighters, who provided food, shelter, and guidance through the treacherous terrain. The raiders had to navigate dense forests, cross rivers, and climb mountains, all while avoiding Japanese patrols and dealing with the harsh realities of war-torn China. The bonds formed between the American airmen and their Chinese allies were forged in the crucible of shared struggle and survival.

The Impact: A Turning Point in the War

The Doolittle Raid, though a tactical success, had a far-reaching impact on the course of World War II. The raid shocked the Japanese military and government, leading to a reevaluation of their defensive strategies and a shift in focus towards protecting the Japanese mainland. This shift contributed to the Japanese decision to extend their defensive perimeter in the Pacific, which ultimately led to the Battle of Midway, a decisive turning point in the war.

For the United States, the raid was a much-needed morale boost in the dark days following Pearl Harbor. It demonstrated that the U.S. could strike back against Japan and that the war in the Pacific was far from over. The raid also galvanized American public support for the war effort, strengthening the resolve to defeat the Axis powers.

Lieutenant Colonel James Doolittle, who had feared that the loss of all 16 bombers might lead to his court-martial, was instead hailed as a national hero. He was promoted to brigadier general and awarded the Medal of Honor for his leadership and bravery. The surviving raiders were also celebrated as heroes, receiving commendations and accolades for their courage and sacrifice.

The Doolittle Raid left an indelible mark on the history of World War II. It was a mission that exemplified the determination and ingenuity of the American military and the resilience of the men who carried it out. The raid's legacy lives on in the annals of military history as a testament to the power of courage, innovation, and the human spirit in the face of overwhelming odds.

Conclusion: A Story of Survival and Heroism

The Doolittle Raid is not only a story of a bold and daring military operation but also a profound narrative of survival and resilience. The men who undertook the mission faced nearly insurmountable challenges, both during the raid itself and in the aftermath as they fought to stay alive in hostile territory. Their survival was made possible by their unwavering determination, the support of their allies, and their refusal to give up, even in the face of death.

The story of the Doolittle Raid continues to inspire generations, reminding us of the extraordinary lengths to which people will go to protect their country, defend their freedom, and support one another in times of crisis. It is a story that underscores the importance of perseverance, teamwork, and the belief that even in the most desperate situations, there is always hope.

The legacy of the Doolittle Raiders endures as a symbol of the bravery and sacrifice of those who served in World War II, and their story remains a powerful example of the indomitable human spirit.

Chapter 37: The Flight of Apollo 12

In the wake of the monumental success of Apollo 11, which saw Neil Armstrong and Buzz Aldrin become the first humans to walk on the Moon, NASA faced the formidable task of building upon this historic achievement. Apollo 11 had fulfilled President John F. Kennedy's ambitious goal of landing a man on the Moon and returning him safely to Earth, but it was only the beginning of NASA's lunar exploration program. The next mission, Apollo 12, was tasked with pushing the boundaries of lunar exploration even further. This mission would not only aim to land on the Moon but also to demonstrate the ability to perform more precise landings, conduct extended scientific experiments, and retrieve valuable samples for analysis.

Apollo 12 was to be the second manned mission to the lunar surface, and it carried the weight of proving that the success of Apollo 11 was not a one-time triumph. The mission was designed to show that NASA could replicate the achievement with greater precision and that the program could pave the way for future explorations of the Moon and beyond. The mission's objectives included landing near the Surveyor 3 probe, which had been sent to the Moon in 1967, conducting extensive surface exploration, and returning with lunar samples for scientific study.

However, the Apollo 12 mission would prove to be anything but routine. From its dramatic launch under the threat of severe weather to the challenges faced by the crew on the lunar surface, Apollo 12 became a story of perseverance, precision, and the unyielding determination of the astronauts and NASA team to overcome adversity and achieve their goals.

The Crew: A Cohesive Team of Experienced Astronauts

The Apollo 12 mission was led by a crew of experienced astronauts, each of whom brought unique skills and expertise to the mission. The commander of Apollo 12 was Charles "Pete" Conrad, a veteran astronaut who had previously flown on Gemini 5 and Gemini 11. Conrad was known for his technical expertise, calm demeanor, and sense of humor, which would prove invaluable during the mission.

The lunar module pilot for Apollo 12 was Alan L. Bean, a former Navy test pilot who was making his first spaceflight. Bean had been a backup crew member for Apollo 9, and his extensive training and dedication made him an ideal candidate for the mission. His role would be to assist Conrad in piloting the lunar module, conducting surface operations, and collecting scientific data.

The command module pilot for Apollo 12 was Richard F. Gordon Jr., another experienced astronaut who had flown with Conrad on Gemini 11. Gordon's responsibilities included piloting the command module, Yankee Clipper, while Conrad and Bean descended to the lunar surface in the lunar module, Intrepid. Gordon would also conduct scientific observations and experiments from lunar orbit, providing critical support to the mission.

The Apollo 12 crew was known for their camaraderie and strong working relationship. They had trained together extensively, developing a deep bond and mutual respect that would serve them well during the challenges of the mission. Their teamwork and trust in one another were essential components of the mission's success.

The Launch: A Harrowing Start Under Threatening Skies

The Apollo 12 mission launched on November 14, 1969, from Kennedy Space Center in Florida. However, the launch was anything but smooth. The weather on the day of the launch was less than ideal, with heavy clouds and the threat of thunderstorms looming over the launch site. Despite these conditions, the decision was made to proceed with the launch, a choice that would soon be put to the test.

Just 36 seconds after liftoff, Apollo 12 was struck by lightning. The electrical discharge coursed through the Saturn V rocket, causing the spacecraft to lose power and triggering alarms in the command module. The situation was dire, and for a brief moment, it seemed that the mission might end in disaster. Inside the command module, the instrument panel lit up with warning lights, and the astronauts were suddenly faced with the terrifying prospect of losing control of the spacecraft.

Fortunately, the crew remained calm under pressure, and the quick-thinking actions of flight controllers on the ground helped to restore power to the spacecraft. Flight controller John Aaron, who was responsible for electrical, environmental, and communications systems, made the critical recommendation to switch the command module's Signal Conditioning Equipment (SCE) to auxiliary power, a move that restored telemetry data and allowed the mission to continue. Aaron's decision, based on his deep understanding of the spacecraft's systems, earned him a place in NASA history as the man who "saved" Apollo 12.

The lightning strike had left the spacecraft rattled, but the crew's composure and the support of the ground team ensured that Apollo 12 remained on course. As the Saturn V rocket continued its ascent, the tension in Mission Control began to ease, and the mission proceeded as planned. The incident was a stark reminder of the unpredictable nature of space exploration and the importance of teamwork, expertise, and quick thinking in the face of unforeseen challenges.

The Journey to the Moon: Navigating the Vastness of Space

With the immediate crisis of the lightning strike behind them, the Apollo 12 crew settled into their journey to the Moon. The spacecraft entered Earth orbit and then performed a translunar injection burn, propelling it towards the lunar surface. The journey to the Moon took approximately three days, during which time the crew conducted system checks, monitored the spacecraft's trajectory, and prepared for the upcoming lunar landing.

The command module, Yankee Clipper, was the crew's home for the majority of the mission. It was equipped with the necessary life support systems, navigation tools, and scientific instruments to ensure the crew's safety and success. The lunar module, Intrepid, was designed to detach from the command module and land on the Moon's surface, carrying Conrad and Bean to their designated landing site.

As the spacecraft approached the Moon, the crew performed a series of burns to enter lunar orbit. This phase of the mission required precise calculations and careful maneuvering to ensure that the spacecraft remained on the correct trajectory. The experience and skill of the crew, combined with the support of Mission Control, were crucial in navigating the complexities of space travel.

Once in lunar orbit, the crew prepared for the separation of the command module and lunar module. Gordon, who remained in the command module, continued to orbit the Moon while Conrad and Bean prepared for their descent to the surface. This phase of the mission required close coordination between the two spacecraft, as well as careful management of fuel, power, and other resources.

The Lunar Landing: A Precision Descent to the Ocean of Storms

The primary objective of Apollo 12 was to demonstrate the ability to make a precise landing on the lunar surface, a critical capability for future missions. The designated landing site was in the Ocean of Storms, a large basaltic plain on the Moon's near side. The site was chosen for its relatively flat terrain and its proximity to the Surveyor 3 probe, which had landed on the Moon two years earlier.

As the lunar module, Intrepid, began its descent to the surface, Conrad and Bean were focused on making a pinpoint landing. The descent was carefully monitored by Mission Control, with real-time data being relayed to the crew. The lunar module's descent engine was throttled to control the rate of descent, while the crew used visual references and navigational data to guide the spacecraft.

The descent was not without its challenges. During the final approach, Conrad noticed that the lunar module was slightly off course, heading towards a crater that could have posed a risk to the landing. Demonstrating his piloting skills, Conrad made a manual adjustment to the lunar module's trajectory, steering it away from the crater and towards a safer landing spot.

The lunar module touched down on the surface of the Moon on November 19, 1969, just 600 feet from the Surveyor 3 probe. The precision of the landing was a testament to the crew's skill and the accuracy of the mission's planning and execution. Conrad's first words upon landing reflected his characteristic humor: "Whoopee! Man, that may have been a small one for Neil, but that's a long one for me."

Exploring the Lunar Surface: Science and Discovery

With the lunar module safely on the surface, Conrad and Bean prepared for their extravehicular activities (EVAs) on the Moon. The primary goals of their surface exploration were to collect lunar samples, conduct scientific experiments, and retrieve parts of the Surveyor 3 probe for analysis. The astronauts were equipped with specialized tools and instruments, as well as the Portable Life Support System (PLSS) backpacks that provided them with oxygen, cooling, and communications.

The first EVA began with Conrad and Bean descending the lunar module's ladder and stepping onto the surface. The astronauts immediately set to work deploying scientific instruments, including the Apollo Lunar Surface Experiments Package (ALSEP), which was designed to measure seismic activity, solar wind, and other environmental factors on the Moon. The data collected from these experiments would provide valuable insights into the Moon's geology and the conditions on its surface.

One of the most significant achievements of the Apollo 12 mission was the retrieval of parts from the Surveyor 3 probe. The probe had been exposed to the harsh lunar environment for over two years, and scientists were eager to study the effects of prolonged exposure to space. Conrad and Bean carefully removed the probe's camera and other components, which were later returned to Earth for analysis. The findings from these studies provided important information about the durability of materials in space and contributed to the design of future space missions.

In addition to their scientific work, Conrad and Bean took the time to document their experiences on the Moon. They captured photographs of the lunar landscape, their activities, and the Earth as seen from the Moon. These images provided a visual record of the mission and offered the public a glimpse of the stark beauty of the lunar surface.

The astronauts conducted a second EVA the following day, during which they continued their exploration and collected additional lunar samples. By the end of their time on the Moon, Conrad and Bean had spent a total of 7 hours and 45 minutes on the lunar surface, covering a distance of approximately 4,300 feet. They had successfully completed all of their mission objectives and had made significant contributions to lunar science.

The Return to Earth: A Safe Journey Home

With their work on the lunar surface complete, Conrad and Bean returned to the lunar module and prepared for the ascent back to lunar orbit. The ascent stage of the lunar module was designed to separate from the descent stage and propel the astronauts back into orbit, where they would rendezvous with Gordon in the command module. This phase of the mission required precise timing and coordination to ensure a successful docking.

The ascent from the lunar surface was executed flawlessly, and the lunar module quickly rendezvoused with the command module. Once the two spacecraft were docked, Conrad and Bean transferred back to the command module, bringing with them the lunar samples and other materials they had collected. The lunar module was then jettisoned and left in lunar orbit, while the command module prepared for the journey back to Earth.

The return journey to Earth took approximately three days, during which time the crew conducted additional scientific observations and experiments. The command module re-entered Earth's atmosphere on November 24, 1969, and splashed down safely in the Pacific Ocean. The crew was quickly recovered by the USS Hornet, the same aircraft carrier that had retrieved the Apollo 11 crew.

Legacy and Impact: The Enduring Significance of Apollo 12

The Apollo 12 mission was a resounding success, demonstrating NASA's ability to conduct precise lunar landings and conduct extended scientific exploration on the Moon. The mission provided valuable data and samples that contributed to our understanding of the Moon and laid the groundwork for future lunar missions. The crew's ability to overcome the challenges of the lightning strike, perform a pinpoint landing, and achieve all of their mission objectives underscored the importance of preparation, expertise, and teamwork in space exploration.

The story of Apollo 12 is a testament to the resilience and determination of the astronauts and the NASA team. It serves as a reminder of the incredible achievements of the Apollo program and the enduring human spirit of exploration and discovery. The mission's success paved the way for subsequent Apollo missions, each of which would continue to push the boundaries of what was possible in space exploration.

Today, the legacy of Apollo 12 lives on in the continued exploration of space, the pursuit of scientific knowledge, and the inspiration it provides to future generations. The mission stands as a symbol of what can be accomplished through perseverance, precision, and the unwavering belief in the power of human ingenuity.

Chapter 38: The Survival of Paul Templer

Paul Templer's survival story is one of the most remarkable tales of human endurance and courage in the face of extreme danger. As a seasoned river guide on the Zambezi River in Africa, Templer was well-acquainted with the stunning beauty and the lurking dangers of one of the world's wildest rivers. The Zambezi River, which flows through six countries and is known for its breathtaking scenery, powerful currents, and abundant wildlife, attracts adventurers and nature lovers from around the globe. However, the river is also home to some of the most dangerous animals on the planet, including crocodiles, elephants, and one of Africa's most feared creatures—the hippopotamus.

The hippopotamus, often perceived as a lumbering and docile animal due to its bulky appearance, is, in reality, one of Africa's most aggressive and dangerous animals. Weighing up to 3,000 pounds and equipped with massive jaws capable of crushing bone, hippos are highly territorial and will attack anything that they perceive as a threat. Despite their size, hippos are incredibly fast in the water and on land, and their unpredictable behavior makes them a formidable presence in the African wilderness.

On a fateful day in March 1996, Paul Templer came face-to-face with the terrifying reality of just how dangerous a hippopotamus can be. What began as a routine day on the Zambezi River quickly turned into a life-or-death struggle that would test Templer's physical and mental limits and ultimately redefine his understanding of survival.

Paul Templer: A Life of Adventure and Passion for Nature

Before the incident that would change his life forever, Paul Templer was living his dream. Born and raised in Zimbabwe, Templer had developed a deep love for nature and adventure from an early age. His passion for the outdoors led him to become a river guide on the Zambezi River, where he spent his days leading tourists on thrilling canoe safaris through the heart of the African wilderness.

As a river guide, Templer was responsible for ensuring the safety of his clients while providing them with an unforgettable experience of Africa's wildlife and natural beauty. His extensive knowledge of the river, its currents, and the behavior of the animals that inhabited the area made him an expert in his field. Templer had encountered hippos many times before and understood the importance of maintaining a safe distance from these unpredictable animals.

Templer's love for adventure was matched by his commitment to conservation and his desire to share the wonders of Africa with others. He believed in the transformative power of nature and was passionate about educating people on the importance of preserving the environment. His work as a river guide was more than just a job; it was a way of life that allowed him to connect with the natural world and inspire others to do the same.

The Fateful Day: A Routine Canoe Safari Turns Deadly

On March 9, 1996, Paul Templer set out on what was supposed to be a routine canoe safari on the Zambezi River. He was leading a group of tourists, along with two apprentice guides, through a stretch of the river that he knew well. The group was paddling in a series of inflatable canoes, enjoying the tranquil surroundings and the sight of wildlife along the riverbanks.

As they navigated the river, Templer and his team were on high alert for any signs of danger. The Zambezi River was known for its abundant hippo population, and the guides were well aware of the risks involved in getting too close to these animals. Despite their precautions, the group soon found themselves in a precarious situation.

As they approached a narrow section of the river, the guides noticed several hippos in the water ahead. Templer instructed the group to paddle away from the animals and steer clear of their territory. However, before they could react, one of the canoes was suddenly attacked by a hippo. The powerful animal lunged at the canoe, overturning it and throwing one of the apprentice guides, a young man named Evans, into the water.

Templer immediately sprang into action, guiding the tourists to safety while paddling towards Evans to rescue him. The situation was chaotic, with the hippo thrashing in the water and the overturned canoe drifting away. As Templer reached Evans, he began pulling him towards his own canoe, determined to get him out of the water as quickly as possible.

The Attack: A Battle for Survival in the Jaws of a Hippopotamus

Just as Paul Templer was about to lift Evans into his canoe, the unthinkable happened. Templer felt a tremendous force hit him from below, and within seconds, he was enveloped in darkness. The hippo had attacked again, this time seizing Templer in its massive jaws. The animal had clamped down on Templer's upper body, and he was now trapped inside the mouth of one of Africa's most dangerous predators.

The pain was excruciating as the hippo's teeth punctured Templer's chest and back, crushing his ribs and tearing through his flesh. He could feel the hot breath of the animal and the rough texture of its tongue as it began to shake him violently from side to side, a behavior known as "rag-dolling," which hippos use to subdue their prey. Templer's life flashed before his eyes as he struggled to breathe, his lungs filling with blood and water.

Despite the overwhelming pain and the sheer terror of the situation, Templer's survival instincts kicked in. He knew that if he was to have any chance of surviving, he needed to remain as calm as possible and try to minimize the damage being inflicted by the hippo. Templer forced himself to go limp, hoping that the animal would lose interest and release him. At the same time, he tried to focus on staying conscious, aware that losing consciousness would likely mean death.

The hippo continued to thrash Templer around, dragging him underwater and then lifting him back to the surface. Templer could feel his body being torn apart by the animal's powerful jaws, but he refused to give up. His mind raced as he thought of his family, his friends, and his desire to live. He was determined to survive, no matter the odds.

A Miraculous Escape: Breaking Free from the Jaws of Death

After what felt like an eternity, the hippo suddenly released Paul Templer from its jaws. Dazed and severely injured, Templer found himself floating in the water, barely able to move. He knew that he needed to get out of the water quickly, as the hippo could attack again at any moment. Summoning what little strength he had left, Templer began to swim towards the nearest canoe.

However, the ordeal was far from over. The hippo, still enraged, attacked Templer again, this time grabbing him by the legs and pulling him under the water. The force of the attack was so intense that Templer's legs were nearly torn off, and he was once again plunged into darkness. The pain was unbearable, but Templer refused to let go of his will to survive.

In a moment of sheer determination, Templer managed to break free from the hippo's grip and swim to the surface. With blood pouring from his wounds and his body barely holding together, he reached the canoe and was pulled aboard by one of the apprentice guides. The other members of the group had managed to reach safety, but Templer's injuries were so severe that he knew he needed immediate medical attention if he was to survive.

The group quickly paddled to the riverbank, where they administered first aid to Templer and prepared to evacuate him to the nearest medical facility. Templer's injuries included multiple deep lacerations, crushed ribs, punctured lungs, and extensive damage to his legs and back. He was losing blood rapidly, and his chances of survival seemed slim.

The Fight for Life: A Grueling Journey to Recovery

Paul Templer was rushed to a local hospital, where doctors worked tirelessly to stabilize his condition and save his life. His injuries were so severe that he required multiple surgeries, including the amputation of his left arm, which had been nearly severed during the attack. The medical team was amazed that Templer had survived such a brutal encounter, but his fight for life was far from over.

Templer spent weeks in the hospital, battling infections, undergoing surgeries, and enduring excruciating pain as his body began the slow process of healing. The physical and emotional toll of the attack was immense, and Templer was faced with the daunting reality of living with a permanent disability. The loss of his arm, combined with the trauma of the attack, left him grappling with feelings of anger, frustration, and fear.

However, Templer's indomitable spirit and determination to live carried him through the darkest moments of his recovery. He was surrounded by a strong support network of family, friends, and medical professionals who encouraged him to keep fighting and to focus on the future. Templer's positive attitude and resilience became a source of inspiration for those around him, and he slowly began to rebuild his life.

The Road to Redemption: Embracing a New Life

As Paul Templer recovered from his injuries, he was faced with the challenge of redefining his life and finding a new sense of purpose. The attack had changed him forever, both physically and emotionally, but it had also given him a deeper appreciation for life and a renewed sense of determination to make the most of every moment.

Templer decided to channel his experiences into helping others, and he became a motivational speaker, sharing his story of survival with audiences around the world. He spoke about the importance of resilience, the power of the human spirit, and the ability to overcome even the most insurmountable challenges. His message resonated with people from all walks of life, and Templer soon found himself in high demand as a speaker at conferences, schools, and corporate events.

In addition to his work as a motivational speaker, Templer became an advocate for conservation and wildlife protection. He used his platform to raise awareness about the importance of preserving Africa's natural habitats and the need for responsible tourism. Templer was determined to ensure that others could experience the beauty of Africa's wilderness while also understanding the risks and responsibilities that come with it.

Templer also wrote a memoir titled *"What's Left of Me,"* in which he recounted his harrowing experience and the lessons he learned along the way. The book received widespread acclaim for its honesty, courage, and inspirational message. Through his writing, Templer was able to reach an even wider audience, sharing his story with people who might never have had the opportunity to hear him speak in person.

Despite the challenges he faced, Templer refused to let his injuries define him. He continued to lead an active and adventurous life, returning to the Zambezi River and even resuming his work as a river guide. Although he had lost an arm, Templer adapted to his new reality with remarkable determination and ingenuity. He learned to paddle with one arm and developed new techniques for navigating the river, proving that he could still excel at the job he loved.

Templer's story is a testament to the resilience of the human spirit and the power of determination in the face of adversity. His journey from near-death on the Zambezi River to becoming a beacon of hope and inspiration for others is a powerful reminder of what can be achieved when we refuse to give up, no matter how difficult the circumstances.

The Legacy of Paul Templer's Survival

Paul Templer's survival story has left an indelible mark on all who have heard it. His incredible journey from the jaws of a hippopotamus to a life dedicated to helping others is a testament to the strength of the human spirit. Templer's experience serves as a reminder that life is fragile, unpredictable, and often filled with unexpected challenges. However, it also illustrates that with courage, resilience, and a positive mindset, we can overcome even the most daunting obstacles.

Templer's legacy extends beyond his personal achievements. Through his work as a motivational speaker, author, and conservation advocate, he has inspired countless individuals to face their own challenges with courage and determination. His story has also raised awareness about the dangers of wildlife encounters and the importance of responsible tourism in protecting both people and animals.

Today, Paul Templer continues to inspire others through his work and his story. His message of hope, resilience, and the power of the human spirit resonates with people around the world, reminding us all that we have the strength to overcome even the most terrifying and life-altering experiences. The survival of Paul Templer is not just a story of survival—it's a story of triumph, transformation, and the enduring power of the human spirit to rise above adversity and embrace life with renewed purpose and passion.

Epilogue

As we reach the end of *Real Survival Stories*, we are left with a profound appreciation for the incredible resilience of the human spirit. The stories shared within these pages are more than just accounts of hardship and endurance; they are powerful reminders of our innate ability to overcome, adapt, and persevere, even in the most desperate of situations. From the vast expanses of the ocean to the remote corners of the wilderness, from the highest mountains to the deepest jungles, each story is a testament to the strength, courage, and determination that lies within us all.

Survival is not just about the physical act of staying alive; it is about the mental and emotional resolve to push forward when every instinct urges us to surrender. Whether facing the frigid waters of the Atlantic, the relentless heat of the desert, or the crushing solitude of a vast wilderness, the survivors in this book demonstrate that the will to live can transcend the most insurmountable challenges. Their experiences teach us that survival is often a battle fought not just against external forces, but also against our fears, doubts, and limitations.

In the face of overwhelming adversity, these survivors found strength in their darkest hours. Some drew on inner reserves of courage they never knew they possessed; others relied on their faith, their love for family, or the sheer force of their will. They adapted, innovated, and endured, proving that survival is as much a state of mind as it is a physical endeavor. Their stories remind us that, no matter how dire the circumstances, there is always a way forward.

As we close this book, let us take with us the lessons these survivors have taught us. Let us remember that we, too, possess the strength to overcome our own challenges, whatever they may be. Let us be inspired by their courage and resilience to face our fears, push our boundaries, and embrace the unknown with the knowledge that we are capable of more than we can ever imagine.

Real Survival Stories is not just a collection of harrowing tales; it is a celebration of the indomitable human spirit. It reminds us that survival is more than just staying alive—it is about living fully, facing life's trials with courage, and never losing hope, no matter how difficult the journey may be.

As you return to the safety and comfort of your everyday life, remember the extraordinary stories you have read here. Let them serve as a reminder that, when faced with life's challenges, you too can find the strength to survive and thrive. For in the end, it is not the trials we face that define us, but how we rise above them.

Thank you for joining us on this journey through the most remarkable survival stories of our time. May these tales inspire you to face your own challenges with courage, resilience, and the unyielding will to survive.

The End.